Theology in Malawi

© Authors 2021 (editorial matter: Kenneth R. Ross and Mzee Hermann Mvula)

All rights reserved. No part of this publication may be reproduced, stored in a retrieval system, or transmitted in any form or by any means, electronic, mechanical, photocopying, recording or otherwise, without prior permission from the publishers.

Published by

Kachere Series
PO Box 1037,
Zomba, Malawi

ISBN   978-99960-53-32-0

eISBN   978-99960-60-92-2

Kachere is represented outside Malawi by:

African Books Collective Oxford (also for e-books) (order@africanbookscollective.com)

www.africanbookscollective.com

Cover: Josephine Kawejere

Index: Hope Kaombe

[Religion in Malawi No. 19]

Theology in Malawi

Prospects for the 2020s

Edited by

Kenneth R. Ross and

Mzee Hermann Y. Mvula

Kachere Series
Zomba
2021

Contents

Introduction: A Seminal Event   6
    KENNETH R. ROSS AND MZEE HERMANN Y. MVULA

Chapter 1
Malawian Christian Theology: Progress and Prospects   11
    KENNETH R. ROSS

Chapter 2
Umunthu Theology and a Paradigm Shift in Theological Education   33
    AUGUSTINE CHINGWALA MUSOPOLE

Chapter 3
Theological Research and Publication   53
    KLAUS FIEDLER

Chapter 4
Fit for Purpose: The Theological Graduate Profile in Light of Malawian Grassroots Priorities   74
    VOLKER GLISSMANN

Chapter 5
Translating "Lord Jesus" as "Bwana Yesu"   94
    WINSTON R. KAWALE

Chapter 6
Situating Malawian Neo-charismatic Apostles in the New Testament   113
    FELIX CHIMERA NYIKA

Chapter 7
A Biblical Perspective on Covid-19 Pandemic and the End of the World   130
    LUKE LIMBITHU

Chapter 8
Response to Covid-19 by State and Church in Malawi: A Critical Reflection   142
    STEWART DAISON KAPINDA

Chapter 9
The Abiding Influence of African Traditional Religion among
    Educated Christian Professionals in Northern Malawi   157
    JOYCE DAINESS MLENGA

Chapter 10
Relevance of Theology in the Age of Secular Humanism   167
    GERARD CHIGONA

Chapter 11
Towards Retaining Young People in the 21st Century African
    Christian Church: Selected Sociological Factors   188
    FRANK BARDEN CHIRWA

Chapter 12
Pain and Trauma: The Experience of Widowhood   206
    GERTRUDE AOPESYAGA KAPUMA

Chapter 13
Cold War between Reverends and Ruling Elders in CCAP, Synod of
    Livingstonia: From Ruling to Assistant Elders   225
    MOSES MLENGA

Chapter 14
The Bible and the Concept of Separation of Powers: Could the Bible
    Constitute the Foundation for Malawi's Good Governance?   240
    MZEE HERMANN Y. MVULA

Chapter 15
The Church in a New Era of Democracy: A Call for Non-Partisan
    Prophetic and Pastoral Functions   258
    TIMOTHY KABULUNGA NYASULU

Report on National Theology Conference Nkhoma University 24-26
    Sept 2020   276

Constitution of Theological Society   285

Notes on Contributors   298
Index   302

Introduction: A Seminal Event

**Kenneth R. Ross and
Mzee Hermann Y. Mvula**

This book is the product of a National Theology Conference that was hosted by Nkhoma University at Nkhoma Mission from 24 to 26 September 2020. Of course, there is nothing unusual about a conference giving rise to the publication of a number of papers but this one carries a special quality for at least three reasons. The first is that for many years there had not been a theology conference at national level in Malawi. Participants therefore came with a great sense of anticipation, many observing that the event was something for which they had long been waiting. The second is that for some time it seemed as if the plans to hold the conference would be thwarted. Its original dates on 5-7 August 2020 coincided with the highest spike in coronavirus infections in Malawi during 2020. There was little option but to postpone the event indefinitely. Mercifully, the rate of infection in Malawi rapidly decreased to the extent that the Government allowed the reopening of schools and colleges in September, which also cleared the way for the conference to be held. Thirdly, it was a very forward-looking conference. It carried the sense of being on the cusp of something new. Hence the subtitle of the book is "Prospects for the 2020s." Conference participants were concerned to set an agenda and open up new possibilities for collaboration and common action on the development of theology and theological education in Malawi.

The conference could not have taken place as it did without the proliferation and expansion of theological education in Malawi during the first two decades of the 21st century. New institutions of higher learning have been founded during this period while older ones have expanded their programmes. The result is that more people

Introduction: A Seminal Event

are teaching and learning theology in Malawi than ever before. However, a significant challenge presented by this remarkable development is a certain fragmentation. There has been little opportunity for faculty members from different institutions to come together, share experiences and help each other to sharpen their skills. This was a key objective of the conference and one that was amply met by the offer of papers from many quarters and by the appreciative and critical engagement that they received when presented. The event convincingly demonstrated the benefits of an academic community that operates at national level, bringing together institutions and individuals from different parts of the country with a common commitment to mutual enrichment. Some 50 theologians from at least 12 institutions took part. By the end of the conference, it was clear that some kind of permanent instrument is needed to promote and sustain such engagement. Appended to the essays collected in this volume are the Conference Report and the draft Constitution of the Theological Society, which looks set to be the organizational outcome. These documents are important in indicating the prospects for theology in Malawi in the 2020s.

Meanwhile, the fruits of the conference have value in their own right as demonstrating something of the direction and vigour of theology in Malawi at this time. Since this was the first national conference to be held for many years, it was decided simply to have an open call for papers, allowing for a presentation on any topic on which someone was working. A revealing outcome was that the papers that were offered divided fairly naturally between three principal areas: biblical studies, faith and culture, and faith and society. The conference therefore split into these three streams for the presentation and discussion of the papers. Much the same structure governs the arrangement of the book, though it is recognized that some papers span more than one area.

First, however, there are a few chapters, mostly originating from plenary sessions of the conference, that take a broad view of the development of theology and theological research and teaching in Malawi. **Kenneth Ross** provides an introductory overview of the history of theology in Malawi, considering major institutional developments, influential scholars and theological emphases that have gained prominence. The next chapter, by **Augustine Musopole**, is more forward-looking, identifying where Malawian theology can find its distinctive focus and suggesting what kind of curriculum might result, with special attention to inter-disciplinary possibilities. **Klaus Fiedler** takes up the question of how high-quality research can be developed, through postgraduate studies as well as writing and publishing by faculty members and others. For his part, **Volker Glissmann** reports on a research project that reveals the expectations of church congregations as regards the qualities of those who have had a theological formation and offer themselves for service as pastors.

Chapters concerned with biblical studies are led by **Winston Kawale's** study of a thorny translation question – how to express the tetragrammaton in Chichewa and the implications for translation of the word "Lord." **Felix Nyika** turns his attention to the adoption of the title "Apostle" by some leaders of Neocharismatic churches in Malawi and explores its validity on the basis of the use of the term in the New Testament. **Luke Limbithu** takes up the topic that has dominated life during 2020, the coronavirus pandemic. He considers a range of questions that are provoked by Covid-19 and asks what light the Bible can shed as we seek to find answers. Another young theologian who attempts to do contextual theology in relation to Covid-19 is **Stewart Kapinda** who brings perspectives from Christian Ethics to bear on the crisis.

When it comes to faith and culture, it is interesting that attention is devoted less to Africa's traditional culture and more to the challenges of cultural change. **Joyce Mlenga** considers ATR not in its original rural setting but rather in the "dual religiosity" practised by educated urban professionals. **Gerard Chigona** traces the rise of secular humanism and explores what it means for the theological task in today's Africa. **Frank Chirwa** is likewise concerned about the impact of modernity on African communities but examines it in terms of the alienation of young people from church life as a result of their exposure to modern culture. For her part, **Gertrude Kapuma** considers the painful experience of widows, who suffer as a result of harmful and hurtful cultural dynamics that too often prevail in both church and community.

As regards faith and society, two contributions focus on the question of power. For **Moses Mlenga** the balance of power between ministers and elders in the Presbyterian system has been disturbed in the CCAP Synod of Livingstonia, with ministers taking more than their share and elders being marginalized. **Hermann Mvula** focuses on the exercise of power by the state. He traces the crucial principle of the separation of powers back to the Old Testament and demonstrates how the biblical foundation has a vital role to play in achieving good governance in today's context, not least in Malawi. Finally, **Timothy Nyasulu** focuses on the one-year period from May 2019 to June 2020 and examines how the churches engaged the political realm in Malawi. He faults them for becoming too partisan, identifying themselves with particular political parties, and calls for a non-partisan approach that is both pastoral and prophetic.

We are confident that the book will make good reading for anyone who would like to know what concerns are motivating Malawi's theologians as we enter the 2020s. It makes no claim to be a systematic theology. Rather it traverses a range of topics that have each claimed their own importance for church and nation at the present time. Each is subjected to thought-provoking analysis and the successive essays open up wide fields for further research. Taken together, they demonstrate the vitality and vigour of contemporary theology in Malawi. The prospects for the 2020s are both enticing and exciting.

Chapter 1

Malawian Christian Theology: Progress and Prospects

Kenneth R. Ross

Formal, written theology represents only a small part of Malawian theology. The great majority of Malawian theology has been unwritten as Malawians through many generations have engaged with the reality of God and the realm of the spirit. This engagement has found expression in symbol, in ritual and in the living of life much more than it has in scholarly books and articles. This does not make it any less theology. When it comes to Christianity, there has, of course, been a theological dimension to Malawians' reception of the Christian message but, again, this has found expression in worship and celebration and life more than in a formal academic context. The faith has been something to sing and celebrate more than something to intellectualize and debate. If you compare the amount of effort Malawians have put into singing their faith to the amount that has been devoted to expressing it in formal academic terms, you will discover a wide difference. Academic theology therefore has to be modest and recognize that its role has been on a small scale in relation to the overall scope of Malawian Christianity. This, however, does not mean that it does not exist nor that it lacks validity.

Theological Education: A Brief History

In fact, from an early stage in Malawi's Christian history there has been a certain prioritizing of theological training. It was the UMCA that led the way in the late 19th century by providing on Likoma Island the theological education required to qualify for ordination.

Similarly, from the early 20th century the three Presbyterian missions all offered theological courses at their central mission stations with missionaries as tutors working with small groups of ordinands. When Harry Kambwiri Matecheta and Stephen Kundecha completed their theological training at Blantyre Mission in 1911, they were proud that the exams they sat were judged to be at the same standard as those of their counterparts in Scotland. The Catholic missions from an early stage prioritized the development of minor seminaries, appointing their most able priests to the staff.

It was the Catholics who were first to create a theological institution at national level when they opened Kachebere Major Seminary in 1939. It was sited in Mchinji District, at the foot of Kalulu Hill, with the idea that it would be convenient for both Zambian and Malawian students and be able to train priests for both countries. It was administered by the White Fathers and meant that priestly formation could be completed in Malawi, rather than students being required to go to Kipalapala Major Seminary in Tanzania. By the 1970s, such was the success of Kachebere that it could no longer accommodate all the students in formation and it was decided to open a new Major Seminary, named St Peter's, in Zomba which was by then becoming established as the academic town in Malawi. From then on students completed the philosophy part of their training at Kachebere and the theology at St Peter's.

Meanwhile the CCAP continued with small-scale ministerial training courses at its various missions until in 1962 the three Synods decided to combine their resources to create a united theological college. It was sited at Nkhoma Mission as a suitably central location and named Nyamukawala (Rise and Shine). The academic standard began to rise. Prior to this, ministerial candidates had usually been mature students with limited formal academic qualifications. Now there were some who had completed secondary school. Numbers remained small with 59 students graduating between 1962 and 1974. The College was

1. Malawian Christian Theology: Progress & Prospects

abruptly closed for political reasons in 1974 and when it regrouped in 1978 it opened in new purpose-built premises in Zomba, close to the recently established University campus, and now including Anglican students as well as those of the three Presbyterian Synods.[1]

Meanwhile in 1973 a Department of Religious Studies had been established within the Faculty of Humanities at Chancellor College, University of Malawi. The proximity in Zomba of the Department, the Seminary and the College provided, as had been hoped, an inviting opportunity for academic collaboration. A Diploma in Theology programme was developed, which formed the basic curriculum at both Zomba Theological College and St Peter's Major Seminary. Syllabi were approved and examinations were moderated by the University, which validated the award of the Diploma. In the 1980s, for the first time, students in both Catholic and Protestant theological formation were undertaking their studies at University level. A further step was taken in 1990 when a Theology Degree programme was introduced at Chancellor College. Students who held a Diploma in Theology could enter this programme at 3rd Year level, gaining their B.A. after a further two years of study. Meanwhile the Diploma Board was expanding with the admission to membership of such institutions as the Likhubula Bible Institute [later EBCOM] in Blantyre, which catered for Evangelical students, the Baptist Theological Seminary in Lilongwe, the St John the Baptist Seminary in the Catholic Diocese of Mangochi and Theological Education by Extension in Malawi (TEEM).[2] As its member bodies sought to raise the level of their programmes, the Diploma Board

---

[1] See Ian Donald Fauchelle, "Theological Education in Malawi: The Contribution of Some Missions and Churches," MA, University of South Africa, 1983.

[2] Kenneth R. Ross (ed), *Church, University and Theological Education in Malawi*, Zomba: University of Malawi & Bonn: VKW, 1995.

became the Board for Theological Studies and began to offer a Degree programme on the same basis as the Diploma.

Much of this development was predicated on the idea that there was one University, mirroring the one party at the political level, which set standards and provided the focus for the development of tertiary education in the country. With the advent of the multi-party era in 1994 it soon became clear that this idea had run its course. A second public University was established at Mzuzu in 1999 and the early 2000s saw the founding of a growing number of private Universities as it became clear that there was huge unmet demand for tertiary education. Several of these were church-based Universities, with the University of Livingstonia in the northern region and the Catholic University at Nguludi leading the way. They included theology among their programmes, thus creating a rapid and exponential growth in theological education in the country, most programmes being validated by the National Council for Higher Education, established in 2011. Institutions now offering tertiary theological education include: Zomba Theological College, University of Blantyre Synod, University of Livingstonia, Nkhoma University, Chancellor College University of Malawi, Mzuzu University, Malawi Adventist University, Malawi Assemblies of God University, African Bible College University, Pentecostal Life University, Catholic University of Malawi, St Peter's Major Seminary, Leonard Kamungu Anglican Theological College, Baptist Theological Seminary, Nazarene Theological College of Central Africa, Theological Education by Extension (TEEM) and Evangelical Bible College of Malawi.

Early Pioneers of Malawian Theology

Much of this enterprise in theological education has been a matter of adopting the curriculum that has been developed in modern times in the Western world and giving Malawians the opportunity to engage

1. Malawian Christian Theology: Progress & Prospects   15

with it. But what about Malawians as creators of theology, rather than simply being on the receiving end?

During the missionary period, Malawians were given little encouragement by their European tutors to venture into theological construction by themselves but there were some who were undeterred. John Chilembwe did not leave any substantial theological writing, but his actions were the product of deep theological thinking. When he addressed, in a letter to the *Nyasaland Times*, the situation faced by Malawians after the outbreak of the First World War, his work has been described by Patrick Makondesa as Malawi's "first pastoral letter."[3] He drew on the Bible and the Christian tradition to advance the social critique that ultimately led to the Rising which, though defeated, had momentous consequences for Malawian history and identity. He advanced what Makondesa has described as "a remarkably early indigenous liberation theology."[4]

Yesaya Zerenji Mwasi, a near contemporary of Chilembwe, was a Tonga who received his theological education at the Overtoun Institution and became one of the first Malawian ministers to be ordained by Livingstonia Mission in 1914. His critique of the racism and paternalism of Livingstonia eventually led him to break away in 1933 to form the Blackman's Church which is in Tongaland. His protest went beyond internal Livingstonia issues to reach a profoundly theological level: "I wish to *naturalize* and *nationalize* God, Christ, faith - in short Christianity. There is no say that Object and Goal of the missionary enterprise is to naturalize and nationalize Christianity - to grow out of its own soil, having its own customs and

---

[3] Patrick Makondesa, *The Church History of Providence Industrial Mission*, Zomba: Kachere, 2006, 126. For the text of the letter see "The Voice of African Natives in the Present War – John Chilembwe," in Kenneth R. Ross (ed), *Christianity in Malawi: A Sourcebook*, 2nd ed., Mzuzu: Mzuni Press, 2020, 246-49.

[4] Patrick Makondesa, *The Church History of Providence Industrial Mission*, 174.

traditions purified by the Gospel of Christ. An exotic Christianity will never take vital root in the life of the natives."[5] This set the theological agenda with which the churches of Africa would be concerned for generations to come.

In the realm of church history, a pioneering figure was Harry Kambwiri Matecheta, Malawi's first Presbyterian minister, ordained in 1911. In 1951 he published his account of the early years of Blantyre Mission.[6] By this time there was an extensive literature, penned by successive generations of missionaries, about this topic. Matecheta was engaged in what his recent editors, Thokozani Chilembwe and Todd Statham, describe as "re-righting" of the history.[7] The European missionaries had focused on their own exploits but Matecheta viewed the Blantyre Mission as an African story. When he describes the building of St Michael and All Angels Church, for example, he does not dwell on the much-celebrated architectural genius of David Clement Scott but points out how remarkable it was that Yao and Ngoni workers collaborated in the construction work.[8] In attempting to write church history as a Malawian story he too set an agenda that would occupy generations to come.

A towering figure in Malawian church life at the time of independence was the Livingstonia minister Stephen Kauta Msiska who became Principal of the CCAP Theological College during its sojourn at Nkhoma in the 1960s and 1970s. Msiska, more than

---

[5] Yesaya Zerenji Mwasi, *Essential and Paramount Reasons for Working Independently*, Blantyre: CLAIM-Kachere, 1999 [original manuscript, 1933], 17.

[6] Harry Kambwiri Matecheta, *Blantyre Mission: Nkhani za Ciyambi Cace*, Blantyre: Hetherwick Press, 1951; translated as Harry Kambwiri Matecheta, *Blantyre Mission: Stories of Its Beginning*, trans. Thokozani Chilembwe, Berlin: Wichern-Verlag, 2016; repr. Mzuzu: Luviri Press, 2020.

[7] Ibid, 15.

[8] Ibid, 17.

1. Malawian Christian Theology: Progress & Prospects

anyone else, reckoned at a theological level with the issues entailed in the transition from expatriate-run mission to indigenous Malawian church. This led him to focus his theological work on the question of the African past. He questioned the replacement theology that had commonly been advanced by the missions, pointing out that this left people with a split between their African identity and their Christian identity. Christianity in his view had to be related at a profound level to the African religious heritage. The God encountered in Jesus Christ, he argued, is the same God of whom Africans have been aware in their traditional religious practice. This he affirmed from a Reformed theological perspective: "For if we were to say that the one supreme God, the Creator, was unknown to the African, we can easily contradict ourselves when we come to teach the Christian theology of divine initiative. Humanity failed to find God. God himself revealed himself to humanity. He loved us first!"[9]

Msiska also drew attention to the understanding of mediation that was prevalent in the African tradition. The longing for God, he observed, was always coupled with an understanding that, as a result of human failure and corruption, there was need for mediation if humanity were to relate to the Creator God. Traditionally, people looked to the spirits and the ancestors to provide mediation but the Christian message now brought the good news that God himself has provided the perfect mediator in the gift of Jesus Christ.[10] He thus develops a theology of continuity where African tradition and Christian faith belong together, the latter being built on the former.

At the same time, he was unsparing in exposing the evil that was found in the inherited tradition and demonstrating its need for redemption. He thus developed a theology of discernment, what he

---

[9] Stephen Kauta Msiska, *Golden Buttons: Christianity and Traditional Religion among the Tumbuka*, Blantyre: CLAIM-Kachere, 1997, 19-20.

[10] Ibid, 33.

termed "golden buttons" – seeking to retain what was good and wholesome and godly in the African tradition while discarding that which was evil and destructive. Without such an exercise in theological discernment he realized that African Christianity would lack integration and integrity. He anticipated the later work of scholars like Bénézet Bujo and Kwame Bediako with their determination to account theologically for the African past.[11] Though his theological career was tragically cut short by political developments, the fragments that have been gathered in *Golden Buttons* set the scene for Malawian theology in a deeply important way.

Development of Malawian Theology

With the development of University-level theology in the 1990s came the establishment of postgraduate programmes, first at Chancellor College and later at Mzuzu University. Prior to this, aspiring Malawian theologians had to find the rare opportunity to study overseas if they wished to take a Masters or PhD degree. Now these became available locally through part-time programmes, allowing students to continue their regular work while studying for a higher degree. This greatly increased the amount of original theological research being undertaken and the number of trained theologians.

Theological production also began to find expression in publication. The Chancellor College journal, *Religion in Malawi* led the way, producing 17 issues between 1987 and 2020. It was complemented by the Kachere Series of books on religion, culture and society from Malawi, launched by the Department of Theology and Religious Studies at Chancellor College in 1994-95. Soon it was publishing several books each year, many of them original contributions to

---

[11] See Bénézet Bujo, *African Theology in its Social Context*, Maryknoll NY: Orbis: 1992; Kwame Bediako, *Christianity in Africa: The Renewal of a Non-Western Religion*, New York: Orbis and Edinburgh: EUP, 1995.

theology. A similar publishing project was begun at Mzuzu University in 2008 when Mzuni Press was launched, producing books on a range of subjects but with a major focus on theology. The privately-run Luviri Press, founded in 2016, also adopted a major emphasis on theology.

The books and articles generated through these initiatives give an indication of the shape and direction of Malawian theology. Three major focal points have been culture, church history and feminist theology. Consideration of aspects of Malawian culture, often including some theological appraisal, has been a prominent feature of the corpus of work that has been generated. Early Kachere publications included J.W.M. van Breugel's *Chewa Traditional Religion*[12] and J.C. Chakanza's *Wisdom of the People: 2000 Chichewa Proverbs*,[13] while early Mzuni Press books included Joyce Mlenga's *Dual Religiosity in Northern Malawi: Ngonde Christians and African Traditional Religion*[14] and Moses Mlenga's *Polygamy in Northern Malawi: A Christian Reassessment*.[15] Meanwhile a substantial contribution has been made by Clement Majawa, first with his *African Christian Reconciliation in the Light of Yao Traditions*,[16] published in 2009, and then his two-volume *Handbook on Borderline between Christianity and Witchcraft*, published in 2017.[17]

---

[12] J.W.M van Breugel, *Chewa Traditional Religion*, Blantyre: CLAIM-Kachere, 2001.

[13] J.C. Chakanza, *Wisdom of the People: 2,000 Chichewa Proverbs*, Blantyre: CLAIM-Kachere, 1999.

[14] Joyce Mlenga, *Dual Religiosity in Northern Malawi: Ngonde Christians and African Traditional Religion*, Mzuzu: Mzuni Press, 2016.

[15] Moses Mlenga, *Polygamy in Northern Malawi. A Christian Reassessment*, Mzuzu: Mzuni Press, 2016.

[16] Clement Chinkambako Abenguni Majawa, *African Christian Reconciliation in the Light of Yao Traditions*, Nairobi: Creations Enterprises, 2009.

[17] Clement Majawa, *A Handbook on Borderline between Christianity and Witchcraft* Vol. 1 (Foundations, Anthropology, Theories and Trends), Nairobi: Scroll Technologies, 2017; Clement Majawa, *A Handbook on Borderline Between Christianity*

As regards church history, ground-breaking contributions have been made, for example, by Patrick Makondesa's *The Church History of Providence Industrial Mission*,[18] and Brighton Kawamba's *The Blantyre Spiritual Awakening and its Music*.[19] In the area of feminist theology, major contributions have included Rachel NyaGondwe Fiedler's *Women of Bible and Culture: Baptist Convention Women in Southern Malawi*,[20] and Molly Longwe's *African Feminist Theology and Baptist Pastors' Wives*.[21] Several Malawian theologians have contributed to the work of the Circle of Concerned African Women Theologians, whose history was written by Rachel NyaGondwe Fiedler.[22]

Systematic theology was conspicuous by its absence until Maximian Khisi's *The Church as the Family of God and the Care for Creation* (2018)[23] and Jones Mawerenga's *Systematic Theology* (2019).[24] Only limited attention has been given to contextual theology, with notable exceptions including James Tengatenga's *Church, State and Society in Malawi: The Anglican Case*,[25] Rhodian Munyenyembe's *Christianity and*

---

and Witchcraft Vol. 2 (Biblical, Theological and Societal Considerations), Nairobi: Scroll Technologies, 2017.

[18] Patrick Makondesa, *The Church History of Providence Industrial Mission*, Zomba: Kachere, 2006.

[19] Brighton Kawamba, *The Blantyre Spiritual Awakening and its Music*, Mzuzu: Luviri Press, 2018.

[20] Rachel NyaGondwe Banda [Fiedler], *Women of Bible and Culture: Baptist Convention Women in Southern Malawi*, Zomba: Kachere, 2006.

[21] Molly Longwe, *African Feminist Theology and Baptist Pastors' Wives*, Mzuzu: Luviri Press, 2019.

[22] Rachel NyaGondwe Fiedler, *The History of the Circle of Concerned African Women Theologians*, 1989-2007, Mzuzu: Mzuni Press, 2016.

[23] Maximian Khisi, *The Church as the Family of God and the Care for Creation*, Mzuzu: Mzuni Press, 2018.

[24] Jones Mawerenga, *Systematic Theology*, Zomba: Kachere, 2019.

[25] James Tengatenga, *Church, State and Society in Malawi: The Anglican Case*, Zomba: Kachere, 2006.

1. Malawian Christian Theology: Progress & Prospects

Socio-Cultural Issues: the Charismatic Movement and Contextualisation in Malawi,[26] Gerard Chigona's *The Catholic Church and Politics in Malawi: The Circle of Silence and Prophetic Engagement (1964-2004)*,[27] and a recent series of articles by Qeko Jere.[28] Biblical studies has attracted few substantial contributions, though exceptions include Hilary Mijoga's *Separate But Same Gospel: Preaching in African Instituted Churches in Southern Malawi*,[29] and Jonathan Nkhoma's *The Use of Fulfilment Quotations in the Gospel according to Matthew*.[30] A 2020 publication that spans Old Testament ethics and contextual theology is Hermann Mvula's *The Theory, Praxis and Pursuit of Constitutionalism in Democratic Malawi: An Old Testament Ethical Perspective*.[31]

---

[26] Rhodian Munyenyembe, *Christianity and Socio-Cultural Issues: the Charismatic Movement and Contextualisation in Malawi*, Mzuzu: Mzuni Press and Zomba: Kachere, 2011.

[27] Gerard Chigona, *The Catholic Church and Politics in Malawi: The Circle of Silence and Prophetic Engagement (1964-2004)*, Balaka: Montfort Media, 2011.

[28] Qeko Jere, "An Evaluation of the Church of Central Africa Presbyterian General Assembly and Poverty Alleviation from a Koinonian Perspective in Malawi," *HTS Teologiese Studies / Theological Studies*, 74/2 (2018), 1-8; Qeko Jere, "Public Role of the Church in Anti-Corruption: An Assessment of the CCAP Livingstonia Synod in Malawi from a Kenosis Perspective," *Verbum et Ecclesia*, 39/1 (2018), 1-10; Qeko Jere, "Perichoretic interaction within the Trinity as a Paradigm for Fostering Unity in the Public Affairs Committee (PAC) in Malawi," *Stellenbosch Theological Journal*, 4.2 (2018), 553-78; Qeko Jere and Vhumani Magezi, "Pastoral Letters and the Church in the Public Square: An Assessment of the Role of Pastoral Letters in Influencing Democratic Processes in Malawi," *Verbum et Ecclesia*, 39/1 (2018), 1-9.

[29] Hilary B.P. Mijoga, *Separate but Same Gospel: Preaching in African Instituted Churches in Southern Malawi*, Blantyre: CLAIM-Kachere, 2000.

[30] Jonathan Nkhoma, *The Use of Fulfilment Quotations in the Gospel according to Matthew*, Zomba: Kachere, 2006.

[31] Mzee Hermann Y. Mvula, *The Theory, Praxis and Pursuit of Constitutionalism in Democratic Malawi: An Old Testament Ethical Perspective*, Zomba: Kachere, 2020.

Critical and Creative Theology

The scale and scope of theological research and publication has vastly increased in Malawi during the last twenty-five years or so. Most of the work that has been produced, however, has been narrow in its focus. Few have been the scholars who have been able to look comprehensively at the Malawian context and offer an overall theological appraisal. When we look for critical, creative and constructive theology that allows us to understand Malawian Christianity against wide horizons, the production so far has been limited but not absent. Here we can offer only three examples.

Perhaps the first Malawian theologian to address this challenge was Patrick Kalilombe, Rector of Kachebere Major Seminary 1964-72 and Bishop of Lilongwe 1972-76. At the same time as Kauta Msiska's theology was getting him into trouble with the Banda regime, so was Bishop Kalilombe's as his development of base Christian communities in the Diocese of Lilongwe exposed him to the suspicion that he was attempting to create a rival political movement. For him it meant an abrupt departure from Malawi in 1976 and a twenty-year exile. Though this was a loss to Malawi and to the Catholic Church in particular, it gave him the opportunity for the theological reflection and writing which, on his eventual return to Malawi, he was able to gather and publish in his seminal work *Doing Theology at the Grassroots*.[32] Like Kauta Msiska he understood the need for a theological understanding of the African past.[33] It was the Chewa rather than the Tumbuka from whom Kalilombe drew his inspiration but he reached similar conclusions: "In the development and functioning of human cultures and spiritualities, such as the African one, has the God of

---

[32] Patrick A. Kalilombe, *Doing Theology at the Grassroots: Theological Essays from Malawi*, Gweru: Mambo-Kachere, 1999.

[33] See Todd Statham "'Like Jairus I call you': Two Theological Attempts to Recover the Malawian Past," *Journal of African Christian Thought* 17 (2015), 40-49.

1. Malawian Christian Theology: Progress & Prospects   23

our Lord Jesus Christ been totally absent? Is it possible that God was at work with the Spirit, inspiring and promoting positive values for the guidance of God's people, even if human sinfulness always tends to put obstacles in front of God's saving work?"[34]

Perhaps the most learned and erudite theologian yet produced by Malawi, he used his re-assessment of the African past as a platform to consider such theological issues as inter-religious relations, the nature of evangelization, contextual theology and the relation of the local and the global in theological construction. The themes to which he returned again and again, according to Victor Mundua, are "the author's missionary vocation, the critical role of the 'grassroots' in theological construction, the integrity of Chewa traditional belief, the combination of Catholic commitment with radical openness to all religious cultures and traditions."[35] Though he built an international reputation as a "third world theologian" and was exposed to many different cultures and contexts, for his theological orientation he constantly returned to his Malawian roots. When considering inter-religious relations, for example, he wrote of his own family at Mua with its Catholic, Dutch Reformed and Muslim members. When he thought of grassroots theology, he was aware that its currency was found not in scholarly articles but in songs, stories, proverbs, artistic and symbolic expressions, drama and celebrations.[36] It was his ability to address the largest questions on the global theological agenda while remaining grounded in the Malawian context, and enabling the one to inform the other, that marked him out as a scholar who broadened the theological horizons.

---

[34] Patrick A. Kalilombe, *Doing Theology at the Grassroots*, 234.
[35] Victor Mundua, "Patrick Kalilombe, Doing Theology at the Grassroots: A Challenge for Professional Theologians," in Bénézet Bujo, *African Theology: The Contribution of the Pioneers*, Nairobi: Paulines, 2012, 63-74, at 64.
[36] Patrick A. Kalilombe, *Doing Theology at the Grassroots*, 195.

Kalilombe, on this basis, did much to set the scene for a Malawian contextual theology. He drew from Latin American liberation theology and the Ecumenical Association of Third World Theologians, of which he was a prominent member, the understanding that theology arises from action. The committed action of Christian witness comes first; theology is a second step as it reflects on the action. For Kalilombe this meant a particular orientation to the Christian community so that its experience would form the basic material for doing theology. However, for him this would never mean a narrow or exclusive approach. He always looked at the Christian community as fully integrated into the wider community. "Ecumenical" for him meant the whole of the inhabited human world so his theological endeavour was always a matter of dialogue and common working with those of other faiths and worldviews.

It also carried a critical and disturbing quality: "that type of theology is neither neutral nor merely theoretical. It is a theology that aims at transforming society by constantly questioning the *status quo* and working to change it. It uses the SEE-JUDGE-ACT methodology."[37] Such questioning was not welcome in Banda's Malawi of the 1970s. Nonetheless Kalilombe continued to champion a grassroots theology that, in his words, "is capable of unleashing a power among those who hitherto have been powerless, so that they can begin to change the *status quo*."[38]

Another Malawian contextual theologian is Augustine Musopole, perhaps the only Malawian theologian who has had the courage to offer a comprehensive and challenging theological vision for his native land. Born in Chitipa, the son of a CCAP minister, after studies at the University of Malawi, University of London and Union Theological Seminary in New York, his career in Malawi included

---

[37] Ibid, 173.
[38] Ibid, 189.

posts as Secretary of the Student Christian Organisation in Malawi, Headmaster of Robert Laws Secondary School, General Manager of CLAIM, the Christian publisher, and General Secretary of the Christian Council before becoming Associate Professor in the Department of Theology and Religion at Chang Jung Christian University in Tainan, Taiwan. Along the way he was thinking and writing on theological issues, particularly those that were pressing in the Malawian context of the late 20th and early 21st century.[39]

When he came to consider what would be involved in the making of a theological vision for Malawi, he began by recognizing that, "the churches in Malawi are still foreign in their spirituality, liturgy, and theology. Africanizing the leadership has not pushed the churches very much towards becoming indigenous. Most of its leadership is in a maintenance mode and lack the theological ability to transform the churches to become truly Malawian. What is required are people of God with theological acumen to create a suitable theology or come up with a confession for the church today in Malawi. The recycling of old theologies will not do."[40] Musopole identified four vital components in this theological task: (a) the doctrine of God; (b) ethnological study; (c) a comprehensive view of salvation; (d) the traditional world view integrated with the biblical worldview.[41] Suggesting a focus on such matters as bondedness, *umoyo*, *umunthu*, community-in-communion, God's providence, celebration of life, power, responsible citizenship, ethnicity, regionalism and national consciousness, Musopole imagined, "a development from no theology to some theology, from foreign theologies to local ones, from

---

[39] See e.g. Augustine C. Musopole, *Being Human in Africa: Towards an African Christian Anthropology*, New York: Peter Lang, 1994.
[40] Augustine C. Musopole, "A Theological Vision for Malawi," *Religion in Malawi* 6 (1996), 3-11, at 7.
[41] Ibid, 3.

uncritical to critical questioning, from knowledge to wisdom."[42] He could see a pathway, which he attempted to follow himself and which he pointed out to others.

During the late 1990s and early 2000s, Musopole was active as a public theologian, bringing his theological vision to bear on the issues of the day, particularly through his regular column in *The Lamp* magazine. Time and again he returned to his preoccupation with *uMunthu* as the basis not only of a viable Malawian theology but of a just and harmonious national life. Whatever topic he was considering his premise was always that, "the focus has to be on the quality of our humanity (*Umunthu*) and life."[43] This was not understood just as a general philosophy but was always grounded in his understanding of the identity of Jesus Christ. "Salvation," he explained, "is renewal of *umunthu* by the Holy Spirit by receiving the authentic *umunthu* of Jesus Christ as the *Namkungwi* of eternal life. This is what the gospel is all about."[44]

From this Christological basis Musopole addressed a wide range of social and political issues with which Malawi was struggling during those years. Corruption, political violence, poverty, civil society, gender, sexual promiscuity in light of the AIDS pandemic, sexuality, leadership style, constitutionalism, the separation of powers, participatory democracy, national development, education, work ethic and the integrity of the natural environment were all subjected to theological analysis and critique.[45] The point to which he returns time

---

[42] Ibid, 6.

[43] Augustine Musopole, "Jubilee 2000: The Christian Message," *The Lamp* 21 (January-February 2000), 1.

[44] Augustine Musopole, "Inculturation and the Gospel in Africa," *The Lamp* 15 (January-February 1999), 14-15.

[45] See the following articles by Augustine Musopole: "The Poor State of Malawi's Economy," *The Lamp* 17 (May-June 1999), 20; "Gender: Defining Men," *The Lamp* 24 (July-August 2000), 16-17; "Abstinence Should be Promoted," *The Lamp* 25

1. Malawian Christian Theology: Progress & Prospects 27

and again is that such issues will not be resolved without a convincing philosophical and theological basis. On the question of how to cultivate a viable home-grown democracy, for example, he writes: "I would like to suggest that a philosophy centred around the concept of *uMunthu* would go a long way to addressing some of the current political confusion that is afflicting us. However, let me say this, that this is *uMunthu* as seen in the face of Jesus Christ, the second Adam (Christo-Munthism)."[46] In this way Musopole attempted to offer a theology that is both inculturated and contextual, deeply rooted in Malawian identity and tradition and closely engaged with challenging contemporary realities while always informed and inspired by the biblical faith.

(September-October 2000), 13; "The Roots of Civil Society," *The Lamp* 26 (November-December 2000), 4; "Honest Men and Women, Honest Pay and Honest Work" *The Lamp* 27 (March-April 2001), 6-7; "Churches and Democracy in Malawi," *The Lamp* 33 (January-February 2002), 11; "Malawi: Threats to Democracy," *The Lamp* 38 (November-December 2002), 10; "A Theology of Governance," *The Lamp* 40 (November-December 2003) 6-7; "Spirituality and Sexuality," *The Lamp* 42 (July-August 2003) 20-21; "Theology, Gender and Culture in Malawi," *The Lamp* 41 (May-June 2003) 24-25; "'MGE': Men for Gender Equality," *The Lamp* 39 (January-February 2003), 31; "uMunthu and the Culture of Violence in Malawi," *The Lamp* 46 (March-April 2004), 20-21; "Politics: Malawi's Privatisation," *The Lamp* 47 (May-June 2004), 18-19; "Democratic Chaos in Malawi: A Theological Quest," *The Lamp* 52 (March-April 2005), 22-23; "Fighting Corruption in Malawi," *The Lamp* 51 (January-February 2005), 22-23; "Malawi, Work Ethic and Poverty Alleviation," *The Lamp* 53 (May-June 2005), 22-23; "Structural Obstacles to Development in Malawi," *The Lamp* 54 (July-August 2005), 22-23; "Education and Class Consciousness," *The Lamp* 56 (November-December 2005), 18-19; "uMunthu and Homosexuality," *The Lamp* 65 (May-June 2007), 11-12; "Police Brutality and Democracy," *The Lamp* 69 (January-February 2008), 11-12.

[46] Augustine Musopole, "A Theology of Governance," *The Lamp* 40 (November-December 2003) 6-7.

Until the mid-1990s theology in Malawi was largely a male preserve, with little encouragement or opportunity for women to offer a theological contribution. A leading figure in changing this situation has been Isabel Apawo Phiri who began her academic career as a Lecturer in Religious Studies at Chancellor College, University of Malawi, from the mid-1980s. Her 1995 book *Women, Presbyterianism and Patriarchy: Religious Experience of Chewa Women in Central Malawi*, based on a University of Cape Town PhD, was the first substantial work of feminist theology to be published in Malawi.[47] She brought a direct challenge to the patriarchal assumptions that shaped attitudes in church and society, both by demonstrating the leadership in religious matters that had been exercised by women in Chewa traditional religion and by questioning the theological basis that kept women in subservient positions, particularly in the CCAP Synod of Nkhoma on which her study was focused.

By this time Phiri was engaged not only in scholarly analysis but also in campaigning to change attitudes, policies and behaviour that upheld patriarchal injustice both in church and society. She therefore operated on the lines of the liberation theologians, deeply engaged in the struggle for justice and doing theology as a reflection on this experience. Her seminal 1996 article "Marching, Suspended and Stoned: Christian Women in Malawi 1995" exposed gender injustice in a way that profoundly challenged prevailing systems and ways of thinking.[48] Such was the heat of controversy that Phiri was obliged to leave Malawi, a source of distress but also an opportunity to develop her theological work on the international stage. This she has done as

---

[47] Isabel Apawo Phiri, *Women, Presbyterianism and Patriarchy: Religious Experience of Chewa Women in Central Malawi*, Blantyre: CLAIM-Kachere, 1997, 2000.

[48] Isabel Apawo Phiri, "Marching, Suspended and Stoned: Christian Women in Malawi 1995," in Kenneth R. Ross (ed), *God, People and Power in Malawi: Democratization in Theological Perspective*, Blantyre: CLAIM-Kachere, 1996, repr. Mzuzu: Luviri Press, 2018, 63-106.

1. Malawian Christian Theology: Progress & Prospects

Professor at the University of KwaZulu Natal, Coordinator of the Circle of Concerned African Women Theologians and Deputy General Secretary of the World Council of Churches. In these roles she has had a wide-ranging theological engagement but always at the centre has been the critical and creative feminist theology that she pioneered in Malawi.

Her starting point is that, "Theological education on the African continent has always been associated with men in the areas of training and literature production."[49] Since the late 20th century this situation has been challenged, particularly by the work of the Circle of Concerned African Women Theologians, with Phiri as one of its leading protagonists. The Circle's mission is to promote theological research, writing and publication on African issues from a women's perspective. This has opened up new approaches and new methods, particularly through the use of gender as an analytical tool. Phiri coordinated the Circle from 2002 to 2007 and has been a constant champion of its re-conception of the theological task and its reform of the theological curriculum.

In common with other Circle theologians Phiri has focussed on culture as a source of theology. This might sound unoriginal since the predominantly male theologians who generated the first written African Christian theology were also much preoccupied with culture. The key point at issue in the first generation was the conflicted identity that many Africans experienced as their Christian faith and their African identity were unreconciled. African women theologians too have brought a focus on culture, "as a way of redeeming African identity and culture which has often been demonized by an aggressive

---

[49] Isabel Apawo Phiri and Lilian Siwila "The Circle of Concerned African Women Theologians: Transforming Theological Education" in Isabel Apawo Phiri and Dietrich Werner (eds), *Handbook of Theological Education in Africa*, Oxford: Regnum Books International, 2013, 966-73, at 966.

Christian missionary agenda to evangelise Africa."[50] However, while there was continuity with the inculturation project of African male theologians, African women theologians also challenged the inculturation project. As a result, "African feminist cultural hermeneutics was developed as a tool of analysis to identify those forms of culture that were life-giving for women and jettison those that were oppressive."[51]

This involves using gender as a hermeneutical tool to expose injustice and provoke fresh thinking. "A gendered approach to African Christianity," Phiri explains, "refers to exposing the injustices that exist in the church, culture and interpretation of the Bible in the relationship between men and women.... We understand gender justice as promoting the humanity of both women and men in the church and using their gifts as revealed by God."[52] Theological education has been deployed in Phiri's work as a key instrument in promoting gender justice. Though the number of women engaged in formal theological education remains small, their numbers and impact are growing. Critical theological reflection is key to exposing unjust cultural practices, violence against women and an inability to deal with human sexuality as challenges that inhibit African churches as they seek to fulfil their calling. Phiri has been one of the leading champions of gender awareness in African theology, reforming

---

[50] Isabel Phiri and Sarojini Nadar, "What's in a Name? Forging a Theoretical Framework for African Women's Theologies," *Journal of Constructive Theology* 12/2 (2006), 11.

[51] Sarojini Nadar and Isabel Apawo Phiri, "HIV Research, Gender and Religion Studies," in Isabel Apawo Phiri and Dietrich Werner eds., *Handbook of Theological Education in Africa*, Oxford: Regnum Books International, 2013, 632-38.

[52] Isabel A. Phiri and Chammah J. Kaunda, "Gender," in Kenneth R. Ross, J. Kwabena Asamoah-Gyadu and Todd M. Johnson (eds), *Christianity in Sub-Saharan Africa*, Edinburgh: Edinburgh University Press, 2017, 386-96, at 386.

theological education so that it equips people to become agents of change in relation to gender injustice in church and society.

Malawian Theology in 2020

By 2020 we can talk about Malawian theology as a serious enterprise. There are at least twenty institutions giving attention to theology in a sustained way. A substantial body of literature has been developed by their faculty members with dozens of books and hundreds of articles reflecting on theological themes from a Malawian perspective. Following in the footsteps of some intrepid pioneers, the last two generations have produced many hardworking theologians and some original ones. Both church and nation are aware of the value of theology, providing both material from which theology can be generated and an audience to which it can be addressed. A generation ago Harold Turner pointed out the potential for theology that he observed in contexts like Africa: "Here at the growing edges of Christianity in its most dynamic forms, the theologian is encouraged to do scientific theology again, because he [or she] has a whole living range of contemporary data on which to work. It is not that these dynamic areas of the Christian world are free from imperfection; but being full of old and new heresies they need theology and offer it an important task."[53] To that task Malawian theologians have begun to turn their attention. Much, however, remains to be done.

It is that remaining agenda that lies in front of us as we enter the 2020s. The flip side of the proliferation of institutions engaged in theological education is that there has been a certain fragmentation. Institutions are little aware of each other and there is little opportunity for collaborative work. A sense of isolation can easily set

---

[53] Harold W. Turner, "The Contribution of Studies on Religion in Africa to Western Religious Studies," in Mark Glasswell and Edward Fasholé-Luke (ed), *New Testament Christianity for Africa and the World*, London: SPCK, 1974, 178.

in, which can be demoralizing and makes it unlikely that inspiring teaching and research will result. The National Theology Conference held at Nkhoma in September 2020 attempted to chart a different direction – one where Malawi's institutions of theological learning are well networked with one another, where opportunities for fruitful collaboration are identified and exploited, where there is a vibrant academy stimulating fresh research, high standards of teaching and good quality faculty development. Of course, these are all goals that can be pursued at institutional level. The question the National Theology Conference has put on the agenda is what could institutions do *together* that would make each one stronger?

Chapter 2

Umunthu Theology and a Paradigm Shift in Theological Education

Augustine Chingwala Musopole

"In order to confront the modern man truly you must have the Scriptures speaking truth both about God himself and about the area where the Bible touches history and the cosmos.... The tragedy of our situation today is that men and women are being fundamentally affected by the new way of looking at truth, and yet they have never even analyzed the drift which has taken place. Young people from Christian homes are brought up in the old frame of truth. Then they are subjected to the modern framework. In time they become confused because they do not understand the alternatives with which they are being presented."[1]

Francis Schaeffer

Introduction

In 2015 there was a conference at Chancellor College, a constituent college of the University of Malawi, on "Re-thinking the Humanities in the Twenty-First Century in Africa." It aimed to address "questions relating to the relevance of the humanities in our modern world. The humanities being constantly portrayed as not important in national development when in actual fact any meaningful development cannot

---

[1] Francis Schaeffer, *A Christian View of Philosophy and Culture; The Complete Works*, Vol. 1, Wheaton: Crossway Books, 1982, xx.

neglect the humanities."[2] Professor Hangson Mpalive Msiska was the keynote speaker of the conference.[3]

In Britain, it was reported in the *Observer*, "A letter to the *Observer*, signed by the directors of major arts institutions and a number of university vice-chancellors, claims that funding cuts and a decision to focus on the sciences have left subjects such as philosophy, literature, history, languages and art facing worrying times." They concluded that without urgent action the country's intellectual heritage is in danger of being diminished. The letter argued that "arts and humanities enrich the country's quality of life and help people to look at the world from different perspectives.... People's complexity comes from their language, identities, histories, faiths and cultures."

Therefore, the major concern was that humanities were no longer considered as necessary as they used to be in higher education in terms of the need for liberal education. This was evident when it came to budgets and hiring of faculty. It should not be forgotten that liberal education was meant for free citizens to enable them to perform their civic duties efficiently from informed positions. The emphasis had now moved to science subjects, technology and other professional studies with a view to the employability of graduates.

However, a study survey of the Kenyan situation showed a different picture in which humanities are still considered important for employment. The survey states, "According to the study, some 81 per cent of employed graduates are from local universities while 17 are from institutions abroad. Firms that took part in the survey say they prefer business and economics studies, engineering, ICT, social and

---

[2] www.cc.ac.mw/news/faculty-of-humanities-international-conference-22-10-2015.

[3] Reader in English and Humanities at Birkbeck College, University of London.

2. Umunthu Theology and a Paradigm Shift

behavioural sciences, humanities and medical science graduates."[4] However, when it comes to theology as a humanities subject, the story was somehow different. Theology had to be removed from degrees to be offered at University by the Commission on Higher Education, in both public and private universities, because no Form Four students chose it.

Therefore, it is not surprising that even Malawian theological colleges that have achieved university status are not seeing an increase in their theological enrolment, and those who have enrolled are keen to add some other courses from other fields for the sake of employability currently or later. The Christian universities themselves have moved their focus to secular subjects which are done without a theological perspective with a view to attracting students within a very competitive market. What are the chances of theological studies making a meaningful contribution to university education in such a market? Is it possible for theological education to go beyond ministerial training so as to find relevance in other fields as well? The present chapter will explore this possibility.

While it seems to me that theological studies have much to contribute to other fields of studies with a view to making them relevant to human existence in a deep and meaningful way, paradoxically, theology itself does not seem to envisage that role nor do the other disciplines see that role for theology. Theology is tolerated rather than considered a serious academic undertaking for national development. Yet, it is my view that without the theological input, all fields of study are bound to prove inadequate in contributing to blessed human development since they become self-serving, not comprehensive, limited, fragmentary and not unitary, being served by humanity instead of serving humanity. Therefore, what is being proposed is a

---

[4] Waihenya Kariuki, "Employer prefer UoN and Kenyatta University graduates, study reveals," *Daily Nation*, 7 May 2020.

paradigm shift in theological self-understanding and theological education. The current academic situation is suffering from fragmentation in its major fields as well as subfields of study. What is needed is a unifying approach that will contribute to human integrity and wholeness. Hence there is need for an interdisciplinary approach to theological education and also all other fields of study.

Theology the Queen of the Sciences

There was a time when theology was considered to be the Queen of the sciences simply because it had to do with God, the creator of heaven and earth; however due to its dogmatism, that is, fixed theological truths based on scholastic education which was founded on Greek logic and modelled on mathematical certitude on the one hand, and on revelation and faith on the other, it was challenged by the Enlightenment, overthrown, and imprisoned within rationalism by Immanuel Kant (1724-1804) who defined Enlightenment in this way:

> Enlightenment is man's emergence from his self-imposed immaturity. Immaturity is the inability to use one's understanding without guidance from another. This immaturity is self-imposed when its cause lies not in lack of understanding, but in lack of resolve and courage to use it without guidance from another. *Sapere Aude*! [dare to know] "Have courage to use your own understanding!"- that is the motto of enlightenment.[5]

This Kantian definition of Enlightenment had its historical roots in Platonic preference for mathematics and Aristotelian love for logical thinking as self-sustaining systems of thought; then through Patristic and medieval scholasticism, and Cartesian modern philosophy's search for certitude; furthermore, the critique of religion for its responsibility for religious wars caused by the Reformation and its insistence on Biblical revelation and authority led to the search for a

---

[5] www.columbia.edu/acis/ets/CCREAD/etscc/kant.html.

2. Umunthu Theology and a Paradigm Shift

new foundation for knowledge. The rise of the scientific method that was introduced by Francis Bacon (1561-1626) provided for an independent foundation for knowledge that was experimentally open to the pursuit of truth, and thus dogmatic theology was removed from its pedestal as the Queen of the sciences. Immanuel Kant restricted all religion to within the "limits of reason." Friedrich Schleiermacher (1768-1834), the founder of liberal theology, wanting to rescue theology from rationalism defined theology not as a thinking, or a doing, but rather as a "feeling of absolute dependence on God." In this way, he introduced a paradigm shift in the manner theology was to be done. However, theology was still held captive to rationalization of religious experience.

Liberalism and liberal theology have dominated the theological scene since the time of Schleiermacher to the present. Theological liberalism tried to fight secular critical thought using the tools of secular liberalism, that is, reason. In reaction there was the fundamentalist movement arising out of the Niagara Falls conference of 1912 that still insisted on the authority of Scripture and its inerrancy. Fundamentalism in Christianity was born following pietism and evangelical revivals in America.

After the First World War (1914-18), the neo-orthodox reaction of Karl Barth (1886-1968) and others rebelled from liberal theology and went back to the Reformed theology of the Reformation based on Sola Scripture and championed revelation while criticizing liberal theology as unattainable. Human beings could never know God through reason and only God could cross the chasm that sin had created and thus redeem humanity. Both fundamentalism and neo-orthodoxy made a tactical move to respond to liberalism in its apologetics, but within the same rationalistic framework. Liberalism having informed atheism and secularism further alienated or restricted theological studies from the university curriculum and replaced it with religious studies. Therefore, theology has been fighting a rear-guard battle within the university; not only theology, but also to some extent religion and philosophy.

Theology based on revelation and dogmatism could not stand critical examination and testing in the same way sciences and social science would since its starting point is the realm of the invisible and hence it requires faith. The existence of God has been contested and has remained the place of ideological and philosophical struggle. Science and social sciences are based on an open method using hypothesis and can be subjected to testing and reinterpretation. Therefore, religion has been tolerated as an existential and historical phenomenon within western human cultures since it refuses to go away and continues to disturb human existence through its revivals and wars. Much of human history is the history of religious conflict and missionary activity which focused on repentance with education, health and economic activities notwithstanding.

Furthermore, science and technology proved to be very progressive and fruitful in changing life for the better on the one hand, even as they have brought about some destructive results for human existence. Theology became an enemy of visible progress and alienated those of a progressive mind-set guided by rational thought and focused on eschatology related to the coming of the kingdom of God. The result was a conflict between what was considered conservative and liberal, theology and science, religion and secularism. Seeking for the unity of the universe as claimed by both has ended in a stalemate. From time to time, the church has tried to adjust itself to modernity, but more as a catch up to it than an active player. It cannot be theology versus science, secularism versus religion, but rather both theology and science, and both spiritual religiosity and secular religiosity, as two sides of the same coin. The challenge is an epistemological one. There is need for a new epistemology based on a new ontology that would resolve this dualistic conundrum. Hence the need for a paradigm shift in contextual theology itself and theological education.

Towards a Different Epistemology

Epistemology has to do with how we know what we know. Western philosophy has championed both rationalism and empiricism. Is there another way? Just as God is love, God is also truth. Just as God cannot be adequately grasped by our reason, and so is also the case with truth. God and truth cannot be completely grasped by reason and reason does not exhaust truth. God and truth have to grasp humanity through an encounter. Truth is both partially grasped by us and also grasps us into itself for growth in it. When truth grasps us, we talk of God's self-revelation to us. When Peter declared Jesus to be the Christ, Jesus told him, "Blessed are you, Simon Bar-Jona! For flesh and blood has not revealed this to you, but my Father who is in heaven."[6] Therefore, this knowledge did not come by his reason, but rather by revelation. When Peter tried to use his own reasoning to interpret the meaning of what it meant for Jesus to be the Christ, he was soon told "Get behind me Satan! You are a hindrance to me. For you are not setting your mind on the things of God, but on the things of man."[7] Therefore, when truth grasps us, it leads to the grasping of God's truth and when we try to grasp it, it often leads to its distortion. Truth comes with many logical systems, and yet western theology has been locked into one and considered it universal. Theology needs to be open to all civilizations and cultures. Therefore, rationality and revelation are two sides of the same coin and condition each other. They are not antithetical to each other. There is need for a new epistemological understanding that takes into account this new way of understanding truth. The new epistemological understanding has

---

[6] Matthew 16:17.
[7] Matthew 16:21-23.

to do with the Holy Spirit whom the Nicene creed describes as the Giver of life. This life is characterized by love as both its ontological foundation and epistemological norm uniting the head and the heart; wisdom and faith as the operational vitality; and then rationality and empiricism as instrumental in the accumulation of all vital knowledge.

Liberalism has brought about a crisis of truth, identity, authority, revelation, meaning and relevance as far as all knowledge is concerned, but much more as theological studies are concerned. Rationalistic perspectives have been critical of the role of Christianity in paving the way for colonialism and has led some African scholars to reject Christianity on rational grounds and also to consider theological studies as irrelevant to matters of national development. Religion has been considered as a private affair. It is like an insurance policy that comes into operation after death and not when one is still alive. However, when we choose to pursue blessed development, and not simply material development, a new paradigm for general education is needed and also for theological education. Blessed development has to do with the flourishing of our humanity in all aspects of our existence and not simply material comforts.

Christian Demographics

Demographically, Christianity has moved to the southern hemisphere from the northern hemisphere. While Christianity is experiencing unprecedented growth in the southern hemisphere, especially in Africa, theological education is facing a challenge. It is the late Tokunbo Adeyemo (1944-2010), the then General Secretary of the Association of Evangelicals in Africa (AEA) who said that theology in Africa is like a river that is a mile wide, but shallow in its depth. This has to do with the Christianity that was brought to Africa by the missionaries.

- Most missionaries were not theologians themselves even though they had a faith and were dedicated to their work;

2. Umunthu Theology and a Paradigm Shift 41

- They adopted western catechetical methods to spread their faith that assumed a rational and not an existential mode;
- They adopted a negative attitude towards the African worldview and spirituality which they evangelized by disparaging it as demonic and to be abandoned through repentance instead of an incarnational gospel;
- Most converts were not theologians since they were converted through the education provided by the "singing" schools that the missionary established. Therefore, they became denominational Christians depending on which school they "sung" from;
- The word theology was limited to those doing ministerial work and not to converts as disciples. It still remains unknown to many Christians who have been exposed to many other forms of knowledge;
- While reformers encouraged all to know theology by translating the Bible in the vernacular their catechesis was narrowly focused and did not become a culture. Rote learning was encouraged since few could read.
- When African scholars assumed the task of doing theology, it remained in the academy and did not trickle down to the members in the pew. It belonged to the theological guilds in the academy as was the case in the West. Ministers and priests resorted to moralizing in their sermons and used little theological thought.
- Even when the laity assumed the kerygmatic task, they engaged in proof-texting and allegorical hermeneutics guided by a gospel of good works; they sung short and emotional songs, and engaged in magical styles of prayer by shouting mantras and given formulas.
- Even though the Bible is narrative, poetic, prophetic, epistolary, and apocalyptic, theology has tended to be didactic and propositional on the one hand and dogmatic on the other.
- Theology lacked its own epistemology and became dependent on other epistemologies, for instance, rationalism, empiricism, even

romantic and philosophical perspectives have proved inappropriate.

- The biblical epistemologies of love founded on the Holy Spirit were relegated to the back burner as attention turned to tongue-speaking and miraculous healing.

Toward an Ecumenical Theology

Given the shifting demographics, African Christianity is being challenged to assume theological leadership on behalf of World Christianity. North Africa once led in this endeavour and impacted the rest of western Christianity. There is need for current day Augustines of Hippo, Cyprians of Carthage, Athanasiuses of Alexandria, and even the Arius, the heretic, to arise to the task of producing a relevant theology for Africa in the twenty-first century based on a relevant ontological and epistemological understanding of love and in relevant styles, be they through song, poetry, art, story, history, discourse. Even more, what is required is an ecumenical theological undertaking rather than a denominational one or one split between Protestant and Roman Catholics as it seems to be the case at the moment. This means that theologians have to deliberately read each other's theological productions and also engage each other. Therefore, there is need for the harmonizing and relating of theological and hermeneutical methodologies and narratives that engage the best insights from all camps.

Much theology has been generated by both Protestant and Roman Catholic camps. Some of the leading African theologians are: John Mbiti, Kwesi Dickson, John Pobee, Charles Nyamiti, Laurenti Magesa, Mercy Amba Oduyoye, James Amanze, Bishop Patrick Kalilombe, Jean-Marc Ela, Fabien Eboussi Boulaga, Engelbert Mveng, Benezet Bujo, Archbishop Desmond Tutu, Tinyiko Maluleke, Allan Boesak, Jesse Mugambi, Philomena Mwaura, Hannah Kinoti, Teresa Kamaara, Harvey Sindima, Isabel Phiri,

2. Umunthu Theology and a Paradigm Shift

Rachel NyaGondwe Fiedler, Klaus Fiedler, just to mention a few. The Paulines Publications of Africa have published a series consisting of three books on *African Theology: The Contribution of Pioneers* which cover the contribution of many theologians even though the majority are Roman Catholics. The series is a very useful resource for doing ecumenical theology in Africa. The Ecumenical Association of Third World Theologians (EATWOT) and its regional affiliates have done much to advance this ecumenical cross-fertilization in advancing contextual theologies. Their publications are a must read for anyone claiming to be doing theology contextually and ecumenically.

While many of us have written papers and dissertations, as well as giving presentations on various aspects of theology, none so far has produced a contextual systematic theology that engaged the African worldview in the context of modernity. There is need for systematic construction to inform the church and the catechetical instruction, if Christianity is to become a culture. Such a systematic theology would need to be interdisciplinary for it to be relevant to the African condition.

Unified Mindset

St. Paul admonished the Church in Philippi, "...complete my joy by being of same mind, having the same love, being in full accord and of one mind."[8] The model of that mind is the one that was in Christ Jesus. Theology might reclaim its status of being the Queen of the sciences, but not in a domineering manner in which it exercised that position in the past over other fields of knowledge. When theology is concerned with truth, it needs to understand that all truth belongs to God, is a characteristic of God, and is as wide and comprehensive as God's nature and love are. There is no one who has all the truth except God and Jesus who embodied it. When thought is captive to

---

[8] Philippians 2:2.

Christ, who claimed to be the truth, it becomes embodied, that is, a way of being and not simply a way of knowledge. This is why truth has to be spoken in love, that is, with integrity and no other way.[9] Hypocrisy is the essence of falsehood as an ontological reality and hence of sin. As such, truth communicates love, and love communicates truth, and both constitute freedom and not autonomy. St. Paul states, "But if anyone loves God, he is known by God,"[10] and also according to St. John such a person knows God. Love is mutual in its subjectivity and objectivity.

Here is the ontological and epistemological circle that I have devised. It states,

> To be is to live, to live is to participate in God, the I AM; to participate in God is to abide in Christ; to abide in Christ is to love; to love is to have umunthu (humanness); to have umunthu is to be wise; to be wise is to know; to know is to do; to do is serve; and to serve is to be responsible; to be responsible is to be free; to be free is to be a being in relation; and to be a being in relation is to be in a community-in-communion; to be a community-in-communion is to be related to the ancestors; to be related to the ancestors is to be related to the cosmos; and to be related to the cosmos is to find life in love and plenitude and at home in the cosmos with God and all things.

This is called ontological and epistemological because it has to do with our own being as to its integrity in the widest sense of that term and directs us to love as the source of all knowledge of life and our existence in the cosmos. Love binds the heart and the head. Thoughts and desires originate from the heart and are processed in the head, and then acted on by the body. Neither life nor knowledge begin with us, but are a gift to us from the one who is the source. As such they are both mysteries that only God can reveal to humanity in whose

---

[9] Ephesians 4:14-16.
[10] 1 Corinthians 8:3.

2. Umunthu Theology and a Paradigm Shift

image we are created and given a capacity to love freely and to know. This is why the Psalmist declares,

> The heavens declare the glory of God, and the sky above proclaims his handiwork. ² Day to day pours out speech, and night to night reveals knowledge. ³ There is no speech, nor are there words, whose voice is not heard. ⁴ Their voice goes out through all the earth, and their words to the end of the world.[11]

God uses his creation to manifest his glory and our scientific study of the same should lead us to declare the glory of God. What we call the marvels of nature are what God has created, and to limit our wonder to these is to engage in idolatry, the worship of the creature instead of the Creator. Psalm 19 ends with the praise of God's word. Revelation in nature and in the Law reinforce each other as two sides of the same coin. St Paul denounces the separation of nature and God's truth when he tells the Romans:

> For the wrath of God is revealed from heaven against all ungodliness and unrighteousness of men, who by their unrighteousness suppress the truth. ¹⁹For what can be known about God is plain to them, because God has shown it to them. ²⁰For his invisible attributes, namely, his eternal power and divine nature, have been clearly perceived, ever since the creation of the world, in the things that have been made. So they are without excuse. ²¹ For although they knew God, they did not honour him as God or give thanks to him, but they became futile in their thinking, and their foolish hearts were darkened.[12]

To deny the reality of God on account of the scientific method is to be futile in one's thinking, to worship the creature instead of the Creator, and to be without excuse for prostituting one's rational abilities to an idol.

---

[11] Psalm 19:1-4.
[12] Romans 1:18-21.

Therefore, the Enlightenment's definition of the limits of knowledge as being determined by rationality proves to be not only terribly limited in its application for grasping the truth, but also totally mistaken and idolatrous, through failing to be grasped by it in love. The Sadducees used the rational route to find fault with Jesus on the matter of the resurrection. Jesus said to them, "You are wrong, because you neither know the Scriptures nor the power of God."[13] They did not have truth on their side since that truth begins with the knowing the Scriptures, and the Scriptures testify to the power of God. The Holy Spirit provides the epistemological key to even rationally understanding the Scriptures and knowing the power of God. Without the Holy Spirit, rationality becomes very limited in leading to truth and, more often than not, distorts it.

The Enlightenment bifurcates the mind and the heart, making the mind the source of thought that then struggles with the desires of the heart to make sense of life. Following the Hebrew Scriptures from which we learn that humanity is created in the image of God in love, through love, with love, by love, and for love, the love encounter is the means to knowledge of both God, humanity, the environment, and to see it as the energy of the cosmos.

- Ontologically, we are loving-beings and this describes our life, our meaning, and our existence;
- As a result, this, epistemologically, love constitutes our self-knowledge, knowledge of others, and knowledge of the environment and our central place in the cosmos.
- Love further constitutes our freedom and not our autonomy; and consequently, we become moral beings accountable to ourselves, to others, to our environment and to God;
- We finally become social beings forming a community-in-communion.

---

[13] Matthew 22:29.

Therefore, love is what humanizes us and has its dwelling in our hearts which is the source of our thoughts, desires and feelings. These are executed by our minds through faith, reason and experience before it becomes wisdom resulting into love again. This way to knowledge transcends the rational and empirical paths to knowledge to which the Enlightenment has made us captive.

New Theological Paradigm

There is need for a paradigm shift in our view of humanity and epistemology with a view to attain a unity or universe of all knowledge. It is a shift from scientific rationalism to a divine scientific ontology through love, revelation, faith, and wisdom. The fear of Yahweh is wisdom and to turn away from evil is understanding.[14] While the Greeks, like the Hebrews, started with the love of wisdom (philosophy) they lost it when mathematics and logic became the touchstone of truth, and not speaking or doing the truth in love. Western philosophy followed suit and distorted western theology in the process. The new theological paradigm has to attend to the following:

(a) Umunthu Theological Perspective

Umunthu or humanness is a critical existential aspect of the essence of our humanity within the African cultural context which the Bible describes as being made in the image of God. It defines the African self-definition and self-understanding in relation to integrity, wisdom, economic productivity, social solidarity and justice, and being a community in communion. However, like all humanity, such an understanding has remained an ideal on account of the evil human heart or eye. The humanness of Jesus as one full of grace, truth and godliness spells authentic humanness that redeems African humanity

---

[14] Job 28:28.

from its failure to attain authentic umunthu. Therefore, uMunthu is authentic humanness as seen in the face of Jesus the Christ who called himself Son of Man. In Jesus we have the incarnate divinity and umunthu. The umunthu of Jesus is the foundation of umunthu theology. Since Jesus came into our worldview with a view to redeeming and fulfilling it, umunthu theology must engage that worldview, but in an interdisciplinary way.

(b) Incarnational Knowledge

By his incarnation God in Christ communicates to us in our own context, that is, our worldview with the purpose of enlightening it in love and truth and fulfilling it with abundant living. Jesus declares his mission in this way,

> For the law was given by Moses; grace and truth came through Jesus Christ. No one has ever seen God; the only one who is at the Father's side, he has made him known.[15]

Jesus who is God's communicative Word came into our environment to make the Father perfectly known.[16] This being the case then, we need to begin our theological reflection with our worldview into which he comes with a view to redemptively fulfil and not to abolish it. To all who receive him and believe in his name, they become children of God, his Father.[17] The mistake made by missionary Christianity was to try to abolish the cultural world with the manger into which Jesus was to be born. He was born in a place smelling of manure as all cultures are. The missionaries made the African worldview with its manure of no use and actually discarded it even though Jesus could not discard it, but rather sought to fulfil it in the

---

[15] John 1:18.
[16] Matthew 11:27.
[17] John 1:12.

same way he restored and fulfilled tax-collectors and sinners to righteousness.[18]

(c) The African Worldview

I want to propose that the African worldview should be required of all disciplines in our universities as a foundational course. It is important to start our university studies knowing who we are with a view to serving our people better.

- The African worldview is human-centred and not God-centred. God is at the periphery overarching all creation. Therefore, God cannot be only at the centre (theocentric) since he is also the same God of the periphery; and the God at the periphery is the same at the centre.

- At the heart of that human existence is uMunthu who is with God (God with us) consisting of love, integrity and wisdom on the one hand; he is engaged in economic productivity, social solidarity and being community-in-communion within historical and cosmic existence on the other.

- Biblical revelation, authority, epistemology, and hermeneutics in dialogue with the African worldview in order to come up with contextual theology. The difference between natural and biblical theology, that is, revelation from below and from above (Emil Brunner vs. Karl Barth).

- Therefore, inter-disciplinary theological studies are the only methodology for engaging theological thought with a view to adequately covering our cosmic knowledge and understanding in our relationship with God.

- The entry point has to be our worldview into which God is made incarnate and how that leads to its fulfilment into blessed development. One dimension of this blessed development is that of human eternal security or salvation.

---

[18] Matthew 5:17.

Critical and Blessed Interdisciplinary Theological Development Studies

Jesus defined his mission as having come so that humanity may have life and have it in all its fullness[19] and the fullness of life had to do with human existential meaning and eternal security from within history and beyond the grave. It is this need felt by every human being that he came to fulfil. The Bible touches on every aspect of our lives like no other body of knowledge and hence its theology is capable of touching on every field of knowledge in the cosmos and thus contributing to their development and relevance.

According to the African worldview and the biblical narrative, humanity is the crown of creation, the face of creation, the voice of creation, and has a priestly role on behalf of all creation. Humanity is capable of using all knowledge to worship and glorify God. Humanity is created in God's image out of love, in love, with love, through love, for love; humanity is a spiritual being having been inbreathed by the living breath of God; humanity is a gendered being, that is, a sexual being who is male and female. Therefore, human sexuality and spirituality are two sides of the same coin and they define each other. The basic education appropriate for our humanity has to do with our self-knowledge and that of God, and the context that defines us. The critical question is: What is the most appropriate theological education for a humanity created in the image of God in love and for love? It is to discover and know what that image means and its purposes in human existence and history. Since the Bible touches on every aspect of human knowledge, theology that is relevant can only be inter-disciplinary. This is how theology came to be called the Queen of all sciences, that is, all knowledge. However, from a love epistemology in which the Holy Spirit plays a critical role, dogmatism has to give way to an open encounter with truth, which is Christ

---

[19] John 10:10.

himself, since all truth is God's truth, and also give way to the teaching of the Holy Spirit.

Below are proposals for inter-disciplinary theological modules for a new paradigm in theological education that takes the African worldview and context, the love epistemology and the role of the Holy Spirit, and the inter-disciplinary orientation seriously.

Theology and Inter-disciplinary Modules

1. Theology, African worldview, and traditions of wisdom
2. Theology, African Literature, self-knowledge and understanding
3. Theology, African history, and Historical agency
4. Theology, economics, and stewardship of creation
5. Theology, African development studies, and blessed development
6. Theology as a science, scientific methodology and practice, (Research and revelation)
7. Theology, technology, and human existence
8. Theology, educational philosophy, policy, and practice
9. Theology, psycho-sociology, and community formation
10. Theology, medical healing and ethics (Securing physical life)
11. Theology, business, marketing, and business ethics
12. Theology, mathematics, and accounting
13. Theology, gender studies, and umunthu
14. Theology, cultural studies, communication
15. Theology, management, governance and politics
16. Theology, legal and moral philosophy
17. Theology, design and creative arts.

The mainstreaming of theology into other fields of knowledge conforms to the Reformed understanding of education; redeems and sanctifies other fields of knowledge; and could contribute to the national struggle with corrupt practices while building communities of integrity in which humanity plays its priestly role on behalf of all creation.

Chapter 3

Theological Research and Publication

Klaus Fiedler

> "Research makes a University to be a University. Otherwise it is just a dignified Secondary School."
>
> *Landson Mbango, Vice Chancellor of Mzuzu University, 2009*

1. Research is the Privilege of the University

In Germany, when a Professor is called to any chair, she is required to represent the subject "in research and teaching." It is research that defines the work of a professor, and research defines the work of any university. Research is not an additional duty to teaching, but research is what makes (university level) teaching possible. So doing research is a privilege, for professor, lecturer and student alike,[1] and teaching based on one's own research makes it attractive.[2]

1.1 A Long Tradition of Research

Not speaking of China and Ancient Egypt, when we look for the origins of Western education, the history of research can be said to have started in the House of Wisdom in Baghdad (c. 820), where the incoming Arab Muslim culture absorbed the classical Greek (and

---

[1] When I came to Makerere as an occasional student, I was fascinated that even undergraduate students, during their holidays, could do research.
[2] Dr Louise Pirouet's lectures on Ugandan Church History based on her local research made me to become a mission historian, not a general missiologist. And when Dr John Mbiti presented his "African Concept of Time," he had all the details at his fingertips.

some Indian) knowledge through translation and started building on it with ever new research.

In 970 this led to the foundation of the first university, Al-Azhar in Cairo, followed by Timbuktu University in Mali. The great process of transmission of Arab Muslim learning to Christian Western Europe did not take place in Egypt or in Mali, but in Spain, where a number of universities developed that preserved the classical Greek knowledge and where new research was done. Muslim Spain excelled in academic freedom, as it welcomed Christian students. They came from all over Western Europe, appreciating the Greek Philosophers (especially Aristotle) through their Arabic translations,[3] and when the Christian universities in Western Europe were founded, the first textbooks were translations and adaptations from the Arabic.[4]

When Muslim learning declined, Western Europe took the lead in creating new knowledge, and we are all aware what universities like Cambridge, Aberdeen or Oxford meant and mean to us, with their university presses for the dissemination of knowledge.

From there Western education found a home in Africa, first at Fourah Bay in 1827 (affiliated to Durham 1876-1967) then in other places like Makerere (1949).[5]

So Western (originally Arabic) learning came to Africa, and we are grateful for that, and equally so for all the research Western scholars

---

[3] They also appreciated paper (learned from the Chinese) and the decimal system (found in India).

[4] For an overview of the translation and transmission process see Klaus Fiedler, *Islamology II* (ODL Module), Mzuzu University, 2010. For a thorough treatment see Phillip K. Hitti, *History of the Arabs*, 1937 and many later editions. There is a free download of the 10th edition.

[5] I had the privilege of studying two years at Makerere in the 1960s, where I got the best part of my education, so that I became a researcher and a scholar, of which, after my studies in Germany, I had neither idea nor plan.

3. Theological Research and Publication

(many missionaries among them) did on the continent in those days of Western contact.[6]

1.2 The Need for Theological Research in Malawi

1.2.1 There is a Good Base

We are deeply grateful for the contribution of our forebears, and therefore it is now time that we make our own contribution to (worldwide) knowledge through our own research, and the way to decolonize education is not to oppose Oxford, Aberdeen or London, but to make our own contribution, and that starts with local research, of which there is already quite a good base.

1. The first local contribution to research was done by giving local information to the classical scholars in the Malawi context like Shepperson, McCracken, Langworthy, Schoffeleers and so many others. They appreciated the local information, but they were all foreigners, working for universities in the Global North. We are grateful for their work, as they laid the foundation.

2. In the field of theology, a further contribution to knowledge was made by Malawian theologians studying abroad.[7] Here names like Handwell Hara, Silas Ncozana, J.C. Chakanza and Isabel Phiri easily come to mind. To study abroad is an on-going process, and depending on the circumstances, the contribution to *Malawian* knowledge varies.

---

[6] A shining example of such research is: D.C. Scott, *A Cyclopaedic Dictionary of the Mang'anja Language*, Edinburgh: Foreign Missions Committee of the Church of Scotland, 1892. This research was led by Scott, but done with many local collaborators.

[7] The very first Malawian to be awarded a doctorate was Fr Harry Chikuse, who completed his doctoral thesis on, "The Validity of Banthu Marriage" at the Theological Faculty of the Pontifical Urban Athenaeum of the Propagation of the Faith, Rome, in 1944.

3. The History Department at Chancellor College strongly emphasized research by both undergraduate students and staff. 245 such papers were presented from 1969 to 1984, maybe 15-20% of them on religious history.[8] No MA programme was in view at that time, but much historical knowledge was generated and has been preserved.[9]

4. Another institution to generate local knowledge was the Diploma Board (later Board for Theological Studies) that related church owned theological training institutions to the University of Malawi through the Department of TRS. Dissertations completed under the BTS are preserved in the respective colleges and more use could be made of them, as many retain solid primary information.[10] These papers need to be secured, catalogued and made accessible.

5. The same applies to the undergraduate research done at the universities, at Chancellor College since 1988, then at Mzuzu University and after that at all the new universities. There is an electronic collection of over 300 papers so far, which has been proven to be highly valuable for further research, but much more should be made available.[11]

6. In the early 1990s, the Department of TRS at Chancellor College started to develop its postgraduate programmes, both MA and PhD. Up to 1995 the whole University of Malawi had graduated three PhDs, so it was easy for TRS to take the lead university wide.

---

[8] A similar situation prevails in the *Society of Malawi Journal*, which has been publishing much in history over the last 74 years.

[9] The papers are preserved in Chancellor College, and a few of them even found their way into the Library of Congress.

[10] I am aware of one publication of such papers: J.C. Chakanza (ed), *Initiation Rites for Boys in Lomwe Society and other Essays*, Zomba: Kachere, 2005.

[11] A BTh from Livingstonia was developed into a book: Kelly Bwalya, *The Life of Dr Wyson Moses Kauzobafa Jele. Missionary to Zambia*, Mzuzu: Mzuni Press, 2017. More should be developed in this way.

3. Theological Research and Publication 57

By 2010 the Department had produced ten PhDs, of which eight have been published.

7. Since 2007 Mzuzu University has been active in postgraduate studies. By now it has produced ten PhDs[12] and four are under examination. During the past decade Chancellor College produced one PhD in Old Testament Ethics. There should be more universities with a PhD programme in Theology.

8. More universities have been doing research at Master's level. Chancellor College started and Mzuzu University followed. But there are also Master's programmes at University of Livingstonia (MTh in Theology and Development), at African Bible College (MA in Christian Leadership), at Catholic University, Blantyre Synod University, and at Malawi Assemblies of God University. Publishing of MAs remains insufficient, I am aware of 10 Chancellor College MAs that have been published, of the 20 Mzuni MAs so far only two are published and one is in the process.

1.2.2. (Much) more Research is Needed

There is a good base, much has been achieved, and Theology and Religious Studies seem to be ahead of other disciplines. Let us use this base not as a point of rest, but as a point of departure. Though research is not confined to the universities, we are grateful to have them, as most research is university related. We are also grateful that in Malawi there are many who are qualified to do research, at all levels,[13] and that there are qualified supervisors to guide and develop them.

1.3. A Significant Local Contribution – Worldwide

With such a good base, let us develop more research to contribute to the progress of Theology in Malawi and beyond. Let our research be

---

[12] Six of them published by 2020.
[13] Foreigners are very welcome to make their contribution as well.

local, but let it also match the international standards and let it be a contribution to knowledge in Malawi and to World Christianity.

1. Develop a new generation of researchers
2. Fill the many gaps that are still to be researched.[14]
3. Develop new perspectives:
   a. Emphasize the local perspective in (history and all other) research.
   b. Emphasize the female side of research.
   c. Emphasize a bottom-up approach to research.
4. Make the curricula research based.
5. Make the curricula locally oriented.

2. The Long View: From Research to Publication

If you want to do major research, be it for a thesis or otherwise, breathe deeply, be grateful for the privilege of research, *and take the long view*. You want to make a unique contribution to knowledge, and that is worth all the effort and all the joy.

2.1 Choice of Topic

There are different ways to find a topic: I found my first field of research from the various sources Prof Noel Q. King had acquainted me with, not for the thesis, but as a contribution to the work of the

---

[14] Some come to my mind: Study of the Roman Catholic Sisters, Brothers and Catechists; Study of the many Pentecostal Churches so far unresearched; Study of the Greek Orthodox Church in Malawi; Histories of various dioceses; Histories of the "New Missions" like Church of the Nazarene, or Evangelical Lutheran Church.

On the BA level: Studies of major congregations; Study of Church Music; Studies in Church Architecture; The Religion of the White Tribe(s) in Malawi; Missionary/Church Medicine Education in the Roman Catholic Church; Special Needs Education --- and so much more!!!

3. Theological Research and Publication 59

Department at Makerere. So available sources and good access to them is a good reason to do research. Another approach is the wish to make a contribution to knowledge about the community to which you belong.[15]

The all-important issue are the sources. Check that you have enough and that you can get access to them. And these sources must be primary sources appropriate for your research.

Research must be precise. Therefore, the topic must be small enough so that you can dig deep, but it must also be broad enough so that it can carry the weight of (maybe) a PhD.[16]

Also consider the usefulness of your research. If you are a lecturer in New Testament, it may be best to do research in New Testament, not in Church History, unless you want to broaden your capabilities.

There is sometimes the idea that it is good to write an MA on a topic, and then develop the same topic into a PhD. That is technically possible, but the few examples I have examined make me strongly advise not to attempt to go that way.

But you may consider the possibility of upgrading: You start as an MA student, and when you have advanced sufficiently, the supervisor my recommend and the university agree that you do not get an MA but proceed to PhD directly, developing your MA research

---

[15] For my research on the Faith Missions, I had the advantage of being an insider and of having an understanding of relevant issues. So I decided to find out which ecclesiology missions have that by definition are *inter*denominational.

[16] "Church and Politics" in Malawi would be too broad a topic, but maybe the "Seventh-day Adventist Church and Politics under One Party Rule" could be an MA topic, and a PhD could cover all SDA history and politics in Malawi.

accordingly.[17] If you see upgrading as a possibility, make sure that your MA topic is big enough for a PhD.

2.2 Deep Primary Research

This is the key for any thesis, for any contribution to knowledge. Here are some pieces of advice, maybe not in systematic order, but taken from real life.

1. Once a student told me: "My research is difficult, nothing has been published on that topic." I tried to explain to him that this is the privilege of research: to work with all the primary sources. I am not sure if I was successful. A few times I received mail from a student studying abroad: "I am starting my research now, please send me literature published in Malawi." Of course, I sent, but you cannot do research based on published material, and if universities abroad allow that, they miss the point.

2. Get *all* available primary sources. It is good to write chapter one with all the technicalities, from the researcher's position to aim and objectives, at the beginning, but then stop writing and start collecting. (For my Heidelberg PhD I worked nearly three years full time collecting information, without ever writing a line of the thesis.) And if you write on Nkhoma Synod, get all the Afrikaans sources. Overall follow this rule: "You must collect 10 times as much as you can put into your thesis."

3. While you are collecting the material, start planning for the dissertation by *envisaging it*. While you collect, look at the materials, read widely, and gradually certain themes will emerge. Structure your thesis along these findings, not along a theoretical proposal.

---

[17] I went through upgrading to my PhD. I know of one such case at the University of Malawi: Ian Dicks, "Towards an Understanding of a Muslim Amachinga Yawo Worldview," 2008 (Ian Dicks, *An African Worldview. The Muslim Amachinga Yawo of Southern Malawi*, Zomba: Kachere, 2012).

3. Theological Research and Publication 61

4. Use oral sources to complement written sources. Conversations with descendants may well give you new insights on the people you find in the archives, and informal conversations with participants in an event may well clarify attitudes better than the minutes. If combined with participant observation, oral information can even be useful on its own.[18]

5. Beware of the questionnaire. Questionnaires are deceptive as they usually gather opinions, not facts. In addition, many answer a questionnaire as they write an examination. In religious research the usefulness of questionnaires is limited. They can be of *some* use when perceptions are to be explored, but in most cases participation, informal conversations and maybe some open-ended interviews where the interviewee never sees the written questions get better and truer results.

6. Go there. Whenever possible, go to the places where your story is or was playing out. You may not get much detailed information there, but you will get better understanding. If you look into history, find the old churches, visit the graveyards and try to find the descendants of important players in your story. If you study Practical Theology, go to live with the people you study, participate and observe.

7. Go to the other end: *Emma DeLany comes to Blantyre*: Find out who she was *before* she came to PIM (and when she returns to the USA, find out what she did thereafter). Also find out what kind of a denomination the National Baptist Convention, Inc. is in America (and how it differs from other Baptist denominations there.)

8. Or take the *Salamanca Education For All Conference 1994* (Get to know enough about it, what it intended and in what context it

---

[18] For a thesis and a book based largely on oral sources, observation and participation, see Hany Longwe, *Identity by Dissociation. A History of the Achewa Providence Industrial Mission*, Mzuzu: Mzuni Press, 2013.

wanted to replace Special Needs Education by Inclusive Education, then find out how that influenced Malawi).

9. Preserve documents if you find them. This starts with your notes. If you are lucky, like Mark Thiesen, you may find four folders of missionary correspondence. They were in poor keeping, he got permission to photocopy them, thus saving them for further research.

10. Your research is of necessity qualitative. Even if you use some statistics, compile a few tables, and add up some numbers, that is not quantitative research. (When a student in a viva claimed that he had used qualitative and quantitative methods, a lecturer challenged him by enumerating the various quantitative methods, and the student had to admit that he had no idea. Nor had I.)

11. If you want to learn from other disciplines, do not go to Social Sciences, but to Social Anthropology, which emphasizes participation, observation, staying together over an extended period, and collecting oral information to produce a "thick description" of social reality.

2.3 Good Control and Use of Secondary Sources

1. Use solid secondary sources for background and context

If you deal, for example, with Livingstonia, base it on John McCracken, *Politics and Christianity in Malawi 1875 – 1940. The Impact of the Livingstonia Mission in the Northern Province*, Zomba: Kachere, ²2008 not on D.D. Phiri's *History of Malawi* and its chapter "The Missionaries." It is a good textbook but it is a tertiary source, based on the secondary sources others produced.

2. Know a good deal of the secondary sources around your area of research

You must be aware of everything that has been written on your subject within Malawi. For outside secondary sources you need to be selective, know enough to relate your research to the on-going argument in the wider academic world. Include under secondary sources unpublished dissertations.

3. Know a good deal of unpublished research in Malawi related to your field

I have a database of about 300 BA dissertations, MA and PhD modules and similar material, but there are many more at the theological institutions, and I hope that one day there will be a National Registry of Theological Research.

4. Not "Literature Review" but "Current State of Research"

These two terms look like covering a similar area, but I prefer Current State of Research, as (1) it includes unpublished literature, knowledge of which is crucial for any new research and (2) it focusses the presentation: Do not just list the books that are there, but show what relationship they have to your research. (3) Include the *few* general books that you intend to relate to specifically in your research, and explain not what is in them but how you want to use them. (4) Do not include all the different pieces of literature that you may use, they will only be mentioned where you use them in the text. (5) Make the presentation of the Current State of Research *attractive by making it short and to the point*. (6) Do not put in any factual information from the books you use [that can be done in the text], but what they yield to your research and how you want to use them, e.g. for the background, for comparison, for a theological framework or for detailed information on a specific aspect.

2.4 Write your Thesis

1. Before I started my research, Louise Pirouet told me: "Klaus, you write a PhD, but in reality you write a book, *so write your thesis as a book*." I am glad that I got this advice early. This is the long view.

The research must yield a contribution to knowledge, and that must be published, and a book is the right way to do this.

2. *Use the final referencing rules from the beginning.* Since you write your thesis as a book, it makes sense to adopt the final writing and referencing style right from the start. We demand a one-page style, with footnotes. Endnotes and bracket references are not allowed. *We insist on footnotes since we want the sources and any other references to be taken seriously.*[19] This referencing style has been codified as Chicago-Mzuni style.[20] The printed page in a dissertation is usually bigger and more generously spaced than in a book, so the *typestyles* must change, but when typestyles are consistently applied in a thesis, to change them for the book is a simple job.[21]

3. Do not follow the common Social Sciences approach: 1. Introduction 2. Literature review 3. Methods 4. Finding 5. Discussion of Findings 6. Summary, Conclusions and Recommendations. This approach is dangerous as too much emphasis is put on theoretical issues and on the literature review. I read an MA, not in Theology, from a British university, up to page 60 I was still waiting for the research, and the whole thesis had less than 100 pages. This approach puts too much emphasis on technicalities and theories, and the result then is not a book, but an academic exercise or maybe a research report.

---

[19] Bracket references make light of sources! (Who looks up in the bibliography what Miller, 1984b:52 means?) And in APA style, if it is not a citation, you just write Miller 2020. Even if any reader wants to check, there is no way.

[20] For the referencing styles, see Hany Longwe, *Academic Research and Writing in Theology and Religious Studies*, Mzuzu: Mzuni Press, 2016, 31-33. Note that this book contains much more usable advice for writing a dissertation than these three pages. (Hany Longwe uses the old name "Kachere Style" instead of "Chicago-Mzuni Style.")

[21] Recommended typestyles for a dissertation are: Normal, Quotation, Bibliography, Footnotes and three (maximum four) levels of Headings. MS Word provides these and they can easily be redefined according to circumstances and requirements.

4. Instead: Put all the technical issues into Chapter 1. Many universities require such a Chapter One (sometimes in form of a proposal),[22] so you better write it, but do not forget: Once we publish the dissertation, chapter one will be discarded and replaced by a general introduction of maybe 2 pages, to attract the readers, not to bore them off.

"Introduction" is the only chapter that has a "technical" heading. All the other chapters have substantial headings, developed from the research you have done.[23] If written in this way, your Thesis can be published easily, discard Chapter One,[24] write a new Introduction and check the rest for readability etc.

5. Chapter 2 can be the background chapter, which is not based on your own research but on good secondary sources. Henry Church wrote on the history of the Free Methodist Church in Malawi and Theological Education, so his chapter 2 was about Methodism in general and how it found its way to Africa. If you have much theoretical discussion, that could also be chapter 2.[25]

---

[22] I wrote two PhDs, for Dar es Salaam and Heidelberg universities, but both neither required a proposal or a (technical) chapter one. I never produced a literature review either, but both dissertations and the books resulting from them books show that I was in command of the literature.

[23] I recommend this even for the last chapter, often called "Conclusion." Better make it a substantive chapter, which portrays major findings, and avoid repetitions. In writing that final chapter, end with a bang, not with a whimper.

[24] Anything important from Chapter One can be put at appropriate places, but in a non-technical way. A few sentences about the researcher and her motivation can be included in the new general introduction, even a sentence or two about the motivation and maybe about the aim, again in a non-technical but narrative way.

[25] An example here is Wezi Makuni Gondwe. Her background chapter is: "The Last Church of God and His Christ as an 'African Independent Church" in which she discusses major typologies of African Independent Churches, finding them often not suitable to Malawi (Wezi Makuni Gondwe, *A History of the Last Church of God and His Christ in Malawi from 1916 to 2015*, Mzuzu: Mzuni Press, 2018, 8-26.)

6. From chapter three onwards you are alone with your sources. You know what others do not know, and you are finding new knowledge that is unique in the world. That is the blessing, privilege and beauty of research.

7. How many chapters? There is no prescribed number or pattern.[26] Structure the thesis from what you are finding into chapters with substantive headings. I have supervised good PhDs with six chapters, but also an equally good one with 13. There is also no prescription on length. A good estimate for an MA is to start with 40,000 words and for a PhD with 80,000.[27] But depending on the topic less may be sufficient, or more may be required, often so in fields like History. Do not worry about the number of words, but avoid being *wordy*. A thesis can be long, but must never be *lengthy*.

8. *Do not get stuck in chapter one!* Supervisors may think that a solid chapter one/proposal is a precondition for a quality dissertation. This is a systematic argument that does not match life. The demand to read five books on how to write a literature review may be well intended, but will delay and frustrate the student, so it is easy to get stuck in Chapter 1 for a long time. It is better to follow those supervisors who see chapter 1 as something that is written concurrently with the research.[28] And a note to supervisors: Your task is not to frustrate students, but to guide and (ultimately) promote them.

9. After writing (or not even writing all of) Chapter 1, do not just write Chapter 2, but start **envisioning** the thesis. (This is best and most

---

[26] Louise Pirouet advised us that all chapters (except Introduction and Conclusion) should be of *broadly* equal length, and when I presented a chapter of two pages to Professor Kimambo, he simply cut it out.

[27] When you make your computer count the words, include footnotes and bibliography, but exclude any appendices.

[28] I expect students to formulate early the aim and objectives, and maybe a hypothesis, and I rarely allow them to write a literature review until much later (but I insist that they know and *use* the literature.)

3. Theological Research and Publication

easily done in a series of close conversations with the supervisor.) Important: The supervisor must find out early if the topic of research is viable, if the student can go deep enough and that the topic is sufficiently big for the thesis.

10. Write the thesis not based on the proposal **but develop it from the findings**. (When I started my theses, I had no idea what I would find, so a proposal would have been quite poor.)[29]

11. *Avoid ideological overload.* It is sometimes good to have a Theoretical Framework, but let it not dominate you. As external examiner I have read a few dissertations on Malawi where I had the feeling that a (preconceived) idea dominated the thesis, and that the facts were aligned to support that thesis. I passed the dissertations because the students had worked a lot (under supervision), but I did not recommend the theses to be published.

12. *Objectivity?* No research is objective. To account for this we include the heading "My position as the researcher." For the same reason we do encourage to write in personal "I" style. Terms like "the present researcher" etc must be avoided, but even if you want to write "objective thesis style", make sure that it does not camouflage your subjectivity.

But: while we cannot achieve objectivity, we must make sure that the facts are correctly represented, that footnotes give the sources (correctly), that facts are not subordinated to "higher" ideas, and that your interpretations are clearly distinguishable from the presented facts.

13. Avoid (all kinds of) plagiarism, at all levels: (1) Plagiarism means copying someone's text without acknowledgment. Such conscious

---

[29] I found that in the early interdenominational Faith Missions the position of women was quite advanced compared to other missions, but that it declined after 1900, in line with the decline of the holiness theology in the Faith Missions (and that some specific missions did not share in this decline). I had no idea about that, so in a proposal I would not have looked for that.

plagiarism is stealing and deserves to be punished. Don't even try. (2) Less immoral and maybe just careless is giving somebody's ideas without acknowledging the source. So take your footnotes seriously![30] (3) Do not even copy yourself! If you have said something once, do not repeat. And if one piece of anecdotal evidence fits two places, you cannot use it twice.

3. Supervisors and their Students

Do not Frustrate your Students!

Delay in answering is probably the most common complaint. Of course, supervisors are (or at least should be) busy people, teaching their students, doing research and representing their chosen field in the academy. But this does not allow a supervisor to make a student wait for weeks (or even months) to get a reply on a chapter submitted.[31] These are the core duties of supervisors, listed in ascending order.

1. *Correct the students*: This is the starting point. And the supervisor should not be slow in marking any text. [It is *not sufficient* for the supervisor to reply: "the chapter is ok, continue with the next." Even a good student needs the supervisor's *detailed* attention, even to mark the small mistakes, which are inevitably there.[32]

---

[30] Don't be hypersensitive. There is no need to give a source for what is common knowledge (like the year of Malawi's independence). And everything that you have moved through and moulded in your mind is yours and does not need a source. (But sometimes it may be good to give a hint on what or who moulded your ideas.)

[31] The worst case I heard from a South African university was that the doctoral supervisor had not replied after a year. That made the student change the supervisor, the university and the research topic.

[32] Students in turn must not abuse a supervisor by submitting sloppy work. I found much sloppiness in orthography and grammar, and much more in referencing. It is not the supervisor's task to get your references straight, If a submitted text is too careless, I send it back without dealing with the contents.

3. Theological Research and Publication

2. *Guide the students*. The supervisor's responsibility is not just to react to submissions by the students, but to guide them on the way, e.g. to draw attention to missed sources, to opportunities to explore, to avoid the pitfalls of generalization etc.

3. *Develop the students:* That is the most important task. Develop them to their fullest potential. The potential differs from student to student, but get the best out of each of them.[33]

4. *Crowning Glory* or *Starting Point*. Louise Pirouet told me that a PhD is a strange thing: For some it is the highest achievement, finalizing it all. For others it is the beginning, and the starting from where they can do so many things.[34] She implied that I should follow the "starting point" pattern.

5. *"Supervision is the Art of the Possible"*. Like Christian Counselling, supervision is not to develop from a pinnacle of truth, but to achieve what is possible. As supervisors we must admit that not every MA is a credit, we must accept that there are also some who just pass, but make sure that your students reach the highest possible level.

6. *Get along with your supervisor:* That is a necessary part of getting your degree. So don't complain about everything. As a student you have

---

[33] Rachel Banda, then not my wife nor related to me, as my student still obeyed me. When she had done her research on the position of Baptist women in Southern Malawi and had written the history of Umodzi wa Amayi there, I felt that she would get an MA for that, but I told her to add a chapter on marriage, and when she had done that, a chapter on preparing girls for marriage. The MA was published as: Rachel NyaGondwe Banda, *Women of Bible and Culture. Baptist Convention Women in Southern Malawi*, Zomba: Kachere, 2006, and Rachel NyaGondwe Fiedler, *Coming of Age. A Christianized Initiation among Women in Southern Malawi*, Zomba: Kachere, 2005.

[34] We should not despise the "crowning glory" approach. Fritz Haus finished his PhD when he was 80. He died a few years later, but he had made a contribution to knowledge, now published as: Fritz Haus, *Carl Hugo and Mary Gutsche and the "German" Baptists of the Eastern Cape*, Mzuzu: Luviri Press, 2019.

the right to "push" your supervisor, to remind him, to get the most out of him. This attitude, different from ideals of African culture, will solve many problems. But if there are serious problems, seek a solution through the postgraduate coordinator, and that may include a change of supervisor or a topic. And if the postgraduate coordinator is the supervisor, you may appeal to the Head of Department.

4. Publish your Research

4.1 The Moral Obligation

As a researcher you gather information from many sources, and you are obliged to return the favour. You may be able to give every archive a copy, but you cannot give one to each interviewee. So publish the research as a book that is available in Malawi *at a reasonable price*. There are famous thesis publishers in America and Europe, but if they sell a copy of your book for 74 $US (plus postage), *you have published in nowhere*, and in no way fulfilled your moral obligation. So publish with a Malawian publisher or with a publisher abroad who can make sufficient copies available in Malawi at a reasonable price.

4.2 A Thesis Written as a Book

As a researcher you have the moral obligation not only to return the knowledge to those who gave it, but also to make your contribution to build up your branch of Theology. Learning, research and publishing all started long ago, and went the long way to come to you here. Now it is time to make your contribution to that never ending circle of knowledge.

4.3 Turn your Thesis into a Book

Start with this soon after the viva. Discard chapter 1, write a short general introduction, go through the text to find all the little things that may need your attention, and make the book ready for publication. Make sure that the text appeals to the "general, educated

3. Theological Research and Publication

and interested Malawian reader."[35] Discard background information that was required for or useful in your thesis, but may be of little value for any general reader or fellow scholar.

Then format the text on A5, and adjust pictures, table and charts accordingly.[36] Adjust the typestyles to the requirements of a book,[37] in cooperation with the publisher. After that you may add an index.[38]

Finally find the money. There are different schemes, depending on the publisher. A typical scheme is that the author (or their friends) has to pay upfront the printing costs for the first print-run of 100 copies.[39] For that the author receives 70 copies, to sell at any price.[40] Selling 50 copies usually brings back the capital invested, ready for the second print run. All books we publish here will also be made available through African Books Collective in Oxford for the Global North as Print on Demand books and as e-Books.[41] Current technology has made it possible that the dissertation you wrote in your little (or big) corner of Malawi will be available worldwide, no longer as a thesis, but as a book.

---

[35] High flying language is no sign of scholarly achievement, but of unfinished cooking.
[36] The page margins are: top 1.5 cm, bottom 1.45, left 1.8, right 1.8, and headers at 0.5 cm.
[37] Normal will still be Normal [typestyle], but it will not be 11/17 but probably 11/13.
[38] These days an index can be generated semi-automatically in MS-Word.
[39] That may be around 200,000 - 300,000 MK.
[40] One of your 70 copies goes to the National Archives as Legal Deposit.
[41] You may claim 20% of the income from ABC as yours.

4.4 Publish Derivatives

Do not rest on your glories once your book has reached the academic world. You are obliged to make contributions beyond that one book. Here are venues:

A reasonable PhD should yield at least 3 publishable articles of 6,000 words maximum each. Plan these early with your supervisor, write them while the external examiner reads your thesis, and publish them after that. An MA should at least yield 2 such articles. If you write Church History, contribute to the online *Dictionary of African Christian Bibliography*.[42]

Beyond that, consider producing a textbook, student guide, or reader, an ODL book or Lecture Notes, and don't be shy to contribute to Wikipedia.[43]

Also think of producing a booklet, like in the *Biographies of People and Parishes Series*[44] or as a help for Counselling.[45] If you have a suitable BA (or MA or PhD module), consider turning it into a booklet.[46]

Supervisors, on any level, keep publications in mind, as that helps to develop the full potential of a student.

---

[42] www.dacb.org.

[43] I am not advocating that you use Wikipedia as a source for your thesis, but that you help that people who use it find the required information and that it is correct.

[44] Like Handwell Yotamu Hara, *From Herdboy to University Lecturer*, Mzuzu: Mzuni Press, 2019.

[45] See Bonet Kamwela, *Married and no Sex Anymore. Mbulu as a Pastoral Problem in Mzimba in Northern Malawi*, Mzuzu: Luviri Press, 2019 or Bonet Kamwela, *Wererani kwa Chiuta Winu*, Mzuzu: Luviri Press, 2020. Both were written as a sideline to his MA research.

[46] Kelly Bwalya, *The Life of Dr Wyson Moses Kauzobafa Jele. Missionary to Zambia*, Mzuzu: Mzuni Press, 2017, is based on a University of Livingstonia BTh.

3. Theological Research and Publication

4.5 Promote Malawian Literature

There is much quest for an African Theology, and that includes Malawi. Such a Malawian Theology must start with publishing. If you want to promote African Theology, promote African publishing, understood as publishing in Malawi. Here are some recommended steps.

1. Buy Malawian books. (Publishing lives by sales…)
2. Fill the libraries with *local* books.
3. Use local books in your teaching.
4. Review the curriculum to make it more research based.[47]
5. Make writing book reports a requirement in your courses.[48]

5. Take the Long View again

Research and publishing is beautiful. We are standing in a tradition of centuries, let us now do our share and make our (local) contribution. So let us become a community of learners and researches, of teachers and publishers. With a worldwide mind let us do the local thing. Let us honour those who taught us, in person or by their books, by furthering scholarship where we are.

And if you are theologians, let us build up Malawian Theology. Not by writing a lonely thesis about it in Aberdeen or Edinburgh, but by doing and promoting local research, teaching and publishing. And let us honour God, the source of true knowledge, by the work we do.

---

[47] To add some titles to the bibliography does not need a full curriculum review, but can be done incrementally.
[48] Mzuzu University requires 10 book reports for an MA and 12 for a PhD.

Chapter 4

Fit for Purpose: The Theological Graduate Profile in Light of Malawian Grassroots Priorities

Volker Glissmann

Introduction

Increasingly, accrediting agencies worldwide assess educational programmes based on their "fitness for purpose" and their "fitness of purpose." For example, the Bologna Process for European higher education uses the two phrases as key consideration to establish an effective contextual curricular design.[1] The Bologna Process is a multi-faced approach about "accountability, access, quality assurance, credits and transfer, and, most notably, learning outcomes" within academic disciplines.[2] This chapter focuses on the contributions of Malawian grassroots reflections on the "fitness for purpose" of theological graduate profiles so that programmes are not only student-centred but also grassroots-centred in their curricular design. Accountability is essential in recognizing that learning contracts exist between students and institutions and their programmes that need to provide students with clear indications of the practical purpose of a programme in terms of skills, learning outcomes and how the learning outcomes prepare for specific occupational fields.[3]

---

[1] European Association for Quality Assurance in Higher Education, 2009, Helsinki, 3rd edition (ENQA 2009).
[2] Clifford Adelman, *The Bologna Process for U.S. Eyes: Re-learning Higher Education in the Age of Convergence*, Washington, DC: Institute for Higher Education Policy, 2009, viii.
[3] It is interesting to write this after as a family we have just finished choosing a university course of study for my daughter. These are the exact same questions that

4. Fit for Purpose: The Theological Graduate Profile 75

Graduates serve communities, and the input of the grassroots communities to the graduate profile is essential for the fitness of purpose.

"Fitness *of* Purpose" basically refers to the suitability (or fitness) of a product for its intended purpose. In education, both at secondary and at tertiary level, questions are raised about balancing of academic, vocational and technical skills. In contrast, in theological education, balancing includes ministerial and spiritual elements concerning the fitness of purpose. "Fitness *for* purpose" refers to the effectiveness of the programme in achieving the programme outcome. Both are important concerning curricular design. Assessments for "fitness of purpose" and "fitness for purpose" are never only determined by institutional self-evaluation but require the input of all stakeholders to evaluate whether a programme is appropriate (fitness of purpose) and effective (fitness for purpose). Fitness of/for purpose offers a unique curricular challenge for theology where often the stated aim is to prepare graduates, among other things, for church ministry. Yet a traditional theological curriculum, which is prominent in many Malawian theological institutions, is fragmented and underemphasizes practical theology as the unifying curricular force.[4]

In 2008 Jaison Thomas published a research about the ideal "graduate profile" or the "ideal leader profile" of graduates of ministerial theological education in some schools in India.[5] He asked three

---

we asked of every programme of study that we looked at as the financial investment is significant.

[4] See Volker Glissmann, "The Fragmentation of Theological Education and its Effect on the Church, Grassroots Theological Education in Malawi and TEE," in Volker Glissmann (ed), *Towards a Malawian Theology of Laity*, Mzuzu: Luviri Press, 2020.

[5] Jaison Thomas, "Church Ministry Formation in Protestant Theological Education: The Contemporary Debate in Kerala, India," PhD, Queen's University of Belfast, 2008.

groups: church leaders, theological educators and students who had just recently joined a Theological College to rank by priorities some theological educational objectives. He then compared the priorities assigned by each group. Unfortunately, at that time, Thomas' research did not include the voice of the grassroots (aka laity) as well as the voice of active ministers in church ministry. The focus here is on the grassroots and their priorities. The findings are the result of a series of qualitative interviews with several laypeople which then will be compared with the conclusions of Jaison Thomas.

No review of theological education or assessment of its fitness for purpose can succeed without the contribution of the voice of the grassroots. Here theological education is understood inclusively as operating on a continuum between grassroots theological education, ministerial theological education and academic theological education.[6] The natural inclination for institutional reviews is to seek input from specialists in the area of theology and theological education. However, these reviews will be faulty and incomplete if they do not consider the priorities of the grassroots who provide the primary audience of all grassroots and ministerial theological discourses. The voices amplified in this paper will help in moving towards formulating Malawian grassroots priorities concerning the purpose of a theological graduate profile.

A few general observations to place this paper into its appropriate, broader context. The grassroots is not a homogeneous group. Instead, it is a diverse group of individuals who have different experiences, aspirations, characters, preferences, and of course, grew up in a specific (and sometimes accumulated other) church and spiritual traditions in their lives. Additionally, the reflection of grassroots participants significantly depends on their level of reflective practice,

---

[6] See Volker Glissmann, "Grassroots Theological Education," *InSights Journal for Global Theological Education* 5/1 (2019), 53–67.

Bible engagement, and participation in church activities, especially leadership. An additional factor is the church tradition that participants belong to as it either explicitly or inexplicitly builds a theology of grassroots participation. The influence of church tradition is evident in the reflection of members of the CCAP. They generally uphold the original Presbyterian idea that the pastor is a designated teaching elder but not one of the ruling elders that make up the church session. All of these make generalizations about the grassroots' perception of a theological graduate profile difficult.

Research Description

The method for the research is a case study. It is a qualitative research whereby in-depth insights were collected from a small sample group (fifteen individuals) through interviews in February and March 2020. Eight participants were interviewed in mini focus groups (LP4, LP5, LP6, LP7, LP10, LP11, LP12, LP13). The focus groups aimed to foster dialogue between the two participants concerning their personal views of lay participation. All interviews were based on a predesigned questionnaire that also included an open question which allowed participants to share additional insights without being limited in scope by pre-determined research questions. All interviews were in English and conducted by myself. The objective was to give a voice to the grassroots church.

Interviews were chosen here because the interview will provide potentially more detailed answers than a questionnaire, especially in a relational culture where the assumption is that the interviewees prefer to express themselves verbally. The research was designed to assess the interviewees' own views and preferences concerning lay or grassroots participation in the churches that they have or are attending. The purpose of the qualitative interview is to describe the interviewees' point of view. All the interviewees reside in urban and semi-urban centres of Zomba and Blantyre. The interviewees also represent a mixture of genders (seven female and eight male), from a variety of churches, including Anglican, Baptist, CCAP, Pentecostal and AIC. However, there was also overlap as some interviewees had experience in more than one church tradition. Members of various CCAP congregations formed the majority of the interviews: 11. The researcher, as well as all interviewees, were laypeople, though a few were elders (or equivalent) in their respective churches. The interview findings are anonymous; all interviewees are only identified as LP (Lay Participation) and a number.

Disclaimer

A research difficulty was the lack of available definitions of the ten characteristics in the original research from Thomas. This shortcoming was only noticed during the interviews. One couple in a focus group interpreted "character" and "role model" as opposites. One rated it as very important while the other as least important. Yet their discussion afterwards showed that they had similar ideas but used different words. The problem might be limited to the term "character." "Character" received: once the least rating (position 10) and two times the second least rating (position 9) and yet at the same time it also received three times the best rating (position 1) and four times the second-best rating (position 2).

Thomas' research does not provide a mathematical model to show the ranking of the priorities. Therefore, the interpretation of the findings cannot take into consideration how close or far apart the original priorities were to each other.

The sample size of fifteen participants will only provide an initial insight. Further research is needed to verify and expand upon the findings of this paper. Additional studies could examine the relation

4. Fit for Purpose: The Theological Graduate Profile

between denominational backgrounds and the people's understanding of lay participation. Thomas researched a distinct ecclesiological setting which is different from the situation in Malawi. For example, church planting and church growth are not equally emphasised in all Malawian churches and seminaries.

Thomas' research is a good starting point and corrective to exclusively ask theological educators to discuss among themselves the direction of theological education. It would be fascinating to do further research and establish a broader empirical base for identifying the characteristics/qualities of a pastor. Fundamentally, it is suspected that there will be cultural and contextual (as well as denominational) differences in the ranking of the qualities. I am using "denominational" here to mean, the "explicit church convictions," like a missional church would both at leadership as well as grassroots level emphasize evangelism and outreach. In contrast, churches which emphasize preaching and biblical exposition as part of their central identity will emphasize these as essential characteristics. In a way, the grading of the importance of qualities will be influenced by a specific echo chamber between pulpit and audience. Though it would be interesting to know how successful, in terms of audience percentage, pulpit monologues are in shaping the overall congregational worldview on specific topics.

Further studies could also investigate if there are differences between urban and rural areas, between younger and older church members, between men and women, between elders, deacons and women's guild members and "ordinary Christians." Interviews conducted in one ecclesiological setting might not be transferable without modification. For a comprehensive graduate profile, the voice of clergy who are involved in church ministry needs is vital.

Research Questions

The research focuses on the grassroots ranking of predetermined categories of qualities in a new pastor (question 1) as well as an open question about other attributes that interviewees would like to add to the list from the first question (question 2).[7]

The research assumes the following definition. A church leader is someone who has been ordained into the pastoral ministry and addressed with a "professional" ecclesiastical title (Reverend, Pastor, Bishop, etc). The grassroots is everyone else in the church. The grassroots includes two distinct groups: lay church leaders (elders, deacons, woman guild, etc) and laypeople without a role or function in the church. The latter are sometimes described as "ordinary Christians," a term also used here until a better and more accurate description is agreed.

Question 1

Imagine your church looks for a new pastor, and you are part of the appointment committee. Which of the following qualities of a graduate from a theological college are most important to you in choosing a new pastor? Could you please rank the qualities from 1-10 (1 being the highest and 10 the lowest rank)?

Most important qualities to look for in a new pastor

1. Administrative Ability
2. Inspiring Preacher
3. Leadership skills
4. Loving concern for People

---

[7] The questions examined here are part of a wider research project which is partially published in Volker Glissmann, "Voices from the Grassroots: Meaningful Partnership," in Volker Glissmann (ed), *Towards a Malawian Theology of Laity*.

4. Fit for Purpose: The Theological Graduate Profile

5. Skills in interpersonal relationships
6. Successful in Church Growth and Evangelism
7. Theological knowledge
8. Person of Prayer
9. Character
10. Role Model

Thomas' grouped these qualities in three groups, as Academic Formation (Administrative Ability, Leadership skills, Theological Knowledge), Spiritual Formation (Character, Loving Concern for People, Person of Prayer) and Ministry Formation (Successful in Church Growth and Evangelism, Skills in Interpersonal Relationships, Inspiring Preacher).

Question 2

Are there other characteristics that you consider essential in a church leader/pastor? Are there qualities from the first question that should be expanded or clarified and included as a separate quality?

Findings

Question 1: Most significant qualities for choosing a new pastor

All 15 participants ranked the qualities from 1-10 (one being the top-rated and ten the least rated). Each interviewee gave 55 points (the total sum of 1-10). The total points allocated were 825 as each interviewee ranked from 1-10 (15 x 55 points). The highest possible score in ranking would have been 15. The lowest possible score in ranking would have been 150.

Characteristics of a "Minister" according to the grassroots

Rank	Quality	Total ranking	Average ranking	Thomas' classification
1	Loving Concern for People	55	3.66	Spiritual Formation
2	Person of Prayer	56	3.73	Spiritual Formation
3	Character	65	4.33	Spiritual Formation
4	Theological Knowledge	71	4.73	Academic Formation
5	Inspiring Preacher	76	5.06	Ministry Formation
6	Skills in Interpersonal Relationships	95	6.33	Ministry Formation
7	Leadership Skills	97	6.46	Academic Formation
8	Successful in Church Growth and Evangelism	97	6.46	Ministry Formation
9	Role Model	102	6.80	n/a
10	Administrative Ability	123	8.20	Academic Formation

There was only one quality that did not receive the ranking ten meaning being of least importance: Loving concern for people. All other qualities received at least once the lowest ranking. The highest number of 10s (seven times) was given to Administrative Ability.[1] The quality with the highest number of 1s (three times each) were: "character" and "person of prayer." Ranking Position 6 is shared by

---

[1] Administrative Ability needs further investigation as ranked lowest here but at the same time administrative abilities were mentioned by the interviewees in elaboration of the qualities in question 2.

4. Fit for Purpose: The Theological Graduate Profile 83

"Success in Church Growth and Evangelism" and "Skills in Interpersonal Relationships."

Evaluation of the Grassroots Findings

The quality "Loving concern for People" is the highest-ranked quality (in position 1, with 55 points), followed by "Person of Prayer" (in position 2 with 56 points), followed by "Character" (in position 3 with 65 points). Position 4 is "Theological Knowledge" which is only six points behind the third position with 71 points. The fifth position ("Inspiring Preacher") is only five points behind the fourth position. The difference between position 1 and position 5 is 21 points (55 to 76 points), while the difference between position 5 and 6 is 19 points (76 to 95 points). Position 6 to 9 are only seven points apart. Between position 9 ("Role Model") and position 10 ("Administrative Ability") is a gap of 21 points.

The classification significance is that the three highest-ranked qualities by the grassroots are all classified by Thomas as "Spiritual Formation." Position 4 is "Theological Knowledge" which is classified by Thomas as "Academic Formation," which is followed by position 5-6 classified as "'Ministerial Formation." Position 7 is a tie at 97 points "Leadership Skills" (Academic Formation) and "Successful in Church Growth and Evangelism" (Ministry Formation). The display in the table is purely alphabetical. Position 5-7 could be classified as "Ministry Formation"' if "Successful in Church Growth and Evangelism" would be listed before "Leadership Skills."

A significant difference between Thomas' findings, and this research is the ranking of the three Spiritual Formation categories in position 1-3 among the grassroots. It is significant that three characteristics that Thomas' classified as part of Spiritual Formation, namely, "Loving concern for people," "Person of Prayer," "Character" were ranked the highest. "Theological Knowledge"(categorized by Tho-

Glissmann

on of grassroots assessments into Thomas' findings

Grassroots Priorities	Seminary Leadership Priorities		Students' Priorities		Church Le Prior
Spiritual Formation	Theological Knowledge (1)	Academic Formation	Inspiring Preacher (1)	Ministry Formation	Person of Prayer (1)
Spiritual Formation	Administration (2)	Academic Formation	Church Growth (2)	Ministry Formation	Character (2)
Spiritual Formation	Leadership (3)	Academic Formation	Interpersonal skills (3)	Ministry Formation	Role Model (3)
Academic Formation	Interpersonal Skills (4)	Ministry Formation	Theological Knowledge (4)	Academic Formation	Church Growth (4)
Ministry Formation	Inspiring Preacher (5)	Ministry Formation	Leadership (5)	Academic Formation	Loving concern (5)
Ministry Formation	Church Growth (6)	Ministry Formation	Role Model (6)	n/a	Inspiring Preacher (6)
Academic Formation	Character (7)	Spiritual Formation	Administrative Ability (7)	Academic Formation	Interpersonal Skills (7)
Ministry Formation	Person (8) of Prayer	Spiritual Formation	Character (8)	Spiritual Formation	Leadership (8)
n/a	Role Model (9)	n/a	Person of Prayer (9)	Spiritual Formation	Administrative ability (9)
Academic Formation	Loving concern (10)	Spiritual Formation	Loving concern (10)	Spiritual Formation	Theological Knowledge (10)

...pose: The Theological Graduate Profile

...of the ranking of the top 3 grassroots priorities: Grassroots Priority

Priorities	Seminary Leadership Priorities (SL)		Students Priorities (S)		Church Leadership Priorities (CL)	
Spiritual Formation	Theological Knowledge (1)	Academic Formation	Inspiring Preacher (1)	Ministry Formation	Person of Prayer (1)	Spiritual Formation
Spiritual Formation	Administration (2)	Academic Formation	Church Growth (2)	Ministry Formation	Character (2)	Spiritual Formation
Spiritual Formation	Leadership (3)	Academic Formation	Interpersonal skills (3)	Ministry Formation	Role Model (3)	n/a

...cademic Formation) is ranked on position four. The sample size is too small here to ...rder of position 3 and 4. It is noteworthy that "Loving concern for people" was ranke... ...sition 10) in Thomas' research by both the students and seminary principals while it ... ...n the church leaders. The Grassroots second priority "Person of Prayer" was ranked ... ...dents and 8th by the seminary leadership, the church leaders though ranked it on ... ...roots' position 1. The grassroots third priority "Character" is ranked 8th by the studen...

by the seminary leadership and 2nd by the church leadership. The priorities of the grassroots are the total opposite of the 1st year students as well as the seminary leadership. Interestingly, the church leadership aligns closer with the grassroots. However, more research (especially a comparison between the four groups in Malawi should be initiated) is needed here before statistically significant conclusions could be drawn from these findings.

Summary of key findings

1) Distinct difference in priorities:
Grassroots: 3 times "Spiritual Formation;"
Seminary Leadership: 3 x "Academic Formation;"
Students: 3 x "Ministry Formation;"
Church Leadership: 2 x "Spiritual Formation" and 1 x non-assigned role model priority.

2) Distinct difference in ranking of spiritual formational characteristics in this (GR – SL – S – CL):
No 1: Loving concern No 1- No 10 – No 10 – No 5
No 2: Person of Prayer No 2- No 8 – No 9 – No 1
No 3: Character No 3 – No 7 – No 8 – No 2

3) A near reversal of priorities between the Grassroots priorities and Seminary and Student Priorities: (GR-SL-S)
No 1: Loving concern No 1- No 10 – No 10
No 2: Person of Pray No 2- No 8 – No 9
No 3: Character No 3 – No 7 – No 8

Question 2: Other characteristics for choosing a new pastor

Two participants (LP9, LP15) out of 15 were satisfied with the list of characteristics given above, while the rest either shared new characteristics or elaborated on specific broader characteristics, like

4. Fit for Purpose: The Theological Graduate Profile

character. All interviewees reflected and commented on concrete examples and issues of concern that they have or are experiencing as grassroots participants.

Summary of Findings

Below the list of additional characteristics of the ideal pastor as identified by the participants:

a) *Elaborations on Character (10 participants elaborated)*

- Humbleness/humility (5 participants: LP11, LP6, LP7, LP12, LP10)
- approachable (2 participants: LP12, LP13)
- truthful, trustworthiness, no gossip (2 participants: LP4, LP5)
- integrity and honesty (including in biblical expositions) (4 participants: LP3. LP4, LP6, LP11)
- listener and advice taker (not a "knowing-it-all" person) (2 participants: LP7, LP12
- fairness (especially when it comes to disciplinary issues – rumours vs. facts and investigation) (1 participant: LP2)

b) *People's person (8 participants)*

Interest in each member (what are the issues facing individuals, families, what is their background) / Commitment to pastoral work (visitation, counselling – spiritual and psychological) / Availability / generally concerned about all members, not just the "pastor's people" (LP1, LP8, LP10, LP11, LP15, LP9, LP 12, LP13)

c) *Communication skills (5 participants)*

Communication skills ("ability to clearly articulate things and say it clearly" – LP11), Ability to speak to and include (and take seriously) all age groups in church/ability to engage and address the audience that is present (LP11, LP3, LP4, LP5).

d) Spiritual concern (4 participants)

Spiritual discernment / spiritual inspiration and someone's spiritual standing (not responding to social position and what an elder might contribute socially or financially. Definitely, not responding to origin "because someone is a 'homeboy'") / "spiritual emphasis not just religious"/ recognition of different spirituality at different age groups) (LP3, LP4, LP5, LP7), "spiritual preaching, not modern self-help talks"(LP3); "a preaching that leads to Christ and is not always about money" (LP7).

e) Biblical interpretative skills (4 participants)

Biblical interpretation skills in general (verses interpreted without considering their literary context, not understandings biblical genres - like parables, and especially biblical interpretation skills in financial giving and promises (seed money, etc) (LP10, LP11, LP6, LP7).

f) Financial management (2 participants)

Transparency and accountability (LP8, LP14).

g) Servant leadership (2 participants)

"A style of leadership that is not concerned about being served but about serving" (LP6, LP7).

h) Ability to connect and understand society (2 participants)

"The gospel speaks to Christians that are in society and engage with society." / "The church should engage theologically with society and its ideas (like ecology, business culture) and especially the ever-changing youth culture" (LP4, LP5).

i) Ecumenically minded (1 participant)

"Ecumenical sympathy, to work together with other churches and show the unity of the wider church" (LP5).

j) Wholistic concern for the whole person (1 participant)

"not just spirituality but practically assisting those who economically struggle" (LP8).

k) Discipleship minded (1 participant)

"church growth and evangelism count for nothing if there is no follow-up with discipleship training" (LP14).

l) Counselling

"counselling is very important for pastors" (LP10).

Theological Graduate Profile

The Graduate Profile is both the essential starting point for pedagogical curriculum design as well as the endpoint of the educational process. Paul Sanders stresses that the process starts from the end, "begin with the end ... clearly defined "graduate profiles" (describing the generic character traits, knowledge, and know-how of the graduating students)."[1] Sanders also describes the graduate profile in shorthand as "overall outcomes" of the curriculum.[2] Institutions are likely to have generic and specific graduate profiles. A generic graduate profile reflects institutional values and priorities which are for all graduates of the institution.

Additionally, particular programmes also have specific graduates profiles reflecting the specifics of the course (like BA in Rural Ministry).[3] Graduate profiles are not exclusively academic, "the

---

[1] Paul Sanders, 'The Role of Academic Leaders in Curriculum Design', in *Leadership in Theological Education: Volume 2: Foundations for Curriculum Design*, ed. Fritz Deininger and Orbelina Eguizabal, Carlisle: Langham Global Library, 2017, 44.
[2] Sanders, 45.
[3] See Sanders, 55; Allan Harkness, "The Role of Academic Leadership in Designing Transformative Teaching and Learning", in *Leadership in Theological*

written profile should also make clear what values, attitudes and behaviours you want to see in your graduates."[4] Bernhard Ott goes so far as to describe them as "general vocational goals."[5] Ultimately, the profile should include "what they need to be and be able to do to serve well."[6] The graduate profile needs awareness of the context from which the students and the context in which they will serve. The question is "what character, attitudes, knowledge and skills should such graduate possess if they are to be successful in that context?"[7] A theological graduate profile recognizes that the graduate will seek employment and therefore needs to be prepared to fulfil the employment requirements of churches. Consequently, institutions must utilize a

> holistic theological curriculum will aim at outcomes that go beyond accumulation of knowledge. 'Orthodoxy' does not automatically lead to 'orthopraxy.' While knowledge is a necessary component of theological education, competencies and character are just as fundamental. Every course syllabus should integrate the "3Cs": Cognition, Competency, and Character.[8]

The graduate profile is there to guide all stakeholders so that the graduate is theologically equipped but is also prepared for people-centred ministry within the church context.

Education: Volume 2: Foundations for Curriculum Design, ed. Fritz Deininger and Orbelina Eguizabal, Carlisle: Langham Global Library, 2017, 149.

[4] Steve Hardy, 'Steps for Curriculum Design', in *Leadership in Theological Education: Volume 2: Foundations for Curriculum Design*, ed. Fritz Deininger and Orbelina Eguizabal, Carlisle: Langham Global Library, 2017, 70.

[5] Bernhard Ott, *Understanding and Developing Theological Education*, Carlisle, 2016, 296.

[6] Hardy, 'Steps for Curriculum Design', 75.

[7] Errol Joseph, 'Contextualized Curriculum Design', in *Leadership in Theological Education: Volume 2: Foundations for Curriculum Design*, ed. Fritz Deininger and Orbelina Eguizabal, Carlisle: Langham Global Library, 2017, 92.

[8] Sanders, 'The Role of Academic Leaders in Curriculum Design', 53.

4. Fit for Purpose: The Theological Graduate Profile 91

The issue of a theological graduate profile, which in many instances is also the profile of a pastor here in Malawi, does not automatically have a unified definition.[9] Thomas's research shows that significant differences around the expectation of the pastoral ministry exist between theological educators, church leaders, students and the grassroots. This chapter is not the space to discuss the ideal pastoral profile that best suits the Malawian church; however, our grassroots finding does not stand alone. A significant research project of the Association of Theological Schools in North America (ATS) with over 5,000 randomly selected interviewees stressed the overwhelming finding that, "our of top five factors 'lie within the area of the clergy's personal commitment and faith and center in the minister or priest as a person.'"[10] Robert Meye continues, "These four items are, in order, 'service without regard for acclaim,' 'personal responsibility,' 'Christian example,' and 'acknowledgement of limitations.' On the opposite (negative) end of the scale, the criteria which draw the severest judgment from clergy and laity alike are 'undisciplined living,' 'self-protecting ministry,' and 'professional immaturity.'"[11] Wilson Chow lists the five negative characteristics: "self-serving ministry, a sense of superiority, immaturity, insecurity, and insensitivity."[12] He further elaborates these points,

---

[9] John O. Enyinnaya, "Graduate Profile as a Tool for Enhancing Spiritual Formation in Theological Education Today," *Ogbomoso Journal of Theology* 6, no. 2 (2011), 69.

[10] Robert P. Meye, "Theological Education as Character Formation," *Theological Education* Supplement 1 (1988), 115. Meye is citing Avid S. Schuller, Merton P. Strommen, and Milo L. Brekke (eds), *Ministry in America*, San Francisco: Harper and Row, 1980, 19.

[11] Meye, "Theological Education as Character Formation," 115.

[12] Wilson W. Chow, "An Integrated Approach to Theological Education," *Evangelical Review of Theology* 19/2 (1995), 222.

1. ***Service without regard for acclaim.*** They expected the minister to be a person who is able to accept personal limitations and is able to serve without concern for public recognition.

2. ***Personal integrity.*** The minister should be able to honour commitments by carrying out promises despite all pressures to compromise.

3. ***Christian example.*** The minister should be one whose personal belief in the gospel manifests itself in generosity, and in general in Christian example that people in the community can respect.

4. ***Pastoral skills.*** People want a minister who shows competence and responsibility by completing tasks and by being able to handle differences of opinion, and who senses the need to continue to grow in pastoral skills.

5. ***Leadership.*** The minister must be able to build a strong sense of community within a congregation, taking time to know the people in his church and developing a sense of trust and confidence between the congregation and himself.[13]

Chow continues to warn that "although public opinion may not always be true and accurate, nevertheless here it represents an expectation from the people whom the minister is called to serve. Such an expectation is actually paralleled by the demands of Scripture. These are the biblical qualifications for church officers. So character formation must be a vital and concrete objective in theological education."[14] This element of Spiritual Formation (Loving concern for People, Person of Prayer, Character) that the grassroots ranks very highly needs to be considered when theological institutions write a graduate profile for their programmes. Theological institutions need to actively

---

[13] Chow, "An Integrated Approach to Theological Education," 222. Also Enyinnaya, "Graduate Profile as a Tool for Enhancing Spiritual Formation in Theological Education Today," 70.

[14] Chow, "An Integrated Approach to Theological Education," 223.

4. Fit for Purpose: The Theological Graduate Profile

engage the grassroots to collect the grassroots contribution to the graduate profile. The above research shows that there is potentially a significant difference also here in Malawi between the four groups.

Conclusion

A key finding of the interviews is the prioritizing of spiritual formational priorities (Loving concern for People, Person of Prayer and Character) among the grassroots for the theological graduate profile. Especially noteworthy is the distinct ranking of these three grassroots priorities contrasting Seminary leadership and Students. The grassroots ranked Spiritual Formation as 1st, 2nd and 3rd priority, while Seminary Leadership ranked it as 7th, 8th and 10th priority and the Students ranked them as 8th, 9th and 10th least priority. Spiritual Formation characteristics, as highlighted by the grassroots, need more robust consideration for the design and development of a theological graduate profile here in Malawi.

Naturally, the open question about important additional qualities for the Theological Graduate Profile (question 2) gives diverse answers. Yet two characteristics dominate the answers, which are a) "elaborations on character" (10 respondents – 66% of the all interviewees) and b) "people person" (8 respondents – 53%). These two priorities correspond to the rated priorities from the first question, namely, "Loving concern for People" (position 1) and "character" (position 2). Position 2 was "Person of Prayer" which is self-explanatory and therefore did not feature in any answer given to question 2. The findings from question 1 and from question 2 show a remarkable sense of continuity, thus highlighting the importance of these grassroots priorities for a Theological Graduate Profile. Furthermore, it is notable that 35 years after *Ministry in America* was published, Malawian grassroots Christians come to a very similar conclusion that emphasizes that the crucial characteristic of a graduate lies in his person and his personal and spiritual conduct.

Chapter 5

Translating "Lord Jesus" as "Bwana Yesu"

Winston R. Kawale

Introduction: Bible Translation as a Missionary Enterprise

One of the most significant missionary enterprises was the translation of the Bible into the languages of the people whom the missionaries wanted to evangelize. It is a process that reflects the central act on which the Christian faith depends and that concretizes the mission which Christ gave his disciples.[1]

Translation has to do with reducing the spoken language to writing. This is because the printed word is the only medium for transferring thoughts and ideas without limitation of time and place. The connotation of available words must be adopted and purified and where the necessary words for new spiritual concepts and values do not exist, they must be found.[2]

According to Wendland, the African or Bantu languages in particular, are an expression of a people's culture, in all of its functional diversity and beauty, and a Bantu tongue is second to none in the world, particularly in terms of its own religious potential.[3] After the early missionaries had reduced the Chichewa language of Malawi to

---

[1] Andrew F. Walls, *The Missionary Movement in Christian History: Studies in the Transmission of Faith*, Edinburgh: T&T Clark, 1996, 28.
[2] G. Gardener, *Recent Development in Southern Africa*, London: T&T Clark, 1958, 224.
[3] Ernst R. Wendland, *Buku Loyera: An Introduction to the New Chichewa Translation*, Blantyre: CLAIM, 1998, 22.

5. Translating "Lord Jesus" as "Bwana Yesu"

writing, they embarked on the work of translating the Bible into Chichewa.[4] This chapter discusses "translating of "Lord Jesus" as "Bwana Yesu," looking at the historical accounts of translation of English Bible versions into Chichewa in Malawi.

The Chichewa Bible Translations

There are four Chichewa versions of the Bible. These versions were translated at different times, by different translators from different denominations and have different formats.

Buku Lopatulika (BL)

The first vernacular Bible to be translated in Malawi was *Buku Lopatulika* (Sacred Bible) by the Protestant missionaries. The first to embark on the Bible translation exercise in Malawi was David Clement Scott of Blantyre Mission. He first translated the New Testament and published it in 1886. After he left Malawi in 1898, representatives of Livingstonia Mission, Blantyre Mission and Nkhoma Mission met in 1900 and formed a translation committee which resolved that a fresh translation be undertaken. Rev William Murray of Nkhoma Mission was appointed as fulltime translator to be assisted by Dr Hetherwick from Blantyre, and by Chichewa mother-tongue speakers Jonathan Sande from Blantyre Mission, and Willebes Chikuse and Ishmael Mwale from Nkhoma Mission.[5] The work was completed in 1919, published in 1922 and distributed in Malawi in 1923. With great joy and excitement, the missionaries at Nkhoma recorded the following minute:

> ChiNyanja Bible 1923: The year 1923 will long stand out as one of great significance because in this year the Bible for the first time appeared in

---

[4] Ibid.
[5] C. Martin Pauw, *Mission and Church in Malawi: The History of the Nkhoma Synod of the Church of Central Africa, Presbyterian, 1889-1962*, Lusaka: RMP, 1980, 211-220.

its entirety in the language of the Nyasa people. We realise our indebtedness to the Lord and express our gratitude to Him for the strength, health and powers of mind imparted to those who were charged with this task and in particular to the head of our Mission to whom, amongst others the work was entrusted. [6]

The *Buku Lopatulika* Bible is a literal or word-for-word translation. It endeavours to stay as close as possible to the original Hebrew and Greek. However, the *Buku Lopatulika* translators used the King James Version along with the English Revised Version. Since William Murray came from South Africa, the Dutch Bible was also consulted. They also used Young's Literal Translation of the Bible.[7] The *Buku Lopatulika* has content titles, cross-references and maps. However, the translators were prevented from adding footnotes due to the Bible Society policy of that time that Bible publications must be produced without note or comment. However, this policy has since been abandoned.[8]

Malembo Oyera (MO)

In Malawi, the Roman Catholic translation Malembo Oyera appeared in 1966. The translation of Malembo Oyera was undertaken by a French Missionary Fr Louis Villy. He arrived in Malawi in 1911, embarked on learning Chichewa and got involved in translating the Bible into Chichewa. With the assistance of Bishop Patrick Kalilombe, Fr Villy completed the translation in 1966.

Fr Villy based his *Malembo Oyera* largely on the Latin Vulgate and the French La Sainte Bible with some references to the Greek text, the English Revised Standard Version and the French Jerusalem Bible.[9] The novel feature of Fr Villy's *Malembo Oyera* translation was that it

---

[6] Cit. Pauw, *Mission and Church in Malawi*, 216.
[7] Wendland, *Buku Loyera*, 24.
[8] Wendland, *Buku Loyera*, 24-25
[9] Wendland, *Buku Loyera*, 25.

5. Translating "Lord Jesus" as "Bwana Yesu"

included an introduction to the Bible as a whole. It also included introductions for each book, as well as detailed explanatory footnotes which were placed at the foot of every page.[10]

Buku Loyera (BL)

Buku Loyera is the third version of the Chichewa Bible. It is an inter-confessional translation with translators drawn from both the Roman Catholic and Protestant churches. This version was published in 1998.[11] Six factors influenced the churches to embark on this new version. These are:

First, both *Buku Lopatulika* and *Malembo Oyera* versions were archaic in nature. The language therein was also archaic. This is because language inevitably changes over time. Certain words fall out of common use and become archaic, known only by the older generation. Yet the Bible has to be read and understood by the young generation.[12] It is the general rule that due to language change, a new translation is needed every quarter century.[13] The two versions could no longer meet this requirement. Consequently, there was need to translate the Bible into contemporary Chichewa.

Second, in the two versions, the verbal styles are compromised by the literal translation procedure. The verbal styles in the two versions reveal that the text was composed by a non-mother tongue speaker of Chichewa. This is evident in the word order and use of conjunctions, demonstratives, pronouns, verb tenses and other rhetorical

---

[10] Wendland, *Buku Loyera*, 26.
[11] Wendland, *Buku Loyera*, 33- 35.
[12] Wendland, *Buku Loyera*, 26.
[13] Wendland, *Buku Loyera*, 27.

expressions such as the idiomatic expressions "*indetu, indetu ndinena ndi inu.*" These do not mean anything in Chichewa.[14]

Third, the word-for-word translation or rendering does reproduce linguistic forms of Hebrew and Greek texts. This is done at the expense of a natural, familiar style in Chichewa and frequently to the detriment of the intended meaning of the original language. For example, in *Buku Lopatulika*, there is the use of the conjunction *ndipo* in imitation of corresponding conjunctions in Hebrew *vav* and Greek *kai*. There is need for an additional more idiomatic, meaning-based popular language version to complement the literal version and to give the ordinary hearers and readers more immediate access to the sense and significance of the biblical text.[15]

Fourth, the two Chichewa versions of the Bible, the *Buku Lopatulika* and the *Malembo Oyera*, are used by Protestants and the Catholics respectively. The Protestants and the Catholics agree on 39 books of the Old Testament and the 27 books of the New Testament. As Wendland observes, if the two camps agree on the significance of the 66 books of the Bible, it becomes agreeable that a joint Bible translation project could help to narrow the gap between the two camps and facilitate the dialogue.[16]

Fifth, there was need to provide enough reading helps for the Bible reader. While the translators were prevented from adding footnotes due to the Bible Society policy that Bible publications must be produced without note or comment, this policy is no longer in use. The *Malembo Oyera* went far ahead in providing an introduction to

---

[14] Ibid.
[15] Wendland, *Buku Loyera*, 28.
[16] Wendland, *Buku Loyera*, 29.

each book, sectional headings, footnotes, cross-references and explanatory notes.[17]

Sixth, there was need to involve both the laity and the clergy in the translation process. This exercise makes the translation relevant and contemporary in nature because it involves the targeted audience.[18] The translators of this version were: from the Catholic Church, Fr Tenthani, Fr Vermeulen, Bishop Kalilombe, Fr Mtingiza, and Mr Chafulumila; and from the Protestant side came Rev Katsulukuta, Rev Kachaje, Rev Mabedi, Mrs Kumange, Mr Gwaza, Prof Pauw, Rev Stytler, and Mr Chadza. Reviewers were Fr Jabin, Fr Salaun and Rev Dr Kawale.[19]

Buku Lopatulika Mu Chichewa Cha Lero

The *Buku Lopatulika Mu Chichewa Chalero* (Sacred Book in Contemporary Chichewa) is the work of the International Bible Society. It is a translation of the New International Version.

According to Lester Chikoya, factors that influenced the International Bible Society to embark on translating the English New International Version into contemporary Chichewa were as follows:[20]

First, it was realized that Chichewa has many dialects. It was, therefore, believed that the *Buku Lopatulika mu Chichewa cha Lero* could provide a common way as regards how Chichewa could be pronounced and written.

Second, it was acknowledged that language changes from generation to generation. It was noted that the changes may be due to use of new terms in the language, borrowing words from other languages,

---

[17] Ibid.
[18] Wendland, *Buku Loyera*, 30.
[19] Wendland, *Buku Loyera*, 30-31, 56n14.
[20] Personal interview, Lester Chikoya, 12 June 2016.

and complete disregard of the use of old words of the language. In this respect, it was decided that the New International Version be translated into contemporary Chichewa so that the contemporary generation should be able to read and understand it.[21] Several groups of people led by Mr Lester Chikoya were involved in this translation. The work based its translation on the original Biblical languages, Hebrew and Aramaic for the Old Testament and Greek for the New Testament.[22]

These four versions have approached the translation of the Bible in different ways and translated the Tetragrammaton differently.

Defining the Term "Tetragrammaton"

Tetragrammaton is the four-letter or consonantal Hebrew word *YHWH* without vowels.[23] This word refers to the proper and personal divine name of the God of Israel.[24] This special covenant name *YHWH* was revealed to Moses at the time of the Exodus (Ex 3:22). The Israelites believed that *YHWH* rescued them from the Egyptian bondage (Ex 20:5; Hos 11:1; 12:9-10; 13:4; Ezek 20:15; Am 2:10; 3:1-2).

Scholars have been unable to reach an agreement on its linguistic meaning. The challenge arises over the major questions as to whether the stem of the verb is simple or causative. If the stem is the simple verb "to be" the conception is that *YHWH* is "ONE WHO IS." This may imply that *YHWH* is the absolute and unchangeable, or self-

---

[21] Introduction, *Chichewa cha Lero*, 2002, ii.

[22] Preface, *Chichewa cha Lero*, i.

[23] B.W. Anderson, "God, Names of," in *International Dictionary of the Bible*, Nashville: Abingdon, 1962, 407-417 [409].

[24] C.J.H. Wright, "God, Names of," *International Standard Bible Encyclopedia*, Vol. 2, Grand Rapids: WB Eerdmans, 1982, 506-7; Anderson, "God, Names of," 409.

existence.[25] The causative interpretation is that YHWH is a causative principle. He is the "sustainer," "maintainer," and "establisher." He is the One who causes to be that which is or which happens.[26] The name YHWH expresses God's character or nature.[27] This interpretation of the Tetragrammaton should be the basis for the translation of the name YHWH.

Approaches to the Translation of the Tetragrammaton into Chichewa

The four Chichewa Bible versions have variably engaged two approaches to translate the Tetragrammaton into Chichewa. The first is transliteration approach, and second approach is translation. Either approach has serious challenges.

Transliteration Approach

To transliterate is to substitute or represent in the closest corresponding words or letters of one language for those of another language. The Tetragrammaton has been transliterated into Chichewa as *Yehova* or *Yahve*.

Yehova

Buku Lopatulika has transliterated the name YHWH as *Yehova*. This is the hybrid English form *Yehovah*.[28] Originally, the divine name YHWH had consonants only without vowels. The vowel points were

---

[25] Wright, "God, Names of," 157.
[26] Ibid
[27] M.J. Harris, "LORD," in *International Standard Bible Encyclopedia*, Vol 3, Grand Rapids: Eerdmans, 1986, 157-158 [152].
[28] Ibid.

added later so that the name was pronounced as *Yehova*.[29] It is sometimes pronounced as Jehovah.[30]

Yahve

Malembo Oyera transliterated *YHWH* as *Yahve*. Again, the vowels were added to the consonants *YHWH*. In Hebrew grammar the consonant "w" is pronounced as "v". That is why there is *Yahve* instead of Yahweh.

There are three objections to the transliteration of the Tetragrammaton:

First, pronouncing the name *YHWH* as *Yehova* or *Jehova*, or *Yahve* is a misleading representation and should remain hypothetical.[31] This is because the divine name had no vowels and adding vowels was doing injustice to how the name should be written. As Anderson observed, this is an artificial name for *YHWH*.[32]

The second objection is that the name *YHWH* is unintelligible to the Chewa people; it does not mean anything at all.

The third objection is that pronouncing this divine name was prohibited among the Jews. Exodus 20:7 clearly forbids the use of the name *YHWH* in vain as *YHWH* will not hold anyone guiltless who misuses his name. In Leviticus 24:16, any simple utterance of the sacred Tetragrammaton was a capital offence. As Harris observes, pronouncing the divine name would reduce God to the status of a pagan deity who was addressed by a personal name.[33]

---

[29] Wright, "God, Names of," 507.
[30] Ibid.
[31] J.A. Motyer, "Jehovah," in *Bible Dictionary*, Grand Rapids: Zondervan, 1987, 502.
[32] B.W. Anderson, "Jehovah", in *International Dictionary of the Bible*, Nashville: Abingdon, 1962, 817.
[33] Harris, "LORD," 157.

Therefore, transliteration is not the best way of communicating the meaning of a word into another language. Therefore, this approach is not acceptable.

Translation Approach

To translate is to express the sense of word, sentence, and speech from one language to another language. The Tetragrammaton has been translated into Chichewa in different ways as follows:

Ndilipo

Wendland reports that when the translators of the *Buku Loyera* were discussing how to translate the Tetragrammaton, there was a suggestion to translate the name as *Ndilipo*.[34] This suggestion was based on the realization that the name seem to come from the simple verb "I am."[35] However, the *Buku Loyera* found this proposal awkward as a designation for someone's name.[36] Therefore, they abandoned the suggestion.

Chauta

Chauta is one of the divine names of God among the Chewa people. The translators of the *Buku Loyera* settled on *Chauta* as the translation for YHWH.[37] The name *Chauta* literally means "Great One of the Bow."[38] *Chauta* is regarded as the provider of rains. *Chauta* is the sustainer and one who maintains the life of people through the provision of rains without which people will have no food.[39] *Chauta*

---

[34] Wendland, *Buku Loyera*, 118.
[35] Anderson, "God, Names of," 410.
[36] Wendland, *Buku Loyera*, 118.
[37] Wendland, *Buku Loyera*, 119.
[38] Ibid.
[39] Winston R. Kawale, "God and Nature in Genesis 1:1-2: 2a and Chewa Cosmogony," DTh, University of Stellenbosch, 1998, 35-43.

is also referred to as *Makewana*, which means "the Mother of all people."[40]

According to Wendland, the *Buku Loyera* translators found *Chauta* to be the closest functional equivalent of *YHWH*.[41] They found that there was theological advantage in adopting an indigenous vernacular name of God.[42] Therefore, *Buku Loyera* has maintained *Chauta* as the translation of *YHWH*. They believe that both *YHWH* and *Chauta* have the same attributes of being able to sustain and maintain people's lives.

However, there are two objections to translating *YHWH* as *Chauta*. First, the Chewa associate *Chauta* with a female god, or goddess.[43] *Chauta* is said to be the wife of the god *Chisumphi* and both *Chisumphi* and *Chauta* are rain gods, responsible for bringing rains at rain ritual ceremonies or shrines.[44] *Chauta* is also referred to as *Namalenga*. In Chichewa, a word that begins with "na" is taken to be a feminine word. Therefore, *Chauta* as *Namalenga* means she is "creator goddess." According to the Chewa people *Chauta* is a female goddess. This is contrary to our understanding of *YHWH*. Among the Jews, *YHWH* was never referred to as a female god. Therefore, to translate *YHWH* as *Chauta* would indicate to the Chewa that *YHWH* is a female god.

Second, translating *YHWH* as *Chauta* means that the name shall be pronounced as such i.e. *Chauta*. As noted above, this is contrary to the tradition attached to the name *YHWH*. Among the Jews, it was prohibited to pronounce the name *YHWH*. In the interest of wider

---

[40] Ibid, 35.
[41] Wendland, *Buku Loyera*, 120.
[42] Ernst R. Wendland and S. Hachibamba, *Galu Wamkota: Missiological Reflections from Southern-Central Africa*, Zomba: Kachere Series, 2007, 381.
[43] Wendland, *Buku Loyera*, 120.
[44] Kawale, "God and Nature in Genesis 1:1-2: 2a," 23.

5. Translating "Lord Jesus" as "Bwana Yesu"

ecclesiastical or theological agreement, it is not proper to pronounce this divine name neither in Hebrew as *YHWH* nor in vernacular as *Chauta*.[45]

Therefore, for these two reasons, the translation of *YHWH* as *Chauta* is faulty.

Ambuye

The translation of *YHWH* as *Ambuye* is found in most of the Chichewa Bible versions. This is the translation of the English word "Lord", which was the translation of the Greek *kurios*, and which was the translation of the Hebrew word *Adonai*. In the ordinary speech etiquette of the Jews, the word *Adonai*, like the word "sir," was customarily used as a title of courtesy and respect in addressing a superior such as a king (1 Sam 24:8; 26:17; Jer 22:18), a father (Gen 31:35), a husband (Gen 18:12) and a master (Gen 24:12; Ex 21:5f). The Jews regarded *YHWH* to be a sacred divine name never to be pronounced as stated above.[46] In order to show respect and reverence to *YHWH* the title *adonai* was used in order to safeguard the name from defamation in all oral reading and also in written form (Ex 23:17; 34:23; Is 3:15; 10:16; Am 8:1; Is 6:1).[47] This substitution of *YHWH* with *adonai* came into force because Exodus 20:7 clearly forbids the use of the name *YHWH* in vain as *YHWH* will not hold anyone guiltless who misuses his name. In Leviticus 24:16, any simple utterance of the sacred Tetragrammaton was a capital offence. As Harris observes, pronouncing the divine name would reduce God to the status of a pagan deity who was addressed by a personal name.[48] Therefore, the divine name *YHWH* was eventually substituted with the term *Adonai*. According to Anderson the term *Adonai* was a title

---

[45] Wendland and Hachibamba, *Galu Wamkota*, 381.
[46] Wendland, *Buku Loyera*, 118
[47] Wright, "God, Names of," 508; Harris, "LORD," 157.
[48] Harris, "LORD," 157.

of honour and respect expressing God's holiness and absolute lordship. Its application to God implies his dignity and dominance (Ps 2: 4; Ps 7:7).[49]

The *Buku Lopatulika, Malembo Oyera, Buku Loyera* and *Buku Lopatulika Mu Chichewa Cha Lero* have translated *Adonai* as *Ambuye* in Isaiah 6:1; Matthew 1: 20, 24; and John 20:28 and other texts.

There are a number of objections to translating *adonai* as *Ambuye*. First, when the *Buku Loyera* translators were discussing the use of *Ambuye* for *YHWH* it was found that translating as *Ambuye* was not really satisfactory and awkward especially when there was a combination of *Ambuye Mulungu* (LORD God) since *Ambuye* is in plural and *Mulungu* is singular. For this reason, the use of the term *Ambuye* in Genesis 2-3 was rejected.[50]

Second, if *Adonai* is to represent or substitute *YHWH*, it should have been consistent throughout the biblical text. Yet, both *Chauta* and *Ambuye* have been used in some texts such as Genesis 2 where *Chauta* is used and *Ambuye* in Isaiah 6.1. Such use is inconsistent.

Third, in Chichewa the term *Ambuye* was appropriately used not by a subject to king nor a wife to a husband, nor a son/daughter to father, nor a subordinate to a leader as was the meaning of *adonai*. Among the Chewa people, the word *mbuye* is used by a slave to his or her owner. The word *mbuye* refers to the slave/owner relationship. It was a slave (*kapolo*)[51] who called his or her slave owner *mbuye*."[52] A slave (*kapolo*) is a person owned by another person. A slave has no rights and can be used in whatever way the owner may wish. A person can

---

[49] Anderson, "God, Names of," 414.
[50] Wendland, *Buku Loyera*, 119.
[51] Steven Paas, *Chichewa/Chinyanja-English Dictionary*, Blantyre: CLAIM-Kachere, 2013, 193, 1052.
[52] Ibid, 298, 972.

5. Translating "Lord Jesus" as "Bwana Yesu"

become a slave by being captured as a prisoner of war (Gen 14:21), or being purchased from another owner (17: 12-13), or by birth for being a child of a slave in the household (Gen 15:3), or as a restitution due to failure to pay criminal damages (Ex 22:3), or by default on debts or self-sale into slavery for dependence on another person to escape poverty (Lev 25:39-43) or by abduction (Dt 24:7).

The Bible does not portray God as a slave owner. Rather, God is referred to as *Adonai*, meaning "Lord" or "master" of His appointees, the prophets, whom He called to serve Him as servants. The designation "servant of God" (*ebed elohim*) refers to a prophet, regarded as a servant who is humble and whose goal is to accomplish the tasks assigned by his master. The possessive "his" recognizes the claim of God upon "his servant" the prophet (1Kg 14:18; 2 Kgs 17:23; 21:10; 24:2). Motyer observes that this designation was never used as "servant of God" but God used it himself when he referred to the prophet as "my servant" (2 Kgs 17:13; Jer. 7:25) and consequently the people used the possessive pronoun and described God's prophets as "his servant" (2 Kgs 17:23; 21:10; 24:2) or "your servant" (Ezr. 9:11).[53] When God warned the Israelites by reminding them of earlier messages given by His prophets He would say "my servants the prophets" (2 Kgs 9:7; 17:13 Jer 7:25; 25:29; Zech 1:6). Through this designation, God approved and confirmed the devotion and obedience of the prophets who faithfully declared his word. Therefore, God is never referred to as slave owner. Rather He is *Adonai*, Lord or Master.

Among the Chewa the term *mbuye* refers to slave owner, and it evokes the slave/owner relationship. *Mbuye* is not applied to the servant/ master relationship. That should be the reason why when "servant-master" concept was introduced in Malawi, the term *mbuye* was not

---

[53] Motyer, "Jehovah," 1278.

used to refer to the servant-master relationship. In Malawi we do not call a master *Mbuye*. There is another word for that.

There are indications that the term *mbuye* was used to translate Lord during the time when there was slave trade in Malawi. The slave traders captured slaves in Malawi and the slaves called the slave traders or owners *Ambuye*. When the missionaries wanted to translate the word "Lord" into Chichewa they used the term which was used for slave-owner relationship *mbuye*. But when the missionaries established the servant-master relationship concept, they did not use the term *mbuye*. They used another word which we will introduce below.

This means that the term *Ambuye* has negative connotations for the Chewa people. If *mbuye* is used for YHWH it would imply that all those who call YHWH as *Ambuye* are his slaves. This could be contrary to the way *adonai* was used for God as outlined above. The Israelites were not slaves of God. It was YHWH who rescued the Israelites from Egyptian slavery (Ex 20:1-2). According to Bartchy, where Paul refers to "slaves of Christ", the phrase is used metaphorically to show self-imposed commitment to Christ.[54] It does not literally mean that we are Christ's captives, but that we have voluntarily and willingly decided to commit our lives to Christ as our Lord, to be his servants not his slaves.

This implies that translating *Adonai* as *Ambuye* is problematic. First it is in the plural, yet we are referring to one God not many gods. Second, it has negative connotations in that the subject who uses the term is a slave of a slave owner, yet God was not a slave owner.

---

[54] S.S. Bartchy, "Slavery," in *The International Standard Bible Encyclopedia*, Vol 4, Grand Rapids: Eerdmans, 1988, 539-546 [546].

Translating "Lord" as *Bwana*

The above discussions do indicate that in Chichewa there is no word or phrase to translate the term Lord which represents Tetragrammaton. What is required is to find a dynamic equivalent and contemporary translation of the term Lord which relates to "servant–master" relationship as observed above.

According to the Chewa economy, servant-master was not part of their life. People did not work for someone else for payment. The servant–master relationship was not part of the Chewa economy. In as far as the Chewa community was concerned, there was total solidarity in that there was observance of community services. The Chewa people used to help each other, and not work for payment. If someone was sick or old, his or her relations would arrange to work for him without pay. It was the responsibility of the community to sustain and "care for the feeble and the poor."[55] If one had a large garden and felt he could not finish it alone, he could ask some people to work for him but not for pay. His wife could brew beer (*mowa*) or sweet beer (*thobwa*) or nsima with meat (*nyama*) for people to drink or eat while they are working for him. Such activity was called either *phala lolima* (sweet porridge for work) or *nsima yolima* (food for work).[56]

Another approach to communal service was that a group of families would agree to work in each other's garden in turns. They would work in one garden this day. The next day they would work in another's garden and so on and so on until that arrangement was completed. This arrangement was known as *chiwira*.[57]

---

[55] Martin Ott, *African Theology of Images*, Blantyre: CLAIM-Kachere, 2000, 498.
[56] Interview, Mayi Nangondo of Mamba Village, 12 June 2014.
[57] Interview, Group Village Headman Gusu, 20 July 2015.

When this was done, it did not occur to the people that they were slaves or servants of the owner of the garden. It was regarded as communal work. Everyone felt that it was responsibility of each person to help one another. The reason behind it was that the produce from the garden was for everybody because, if anything happened everybody would benefit from it. If someone had no food, one would ask for help from someone for whom one had worked and would not buy that food. If there was a funeral or a wedding in the village, food would be collected from each family for the function without asking for pay. Therefore, among the Chewa there was no concept that one was a servant of the other.

There are indications that the concept of a servant (*wantchito*) to work for someone for payment came with the arrival of missionaries who had to employ someone to work for them and be paid for the work done.[58] The Chewa had no such arrangement in their economy. When this was introduced, they did not find any Chichewa vocabulary for that service. They did not use the word *mbuye* because it did not fit the servant-master relationship. *Mbuye* was for the slave–owner relationship yet this new phenomenon was for the servant–master relationship. The workers could voluntarily work for someone else for pay and would decide to stop working if they wished to do so. They were not slaves in that service. In view of not finding any Chichewa vocabulary for such service the only possible way was to borrow from another language.[59]

By this time there were interactions between the missionaries in Malawi and Kenya.[60] There are many Kiswahili words which have been borrowed into Chichewa. One of these words is *ndege*, a Swahili

---

[58] Steven Paas, *Chichewa/Chinyanja-English Dictionary*, 565, 1041.
[59] Wendland, *Buku Loyera*, 9, 45.
[60] Thomas Jesse Jones, *Education in East Africa*, London: Phelps-Stokes, 1960, 125.

word for bird which they have used to translate aeroplane.[61] The Chewa of Malawi have also borrowed the Kiswahili word *bwana* for boss, master or Lord.[62] In Chichewa, servants call their masters *Bwana*. The title is used for every master at the workplace, and it is used for District Commissioners who are referred to as "Bwana DC".[63] Like the title *Adonis*, the term *Bwana* is a title of honour and respect. If the title *Bwana* is used for *Adonai* to substitute *YHWH* it would imply giving honour and respect to God and would express God's dignity, dominance, absolute lordship and holiness. In Kiswahili, "Lord Jesus" is translated as *Bwana Yesu*. In Chichewa, the translation could be the same.

It is, therefore, submitted that the divine name *YHWH*, which the Israelites substituted with the term *adonai* in order to give respect to the sacred divine name, be translated in Chichewa with a Kiswahili borrowed title *Bwana* which will give the divine name *YHWH* the dignity and holiness it deserves.

Conclusion

This chapter has noted that transliteration of *YHWH* presents problems. It was observed that *Yehova* or *Jehovah* or *Yahve* was unintelligible and does not make sense in Chichewa. Translating *YHWH* as *Chauta* was seen to be problematic because the name *Chauta* refers to a female God. Therefore, to translate *YHWH* as *Chauta* would indicate to the Chewa that *YHWH* is a female God. Secondly, translating *YHWH* as *Chauta* and pronouncing it, is contrary to the tradition attached to the name *YHWH* since pronouncing the name was prohibited.

---

[61] Paas, *Chichewa/Chinyanja-English Dictionary*, 382.
[62] Paas, *Chichewa/Chinyanja-English Dictionary*, 31, 905, 919.
[63] Paas, *Chichewa/Chinyanja-English Dictionary*, 31.

Translating *Adonai* as *Ambuye* is problematic. First, the word *Ambuye* is in the plural yet we have one God. Second, in Chichewa the term *Ambuye* is used by slaves referring to their owner. This is contrary to the way *Adonai* was used for God who rescued the Israelites from slavery. The term *Ambuye* has negative connotations in that it refers to the slave/owner relationship, whereas *Adonai* refers to the servant/master relationship.

It has, therefore, been proposed that the Tetragrammaton be translated as *Bwana* – a title used by a servant to his master or boss, and that this title will give the divine name *YHWH* the dignity and holiness it deserves. It is hoped that future Chichewa Bible translators will take this proposal seriously.

Chapter 6

Situating Malawian Neo-charismatic Apostles in the New Testament

Felix Chimera Nyika

Introduction

Apostles are alive and well in Malawian Neo-charismatic churches. We have Apostle Stanley S. Ndovie Apostle Madalitso Mbewe and Apostle C.J. Tsukuluza to name but the famous few.[1] The problem, however, is that mission-initiated Protestantism has fostered the traditional Protestant view of apostles as those who were commissioned as such by Jesus and were entrusted with encapsulating his teaching into Scripture so that only the Twelve, Paul, Barnabas, and James qualify as apostles.[2] Does the New Testament itself define apostolic office in such a restrictive way? I argue in this chapter from a biblical theology standpoint that contrary to the restrictive Protestant view of apostleship, a word-study of *apostolos* and *pempō* show that the essence of apostleship was in the commissioning of the sent and that the New Testament shows a variety of apostles differentiated by the salvation history transforming event of Pentecost so that there are pre- and post-Pentecost apostles, and that the presence of false apostles militates against the idea of a restricted apostleship as traditionally understood. I conclude with a brief analysis of my

---

[1] For a study of Malawian Neocharismatic apostles and their self-conception, see my *Apostolic Office amongst Malawian Neocharismatics: A Contextual, Biblical-Theological, and Historical Appraisal*, Mzuzu: Mzuni Press, forthcoming 2021.

[2] See Wayne Grudem, *Systematic Theology: An Introduction to Bible Doctrine*, e-book, Grand Rapids: Zondervan, 2000, 791.

thoughts on what apostleship entails. Due to limitations of space, I have neither delved into all the passages that use the words *apostolos/apostellō* and *pempō*, nor all passages that harbour the concept of apostleship, nor defended the continuation of apostolic office today.

Etymology of apostolos/apostellō and pempō – Conceptualizing the Apostolic Task

The word apostle was used with the word boat (*ploion*) in Classical Greek for naval expeditions. Later *apostolos* was used to refer to a crew of men sent out for a specific purpose – whether a band of colonists and their settlement or the commander of an expedition – and carried with it an adjectival passive character so that it denoted the quality of being sent. Though Rengstorf asserts that *apostolos* was never used of an emissary in the Greek language, which has many other words suitable for the purpose such as *angelos* or *kēryx*, surmising that its use by the Christian church was innovative; however, the evidence proffered by BDAG contradicts such an assertion.[3] In Hellenistic Judaism, Philo does not use the word but Josephus uses it twice in the sense of sending emissaries when he refers to a Jewish delegation to Rome on a sea-voyage. The LXX uses the word only once in 1 Kings 14:6, where Ahijah the prophet says to Jeroboam's disguised wife who has come to inquire of the fate of their ill son, that Ahijah has been "charged with unbearable news" for her. The LXX translates the passive participle שלוח (*šā luăchă*) as *apostolos* – which is the word "charged" in the English Standard Version (ESV) – thereby

---

[3] See Karl H. Rengstorf's "ἀπόστολος" in Gerhard Kittel (ed) and Geoffrey W. Bromiley (trans), *Theological Dictionary of the New Testament*: Volume I, Grand Rapids: Eerdmans, 1964, 407-445.

6. Situating Malawian Neo-charismatic Apostles in the NT   115

giving *apostolos* a technical and theological sense as it points to Ahijah's prophetic commission.[4]

Since Jesus probably did not use the Greek term apostle for his disciples but must have used a Hebrew or Aramaic equivalent, the traditional view has been to locate the background of the word in the Rabbinic institution of the *šā·liăch*. However, there are difficulties with this view since it is doubtful that Jesus actually used the word *apostolos* when commissioning his disciples as an examination of the parallel texts in Mark 3:14 and Luke 6:13 attests. Moreover, it is anachronistic to speak of the institution of *šā·liăch* as a background since the use of the nominal form of *šā·liăch* cannot be dated to literature earlier than the second century AD.[5]

The word *apostolos* is a derivative of the verb *apostellō*, which carries the basic meaning of "send" (*things or persons*), "send away," "chase away," and "send off."[6] Together with its cognate *exapostellō*, *apostellō* is used by the LXX more than 700 times to translate the Hebrew word *šā·lăch* which means "to stretch out/send," but with the authorization to fulfil a particular task (Jos 1:16; 1 Kin 5:9; 20:9; 21:11; 2 Kin 19:4; Jer 34:3). It seems the emphasis of *apostellō* then is on the authorization to fulfil a particular task. Only five other times is *šā·lăch* translated by *pempo* (send) in the LXX, though *pempo* occurs 26 times in the LXX. In 1 Kings 14:6 – in translating the passive participle of *šā·lăch*, *šā·luăch* – the LXX uses the word *apostolos*. It is not far-fetched to see that Jesus' background for apostleship, though he may not

---

[4] See Karl H. Rengstorf "ἀπόστολος" 407-445.
[5] Colin G. Kruse, "Apostle" in Joel B. Green, Scot McKnight, and I. Howard Marshall (eds), *Dictionary of Jesus and the Gospels*, electronic edition, Downers Grove, Ill: Inter-Varsity, 1992.
[6] See Erich von Eicken and Helgo Lindner "apostellō" in Colin Brown (ed), *The New International Dictionary of New Testament Theology*: Volume I, Grand Rapids: Zondervan, 1975, 126-127.

have used the Greek word *apostolos* but probably an Aramaic equivalent, is to be found in the OT prophetic commissioning.

Pempo is a less problematic word as its general sense is "send" and as it is used of human beings or other beings possessing a personality and of things in Homer, inscriptions, papyri, the Septuagint, *Epistle of Aresteas*, Josephus, and the *Testament of the 12 Patriarchs*.[7] When used in the former sense, it can refer to the sending out of God's envoys. When his enemies sent officers to arrest him, Jesus said he would soon be going to him who "sent" (aorist active participle of *pempō*) him (John 7:33). His judgement is not his alone but also of the Father who "sent" (aorist active participle of *pempō*) him just as he does not bear witness of himself but the Father who "sent" (aorist active participle of *pempō)* him (John 8:16, 18). The Father who "sent" (aorist active participle of *pempō*) Jesus is not only true (John 8:26) but he who "sent" (aorist active participle of *pempō*) him is also present with him (John 8:29).

The etymology of these Apostolos and *pempō* show that apostleship has more to do with authorization to fulfill a particular task rather than restricting apostolic office to the Twelve, Paul, and James or other restrictive combination of those that saw the historical Jesus.

A Variety of Apostleships

Apostleship in the NT encompasses a wide semantic range from occasional envoys sent on a particular mission like "apostles of the churches" sent to Corinth to collect the church's gift towards the Judean relief effort (1 Cor. 8:23) to those whose commissioning is vocational. The concept is also used to denote both the function of

---

[7] "pempō" in William F. Arndt and F. Wilbur Gingrich (eds), *A Greek-English Lexicon of the New Testament and other Early Christian Literature*, 2nd ed, Chicago: University of Chicago, 1979, 641-642.

being sent and the office. In the occasional sense of apostleship, the function is usually stressed; in the vocational sense, the office is in view. Moreover, pre-Pentecost and post-Pentecost notions of apostleship seem to be mediated differently. All these facts militate against seeing apostleship as just a single concept that applies to the office of the Twelve and Paul. The NT evidence forces us to see apostleship as a very wide concept that encompasses both function and office.

Pentecost – The Watershed Moment in Apostleship

The rays of vocational apostleship of the Gospel seem to be refracted by the prism of the cross of Christ as there is a transition from the pre-resurrection Jesus to the post-resurrection Jesus so that the physical commissioning of the former period takes on a spiritual dimension after his resurrection. Specifically, after the Paraclete has come on the Day of Pentecost, the instructions of Jesus are mediated through him so that he is now the one who sends on mission and marked a new epoch in redemptive history of eschatological import. This new epoch in salvation history is observed in that the ascended Lord Jesus was crowned and sent the Holy Spirit who empowers the church for witness by not only internalizing the revelation of God among His people but also by the democratization of the charismata (Acts 1:8; 2:1-4; Rom. 12:4-8; 1 Cor. 12:1-31; Eph. 4:7-13) thereby advancing the kingdom of God.[8]

Pentecost also has eschatological import as Luke locates it in Jerusalem whence eschatological salvation is expected (Luke 24:49b; Acts 1:2, 6-8; 2:17); he uses the word *epangelia* for "promise" in Acts 1:4 ("the promise of the Father") which he uses elsewhere for the Abrahamic covenant ("the promise is for you and your children",

---

[8] See Willem A. Van Gemeren, *Interpreting the Prophetic Word: An Introduction to the Prophetic Literature of the Old Testament*, Grand Rapids: Zondervan, 1990, 357-360.

Acts 2:39; cf. Gen. 17:7-10) thereby signifying that the outpouring of the Spirit is inaugurating a new covenantal era; his use of the introductory formula "in the fulfillment of the day ..." (Acts 2:1) to speak of Pentecost, parallels OT terminology that he ascribed to the birth of the Messiah (Luke 2:6) and Jesus' resoluteness to die and rise in Jerusalem – both of which are key events in salvation history – he is implying that Pentecost is a similar type of event; he clearly demarcates a line between Pentecost and the time prior to it when he narrates that the only Spirit-filled people are Jesus, John the Baptist, and the latter's parents before Pentecost while there is a democratization of Spirit-filling after it; he shows that John the Baptist's expectation that Jesus would baptize with the Spirit and fire is only realized on the day of Pentecost (Luke 3:16; Acts 2:17); his description of Pentecost is akin to Philo's giving of the law (*The Decalogue 32-33*) thus equating the two events so that it can be said that he considered Pentecost to be the giving of a new law; and, his list of the nations in Acts 2:5 has (1) eschatological overtones as it was the Old Testament expectation that diaspora Jews and all the nations would be regathered to Jerusalem to enter into a new and everlasting covenant with God and (2) is intended to portray Pentecost as a reversal of Babel (Gen. 11:1-9) especially by his use of similar verbiage to the latter passage.[9]

Pre-Pentecost Apostles

In this category are the apostles sent by God, the apostles of the Lamb, and the apostles to the nations.

---

[9] See Graham F. Twelftree, *People of the Spirit: Exploring Luke's View of the Church*, Grand Rapids: Baker, 2009, 75-78.

Apostles of God

These apostles are those that are sent on a mission by God such as Jesus Christ, John the Baptist, and angels. The most significant apostleship in this category is that of Jesus as the sent-one of God whose mission is unique insofar as his vicarious atonement and other functions made efficacious by his deity. Though he stands in the šā·lāh tradition of the Old Testament, he surpasses it as he is also the fulfilment of many of its prophecies. His self-understanding as an apostle is clearly evidenced in Matthew 15:24 when he informs the Canaanite woman during his ministry in Tyre and Sidon that he was sent (aorist passive of *apostellō*) only to the lost sheep of Israel. He was sent to serve men even to his death (20:28) and is figuratively sent (aorist indicative of *apostellō*) by his Father to murderous farm tenants (21:37). He is also sending (present active indicative of *apostellō*) prophets, wise men, and scribes to Israel (23:34), but Jerusalem is a city that kills prophets and stones those sent to it (plural passive participle of *apostellō*) (23:37). However, Jesus' apostleship has a limited scope since he was "sent only to the lost sheep of Israel" (Matt 15:24) and scarcely evangelized non-Jews.[10] The unique apostleship of Jesus is the basis of the apostleship of the Twelve whom he endows with authority "over unclean spirits, to cast them out, and to heal every disease and every affliction" as he did during his pre-resurrection mission (Matt 10:1).

John the Baptizer is understood by Jesus as the "sent" (aorist active indicative of *apostellō*) messenger who prepares the way of the Lord (Luke 7:27). Apostleship in John begins in the prologue (1:1-18) with John the Baptizer who was "sent" (perfect passive participle of *apostellō*) by God to bear witness to the Christ (1:6), "sent" (aorist passive participle of *pempō*) to baptize with water (1:33), and "sent"

---

[10] Colin G. Kruse, "Apostle."

(perfect passive participle of *apostellō*) ahead of Jesus (3:28). In Luke, the *apostellō* motif begins with angel Gabriel's self-enunciation that he stands in the presence of God and was "sent" (aorist passive indicative of *apostellō*) to speak to Zechariah, John the Baptizer's father (Luke 1:19).

The Twelve Apostles of the Lamb

There is continuity between Jesus' apostleship and that of the Twelve as observed above. The Twelve symbolize the new Israel that Christ has become the embodiment of through his fulfilling roles that Israel had failed to fulfil. This is also seen in the replacement of Judas Iscariot with Matthias so that their symbolic number is maintained (Acts 1:15-26). They have such a unique role that they are distinguished from later apostles as the Apostles of the Lamb who make up the foundations of the wall of the New Jerusalem (Rev 21:14). Initially, the Twelve have a similarly limited scope of apostleship as Jesus, only to the Jews during their Galilean mission (Matt 10).[11] When he commissions them, Jesus tells his disciples that the harvest is plentiful but the labourers are few so they should earnestly pray to the Lord of the harvest to "send out" (aorist active subjunctive of *ekballō*) labourers into the harvest (9:38). It is in response to that prayer that Jesus chooses and empowers (10:1) twelve of his disciples, whom Matthew designates apostles (genitive plural of *apostolos*) (10:2-4), to "send" (aorist indicative active of *apostellō*) them on a mission amongst the Jews (10:5-11:1). Matthew uses the word *apostolos* only here in his gospel and does not attribute

---

[11] This evidences Jesus' understanding of his disciples along the *šā·lîăḥ* paradigm, see Colin G. Kruse, "Apostle."

it to Jesus as do the other synoptic writers (cf. Mark 3:14 and Luke 6:13).[12]

However, the Great Commission (Matt 28:18-20) takes the mission of the Twelve further as now the resurrected Jesus has universal authority which enlarges their mission to a universal one. Further, the mission will now incorporate the making of other disciples globally who would be taught and assimilated into the apostolic community. There is really no difference between this grander universal mission and the localized mission in Galilee (Matt 10), except the geographical scope of the mission. The activities remain the same as do the instructions. Moreover, the Great Commission is addressed to the remaining eleven disciples who are representative of the whole church. Essentially then the apostolic commission does not cease until the end of the age is reached through apostolic operations by which "this gospel of the kingdom will be proclaimed thought the whole word as a testimony to all nations and then the end will come" (Matt 24:14). One can adduce then that the Great Commission is predicated on the assumption of the continuation of the ministry of the apostles.

The 70/72 Apostles to the Nations

This group – symbolic of the table of nations in Genesis 11 – is sent with the same instructions issued to the Twelve so that they too are apostles. Jesus appoints and "sends" (aorist active indicative of *apostellō*) 70 or 72 others in pairs ahead of himself into towns that he is about to visit (Luke 10:1). These 70/72 are symbolic of the mission to the Gentiles as the number seems to be an allusion to the table of the nations in Genesis 10. Though they are not given the appellation "apostles," they are functioning in such a capacity given the similar

---

[12] Both Mark and Luke have the phrase "whom He named apostles," which better manuscripts omit as shall be discussed below in the Mark section.

instructions to the apostles. Jesus informs them that the harvest is plentiful but the labourers are few so they should pray to the Lord of the harvest to send (aorist active subjunctive of *ekballō*) labourers for the harvest (Luke 10:2; cf. Matt 9:37-39; John 4:35). He is "sending" (present active indicative of *apostellō*) them out as lambs amidst wolves (Luke 10:3; cf. Matt 10:16). They are to neither carry nor make provisions for their journey (Luke 10:4), but accept hospitality from sympathizers (Luke 10:5-8), heal the sick and proclaim the gospel (Luke 10:9), and pronounce judgement on towns hostile to the gospel (Luke 10:10-12). To hear the message of the 72 or 70 and to reject it is tantamount to hearing and rejecting the Father who "sent" (aorist active participle of *apostellō*) Jesus (Luke 10:16). It should also be noted that this mission was not a Lucan creation but is very much historical.[13]

Post-Pentecost Apostles – A New Sender

After his resurrection, Jesus promises his disciples that they would be filled with power to be global witnesses when the Holy Spirit will come upon them (Luke 24:49; Acts 1:4-8; John 20:21-23; cf. Matt 28:16-20). At his ascension to the right-hand of the throne of the Father, he sends the Holy Spirit together with the Father (John 14:16-17; 16:13-15). From then onwards the Holy Spirit is the sending agent of the Father and the Son just as Jesus was the sending agent of the Father; he is in effect the commissioning agent of mission (John 14:12, 25-26; 16:7). Sending in this era of the Holy Spirit is supernatural and can be through visions (Acts 9:1-9; 26:19) and prophecy (Acts 13:1-2). In this category are Paul and his apostolic team, James, and other unnamed apostles.

---

[13] See Colin G. Kruse, "Apostle."

Paul, Barnabas, and the Pauline Apostolic Team

The commissioning of these apostles is not specified, except in the case of Paul who was called to apostleship on the Damascus Road when he encountered Jesus in a vision (Acts 9:3-19). This was later confirmed by the church in Antioch when both he and Barnabas were commissioned by the Holy Spirit through a prophecy that sparked their first mission (Acts 13:1-3). Barnabas, whose name was changed by the apostles from Joseph to denote his generosity (4:32-37), is "sent" (aorist active indicative of *exapostellō*) by the apostles in Jerusalem to Antioch (11:22). While at Antioch during a season of prayer and fasting, the Holy Spirit speaks through a prophet(s) that Barnabas and Paul should be "set apart for the work to which I have called them" whereupon the prophets and teachers "send them off" (aorist active indicative of *apoluō – send, cause another to depart*) (13:13). Luke summarizes the event as their "being sent (aorist passive participle of *ekpempō*) out by the Holy Spirit" (Acts 13:4). Luke finally adumbrates Barnabas' and Paul's ministry when he specifically calls them apostles during their ministry in Iconium (14:4) and Lystra (14:14).

This group grows to include Timothy, Epaphroditus, Epaphras, Tychicus, Silvanus/Silas, Titus, and Artemas all of whom function as apostles. Timothy is notable in this group as Paul is "sending" (aorist active indicative of *pempō*) Timothy – his "beloved and faithful child in the Lord" – to Corinth to remind the believers of Paul's ways in Christ (1 Cor. 4:17).[14] Further cementing the idea that Timothy is an envoy, the Corinthians should "put [him] at ease" among them since "he is doing the work of the Lord" just like Paul and so should not

---

[14] Fee asserts that "this verse implies that Timothy is going in Paul's stead, and therefore that he is to be regarded by them as though Paul himself were present among them," Gordon D. Fee, *The First Epistle to the Corinthians*, The New International Commentary on the New Testament, Grand Rapids: Eerdmans, 1987, 188.

be despised (1 Cor. 16:10-11).[15] Others place Apollos also in the category of apostle and, as a companion of Paul's, he may be grouped here.

James, Andronicus and Junia

These three are given the appellation apostle in the NT, though their commissioning is not mentioned. Probably their calling to apostleship was before Paul's (1 Cor. 15:7; Rom. 16:7). Though others see Andronicus and Junia not as "apostles of Christ" but as "apostles of the churches," probably such a distinction emanates from a too restrictive definition of apostleship that is not warranted by the NT text. For example, Ellis asserts that this couple cannot be "apostles of Christ" – which he understands as they had seen the historical Jesus – because: (1) they are not as famous as Peter, James, or Paul himself and yet are called "outstanding amongst the apostles"; and, if they were "apostles of Christ" the phrase "who were in Christ before me" is a tautology.[16] However, their fame may not be the only thing that makes them "outstanding amongst the apostles." Moreover, the appellation "apostles of Christ" need not have its main criteria as those who saw Jesus as this is not the core of apostleship as much as the sending itself. As has been shown, many functioned as apostles who did not see Jesus in the flesh but may have had revelations of Jesus calling them as did Paul.

Unnamed Apostles

These include the 500 apostles to whom the resurrected Christ appeared (1 Cor. 15:7), the unnamed brother travelling with Titus and

---

[15] Fee calls Timothy "Paul's personal delegate," Gordon D. Fee, *The First Epistle to the Corinthians*, 822.

[16] See Earle E. Ellis, "Paul and His Coworkers," in Gerald F. Hawthorne, Ralph P. Martin, and Daniel G. Reid, *Dictionary of Paul and His Letters*, electronic edition., Downers Grove, IL: InterVarsity Press, 1993, S. 183.

the "apostles of the churches" (2 Cor. 8:16-24), and those that preached the gospel to Peter's readers (2 Pet. 3:1, 2). These 500 apostles are not named and they are probably a larger group of apostles which included the Twelve. Fee posits three options commentators have chosen as to who comprises "all the apostles": (1) Peter, the Twelve, and James, so that "all the apostles" means Christ appeared to all of them at once; (2) "all the apostles" is referring to the Twelve in a second commissioning appearance to them; and (3) another group of apostles not mentioned before.[17] Fee sees the last option as the most viable one, explaining that Christ's appearance to the disciples in Acts 1:6-11 would have included not only Peter, the Twelve, and James but also others who later came to be known as apostles so that the term "apostle" here is used in a more functional than an official way.

Paul's co-workers accompanying Titus to Corinth to collect the church's gift towards the Judean relief effort are commended as "apostles of the churches" (8:23) with one of them having been appointed (*cheirotoneō*) by the churches for this particular task (8:18-19).[18] Since 2 Peter is a general letter sent to many Gentile congregations, one would not be wrong to surmise that the Apostle Peter expected that other apostles had planted these churches.[19] Though Ellis terms these as "apostles of the churches" – commissioned missionaries who did not see Jesus and thus were of a lower level of apostleship than the "apostles of Jesus Christ" who saw Jesus – and would include Epaphroditus (Phil 2:25), and Andro-

---

[17] Gordon D. Fee, The First Epistle to the Corinthians, 731-732.
[18] See Paul Barnett, *The Second Epistle to the Corinthians*, The New International Commentary on the New Testament, Grand Rapids: Eerdmans, 1997, 426.
[19] See Richard J. Bauckham, "2 Peter," in Ralph P. Martin and Peter H. Davids, *Dictionary of the Later New Testament and Its Developments*, electronic edition., Downers Grove, IL: Inter-Varsity Press, 2000, c1997.

nicus and Junia (Rom. 16:7); however, if post-resurrection apostleship is mediated by the Holy Spirit through the church, as with Paul and Barnabas (Acts 13:1-2), these need not be deemed lesser than the "apostles of Christ," especially since they have similar functions. Ellis also relegates this group to a lower level on the basis that they did not see Jesus yet he himself asserts that the title "brother" is used by Paul to refer to "those whose ministry takes on a travelling missionary character (2 Cor. 2:13; 8:18, 22-23; cf. Acts 10:23; 11:12)" which, when shod of its "having-seen-Jesus" criteria, will locate such "brothers" in the realm of apostleship.[20]

The Presence of False Apostles

The presence of false apostles (2 Cor. 11:13; Rev 2:2) in the NT seems to militate against the view that there was a closed circle of apostles restricted to the Twelve, Paul, James, Barnabas, Andronicus, and Junia – or indeed whatever restrictive combination can be thought of. Paul's polemic in 2 Corinthians is against super-apostles (*hyperlianapostolos*) compared to whom he does not deem himself inferior though they may be more skilled in rhetoric (11:5-6).[21] They challenge Paul's apostleship and accuse him of being unimpressive in presence and speech (10:10). They boast that their *modus operandi* is like Paul's, but they are really "false apostles (*pseudapostolos*), deceitful workmen, disguising themselves as apostles of Christ" (11:13) who "enslave, devour, take advantage of, put on airs, or strike [the Corinthians] in the face" (11:19-20). The threat of such "apostles" points to the fact

---

[20] See Earle E. Ellis, "Paul and His Coworkers," S. 183.
[21] See Colin Kruse, *The Second Epistle of Paul to the Corinthians: An Introduction and Commentary*, The Tyndale New Testament Commentaries, Grand Rapids: Eerdmans, 1987, 48-49.

that apostleship in the early church was not thought of as confined to the Twelve and Paul.[22]

If the apostles were a small closed circle, then the issue of false apostles who are not even named would not have been an enormous problem as they could be easily identified. It was because there were many apostles that were not as widely known that false apostles could arise. The fact that Paul recognized their apostleship (2 Cor. 11:5) and credentials (2 Cor. 3:1) indicates that apostleship was indeed not a tightly limited phenomenon.[23] Moreover, Paul does not appeal to the fact that these apostles were not party to a closed apostolic circle of the Twelve and others, which would have been a very convincing argument if it were true.

The Essence of NT Apostleship

So how should we conceive of apostolic office in the NT? Several conclusions stand out from a survey of the office in the NT:

Definition of an Apostle

An apostle is an envoy who is sent with Christ's cosmocratic authority (Matt 28:18) to fulfil Christ's global kingdom mission (Mark 1:14, 15; Matt 24:14) by laying the foundational truth of Christ's messiahship (Matt 16:15-19) on which Christ builds his church on earth (1 Cor. 3:10-15) in the context of spiritual warfare against Satanic forces (Matt 16:18; Eph. 6:10-19) to which the church demonstrates the manifold wisdom of God (Eph. 3:10).

---

[22] Kruse notes that such criteria for evaluating apostleship were very important in the early church in which there where many claims to apostleship, Colin Kruse, *The Second Epistle of Paul to the Corinthians*, 51.

[23] Ellis points to this fact but sees these false apostles as those who had seen Jesus and had turned rogue, Earle E. Ellis, "Paul and His Coworkers," 183.

The Work of an Apostle

In laying the foundational truth of Christ, apostles preach the gospel with or without attendant miracles so that non-believers are converted (Acts 3:1-26; 2 Cor. 12:12) and churches established (Acts 14:21-22; 2 Pet. 3:1, 2), appoint local church leaders (Acts 14:23; Titus 1:5), mentor other leaders and apostles (2 Tim. 3:10, 11), and give spiritual oversight to local churches to mobilize them for Christ's mission (1 Pet. 5:1-4; Eph. 4:11-13). Since such ministry is done in the context of spiritual warfare, apostles suffer persecution from elements that oppose Christ's mission (Acts 4:13; 2 Cor. 10:15-16) in their God given spheres of influence (Gal. 2:7-9; 2 Cor. 10:15-16).

The Place of Apostles

Apostles work with prophets in laying the foundational truth of Christ (Eph. 2:19, 20) as well as in sharing the Holy Spirit's revelation of the mystery of the church (Eph. 3:4, 5). Apostles are higher in rank to prophets in the hierarchy of offices in the church (1 Cor. 12:28; Eph. 2:20; 3:4, 5). Prophets build up the church through the charismatic gift of prophecy (1 Cor. 14:3), foretell the future (Acts 11:27-28; 21:4, 10-11), and give direction to the Holy Spirit's leading in a church (Acts 13:1-2). Apostles – together with prophets, evangelists, pastors, and teachers – complete the five offices of Christ that prepare and mobilize the church for the mission of Christ (Eph. 4:11-16).

The Gender of an Apostle

Women can also be apostles as evidenced by the presence of Junia amongst the apostles (Rom. 16:7) as well as, to a lesser extent, the similar apostolic work of Priscilla and Aquila (Acts 18:18, 26; Rom. 16:3; 1 Cor. 16:19; 2 Tim. 4:19). Paul sends greetings to Andronicus and Junia, probably a husband-and-wife apostolic team, whom he refers to as kinsmen and fellow prisoners, "well known amongst the apostles," and who were in Christ before him (Rom 16:7).

Conclusion

The evidence from the NT shows that an apostle is one who is sent with the full authority of the sender to act on his or her behalf. The concept of apostleship as found in the NT is quite robust and ranges from the occasional to the vocational. To maintain that NT apostleship was limited to the Twelve, Paul, and a select few who had seen Jesus, is to ignore the robustness of the concept in the NT. So, when Apostle Ndovie or Apostle Tsukuluza asserts that he has been commissioned by God through a vision or some other charismatic experience to proclaim Christ and plant churches, he is within the gamut of NT apostleship. Moreover, we should situate these apostles within the category of post-Pentecost apostles who are sent by the revelation of Jesus through the Holy Spirit.

Chapter 7

A Biblical Perspective on Covid-19 Pandemic and the End of the World

Luke Limbithu

Introduction

On 11 March 2020, the World Health Organization (WHO) declared coronavirus 2019 (COVID-19) to be a global pandemic.[1] This declaration has caused fear, anxiety, nervousness, and panic across all classes of people in the world. Politicians are helpless, medical professionals feel terrified as their own lives are on the line, business owners are scared that their businesses will crumble, religious leaders are looking for answers. Fear is the environment in which the world finds itself. The greatest minds of the world are grappling with this elusive deadly enemy. Most media outlets around the world are full of heart-breaking news of sickness and death caused by the Covid-19 pandemic. The human family has more questions than answers especially since scientists for most of 2020 were unable to find any remedy for this lethal virus.

This chapter seeks to find biblical answers to the following questions raised by individuals and groups: What is the biblical view of coronavirus? Is this pandemic a sign of the end of the world?[2] Is the

---

[1] World Health Organization, www.who.int/emergencies/diseases/novel-corona virus-2019/coronavirus-disease, [15.4.2020].

[2] Madeline Kalu, Does COVID-19 Fulfill Biblical Plague Prophecies, www.christi- anity.com/wiki/bible/does-covid-19-fulfill-biblical-plague-prophecies.html [7.5.2020].

coronavirus God's judgment on our society?[3] Should religious groupings adhere to restrictions imposed by medical experts and state authorities?[4] Is coronavirus God's call for us to have a day of rest per week from all our activities to allow humankind and nature to replenish?[5] If such questions are not addressed there is significant risk that the efforts of health authorities to contain the pandemic will be frustrated.

The Old Testament View of Diseases [Covid-19 Pandemic?]

This section explains how Old Testament teaching is relevant to the coronavirus. Scientists have found that the coronavirus is a large family of viruses which may cause illness in animals or humans. In humans, several coronaviruses are known to cause respiratory infections ranging from the common cold to more severe diseases such as Middle East Respiratory Syndrome (MERS) and Severe Acute Respiratory Syndrome (SARS). The most recently discovered is coronavirus which causes the coronavirus disease known as Covid-19.[6] There is no direct reference to the term coronavirus in the Bible. However, this disease can be regarded as one of the plagues or

---

[3] Paul Williams, Is Coronavirus the end of the world? www.youtube-.com/watch?v=wQUoS9wQPyQ [10.4.2020].

[4] Australian Government Health Department, Limits on public gatherings for coronavirus COVID-19, www.health.gov.au/news/health-alerts/novel-coronavirus-2019-ncov-health-alert, [22.5.2020].

[5] Hazon Videos, greensabbathproject.net, www.youtube.com/watch?v=c3BN_GnU5vI, [8.6.2020].

[6] World Health Organization, Coronavirus pandemic, www.who.int/-emergencies/diseases/novel-coronavirus-2019/coronavirusdisease,answers?gclid-=EAIaIQobChMI2aS61sbE6QIVNYBQBh133wZhEAAYASAAEgJuhfD_BwE&query=coronavirus, [15.4.2020].

pestilences, which do occur in the biblical narrative.[7] This is because of the way it is contracted and spread.

In the Old Testament the Hebrew term for plague or pestilence is *hp'GEm;* (maggēpâ, [Numbers 14:37]), and it occurs in Numbers 14:37; I Samuel 6:4; and II Samuel 24: 21,25. In both usages it is translated as "a blow," "slaughter," "plague," "pestilence," and "torment."[8] The same word pestilence is also referred as rb,D, (*deber*, and as used on Leviticus 26:25, and Numbers 14:12, it is translated as "pestilence." [9] This term is also identified in the Old Testament as @v,r, (*rešep*, as used on Psalm 78:48; Job 5:7; Deuteronomy 32: 24; Habakkuk 3:5, it is translated as "flame of love," "flame of a bow" and "pestilence." Naudé and Harrison, say that in some cases this term is used metaphorically for a devastating disease. They say its symptoms include high fever, shivering, pneumonia, and haemorrhage from mucous membranes. This was one of the most serious threats that God could level against disobedient Israel.[10] The terms *hp'GEm;* (*maggēpâ*), rb,D, (*deber*), and *rešep*, as used above underline the

---

[7] Plague or pestilence is an epidemic of varying intensity and widespread incidence that occurred through history of the world. It is also caused by a virus that spread fast and can be deadly and challenging to manage. (Marcantonio Raimondi, "Plague," *Encyclopaedia of Plague and Pestilence from Ancient Times to Present*, [3]2008, 199.)

[8] R.K. Harrison, *New International Dictionary of Old Testament & Exegesis*, vol. 2, Grand Rapids: Zondervan, 1997, 847.

[9] Ibid, 915.

[10] Jackie A. Naudé and R.K. Harrison, *New International Dictionary of Old Testament & Exegesis*, vol. 3, General Editor Willem A. van Gemeren, Grand Rapids: Zondervan, 1997, 1204-05.

seriousness of this threat.[11] This indicates that pestilences in the Old Testament had nothing to do with eschatological events.[12]

The New Testament View of Diseases [Covid-19 Pandemic?]

This part of the chapter explains how the New Testament makes reference to Covid-19 Pandemic. The Greek term for plagues or pestilences is *loimoi*, (*loimoi*, [Mathew 24: 7]) "pestilences," or "plagues." This word *loimoi* is also used in Luke 21:11.[13] This term is translated as "hunger" or "famine," (Luke 21:11), and it is also translated as "plague," or "pestilence" (Luke 21:11). In both Matthew and Luke, the term *loimoi* is used in reference to an event that will happen before the coming of Jesus Christ. Therefore, the term *loimoi* as used in the books of Mathew and Luke is translated as, "famine," "hunger," "plagues," or "pestilences." Therefore, *loimoi* can be identified with today's coronavirus. However, in the New Testament these "pestilences" are not the end of the world but events happening before the second coming of Jesus Christ.

State Restrictions and the Biblical Mandate to Gather Together for Worship

Following the outbreak of the Covid-19 pandemic in Malawi, medical experts advised state authorities to suspend regular meetings in large groups of more than one hundred people for all activities including

---

[11] R.K. Harrison, *New International Dictionary of Old Testament & Exegesis*, vol. 1, Grand Rapids: Zondervan, 1997, 915.

[12] Eschatology means end time events, or event happening before the coming of Jesus Christ.

[13] William D. Mounce, *The Analytical Lexicon to the Greek New Testament*, Grand Rapids: Zondervan, 1993, 303.

worship.[14] Some believers have questioned their leaders for obeying such restrictions.[15] Their argument is that in the Bible the scriptures say that, "not forsaking the assembling of ourselves together, as *is* the manner of some, but exhorting *one another,* and so much the more as you see the Day approaching" (Hebrews 10:25 NKJV). Luke in the Book of Acts says, "Peter and the *other* apostles answered and said: "We ought to obey God rather than men" (Acts 5:29 NKJV). These believers have used these texts to argue that medical experts and the state should not stop Christians from gathering in large groups in order to avoid contracting or spreading of the disease.

While the foregoing statements might be true, the same scriptures say that believers should obey those in state authorities because they are ordained by God. The book of Romans states:

> Let every soul be subject to the governing authorities. For there is no authority except from God, and the authorities that exist are appointed by God. Therefore whoever resists the authority resists the ordinance of God, and those who resist will bring judgment on themselves. For rulers are not a terror to good works, but to evil. Do you want to be unafraid of the authority? Do what is good, and you will have praise from the same. (Romans 13: 1-3 NKJV).

The scriptures further say, "Fear God. Honour the king" (I Peter 2:17 NKJV). The inspired word of God further says, "…Be of good comfort, be of one mind, live in peace; and the God of love and peace will be with you" (II Corinthians 13:11 NKJV). What these texts are saying is that believers just like any citizen are to live in obedience to the authorities because they are ordained by God. Therefore, it is imperative for believers to obey both medical experts and state

---

[14] The announcement made by the then State President of Malawi, Prof. Arthur Peter Mutharika on Malawi Broad Casting Television (MBC TV), 23.3.2020.

[15] Unpublished statements made by people of different religious groups following the announcement by the State President of Malawi Prof. Arthur Peter Mutharika restricting gatherings of more than one hundred people.

authorities because those in different positions of authority are also placed there by God.

On the other hand, it is a different matter if government decides to shut down churches as an act of persecuting Christians for obeying the law of God. Then the believers can protest and defy those in authority. In the case of Peter in Acts 5, he was told not to preach the gospel which is not the case with Covid-19 pandemic restrictions. If the church would defy medical advice on coronavirus, then it would run the risk of exposing the believers to the pandemic. Members ought to understand that this is a health issue and following health rules does not mean little faith in God. Even Jesus himself refused to jump over the pinnacle of the temple when tempted by the Devil. Matthew reports that Satan told Jesus saying, God would give charge of angels to take care of Him. But Jesus responded, "It is written again, you shall not tempt the Lord your God" (Mathew 4:4-7 NKJV). The response of Jesus to Satan indicates that, in human form as he was, if he jumped from the pinnacle of the temple to the ground he would have died. Similarly, believers should not be taking unnecessary risks believing that God will take care of them. Therefore, defying medical advice on Covid-19 pandemic would amount to taking the risk of contracting the disease.

Coronavirus and the End of the World

There have been other pandemics that affected the whole world in the past, but in the recent past the advent of Covid-19 pandemic has been the first disease in our generation to have huge impact on our lives followed by lockdowns worldwide.[16] This has made some religious believers to conclude that the coronavirus pandemic marks

---

[16] Lockdown is the law that restricts movement of human beings and goods. Including shutdown of companies and factories and people restricted to stay home.

the end of the world.[17] Others have suggested that the coronavirus is the antichrist predicted in the Bible.[18] This section discusses the connection some people are making between the coronavirus pandemic and the end of the world.

Because of the Covid-19 pandemic people around the world have been quarantined to contain the spread of the disease.[19] The lockdown among other things brought many restrictions to people and companies. It brought shut-down of production in factories, restriction of travel, less or no vehicles were allowed to drive in some places, movement of people was restricted and controlled.[20] MacArthur says that in these countries people are not allowed to meet in their places of worship. Because such restrictions are happening for the first time in the lives of some believers, and that they have never seen something of this magnitude in their lifetime, their interpretation has been that this is the end of the world.[21]

The gospels of Matthew and Luke indicate that pestilences are signs that the coming of Jesus Christ is near.[22] According to Matthew and Luke, pestilences in themselves are not the end of the world but signs of the coming of Jesus. The Epistle of John explains who the antichrists are. He says, "little children, it is the last hour; and as you have heard that the Antichrist is coming, even now many antichrists have come, by which we know that it is the last hour" (I John 2:18

---

[17] Unpublished sources.
[18] Ibid.
[19] Phil Johnson, "Interview with John MacArthur," www.youtube.com-Thinking Biblically-About-the [5.6.2020].
[20] Dough Batchelor, "Sunday Law News Report," www.youtube.com/watch?v=KCJ9L5UFtdc, [June 23, 2020].
21 Phil Johnson, "Interview with John MacArthur," www.youtube.com-Thinking Biblically About the COVID-19 Pandemic, [23.6.2020].
[22] Matthew 24:7 (NKJV); Luke 21:11(NKJV).

NKJV). In this text John acknowledges the presence of the antichrists and he describes them as the ones that deny the divinity of Jesus. He further says that they are the ones who deny the Father and the Son (1 John 2: 22 NKJV). He describes the antichrist as, every spirit that does not confess that Jesus Christ has come in the flesh (I John 4:3 NKJV). In addition to that, John says that the antichrists are deceivers gone out into the world who do not confess Jesus Christ as coming in the flesh (2 John 1:7 NKJV). John says that the antichrist is the one who denies the divinity of Jesus Christ, he also describes him as the one who does not confess that Jesus Christ came to us in human form.

The apostle Paul in his Second Letter to the Thessalonians, alludes to the idea of antichrist when he says, "…Let no one deceive you by any means; for that Day will not come unless the falling away comes first, and the man of sin is revealed, the son of perdition, who opposes and exalts himself above all that is called God or that is worshiped, so that he sits as God in the temple of God, showing himself that he is God" (2 Thess 2:2-4 NKJV). Although Paul does not directly mention the word antichrist, what he is saying implies or insinuates the idea of antichrist. The coronavirus pandemic is not the antichrist. This disease has only brought restrictions like how we interact with each other. The health authorities are only limiting us as regards how many can gather at once for worship but have not banned worship. The Covid-19 pandemic just like many other pestilences that have come in the past is just one of the signs of the end of world but not the end of the world.

Coronavirus and Calls for a Green Sabbath Day

This section explains calls made by organizations and individuals requesting those in authority to consider instituting or legislating a world day of slowdown or rest so that humankind and nature can rest. Organizations and individuals are calling for "one emission-free day per week."[23] These calls come because in countries where they had lockdown, at the end of it people noticed that the atmosphere was clear, there was fresh air and for the first time in many years they were able to see and hear birds.[24] So they believe that one day per week will bring a change to humanity and nature. They insist that people should have time to rest and socialize, something which is missing at the moment. They also maintain that nature will have a day per week to recover. Hence they are calling for "at least one carbon footprint-free each week on any day of the week."[25] Israel agrees with them and is calling for observance of Shabbat (Sabbath) each week for nature and people to rest.[26] Some are calling for "one common day of rest,"[27] and Kumar suggests that it should be Sunday.[28]

A study provided by McGrath shows that "in New York early results shows that carbon monoxide mainly from cars has been reduced by nearly 50% compared with last year."[29] This is because in 2018 there was no lockdown hence carbon monoxide from cars and industries

---

[23] greensabbathproject.net, www.youtube.com/watch?v=c3BN_GnU5vI, [5.5.20 20].

[24] Musona, *The Lockdown Experiences*, Basanti Colony, Odisha: Poets Pen, 2020, 128.

[25] greensabbathproject.net, www.youtube.com/watch?v=c3BN_GnU5vI, [5.5.20 20].

[26] Caroline Rothstein, "We need Shabbat now more than ever in the Days of Coronavirus," www.jpost.com/diaspora/we-need-shabbat-now-more-than-ever-in-the-days-of-the-coronavirus-623236, [2.4.2020].

[27] Joseph Tortelli, *If History Rhymes*, https://newbostonpost.com/2020/04/01/if-history-rhymes/, [1.4.2020].

[28] Satish Kumar, "Slow Sunday: The Simple Solution to Global Warming," www.theguardian.com/environment/cif-green/2009/sep/17/low-carbon-sunday [17.9.2009].

[29] Matt McGrath, "Coronavirus: Air pollution and CO_2 fall rapidly as virus spreads," www.bbc.com/news/science-environment-51944780, [19.3.2020].

was very high. Valenzuela says that we should be living and working in a way that does not tax the planet to a breaking point, by having a day off.[30] His view is that the current trend is taxing for the people and our mother planet. Field agrees when he says that we need a day of rest for ourselves and nature to recover.[31] In addition to that, Schorsch concurs and says, "The Sabbath in an era of climate change – an ancient Jewish practice may help to save us all."[32]

Conclusion

This chapter has established that pestilences akin to the Covid-19 pandemic in the Old Testament were God's punishment against disobedient Israelites and sometimes other nations who surrounded the Israelites. This study shows that the difference between the Old Testament and the New Testament pestilences is that in the New Testament, unlike in the Old Testament, pestilences are signs that the coming of Jesus Christ is near. This suggests that there is nothing we can do to stop them. This chapter has also found that believers of different religious groups should adhere to guidance provided by state and medical authorities in time of pestilences. In addition to that, this study also indicates that pestilences like Covid-19 pandemic are not the end of the world but signs of the end of the world. The chapter affirms the significance of a day of rest for humankind and nature to recover as was established by God in the beginning.

This study also asserts that God is the only one who declares the end from beginning, and from ancient time things that are not yet done.

---

[30] Michael Valenzuela, philstar global, www.philstar.com, [5.5.2020].
[31] Robert Field, "Why God Took Sunday Away," https://4the10.net/why-god-took-sunday-away.html, [6.5.2020].
[32] Jonathan Schorsch, "The Sabbath in an Era of Climate Change," www.tabletmag.com/sections/belief/articles/the-sabbath-in-an-era-of-climate-change, [4.2.2020].

This chapter has established that God will not do anything unless he reveals his secrets to his servants the prophets. This study reveals that with pinpoint accuracy Jesus precisely declared how the world will end. However, areas that might need further study are to establish the reasons why some believers would think to defy expert medical advice and still imagine that they are obeying God. It can also be of interest to find out how a single day of rest could be agreed upon by different religious groups who currently observe different days of worship.

References

Australian Government Health Department, Limits on public gatherings for coronavirus COVID-19, www.health.gov.au/news/health-alerts/novel-coronavirus-2019-ncov-health-alert/how-to-protect, [22.5.2020].

Batchelor, "Dough, Sunday Law News Report," www.youtube.com/watch?v=KCJ9L5UFtdc, [23.6.2020].

Burke, John, greensabbathproject.net, www.youtube.com/watch?v=c3BN_GnU5vI, [5.5.2020].

Field, Robert, "Why God Took Sunday Away," https://4the10.net/why-god-took-sunday-away.html, [23.6.2020].

Harrison, R.K., *New International Dictionary of Old Testament & Exegesis*, vol. 1, Grand Rapids, Michigan: Zondervan, 1997.

Hazon Videos, greensabbathproject.net, www.youtube.com/watch?v=c3BN_GnU5vI [8.06.2020].

Johnson, Phil, "COVID-19 Pandemic," www.youtube.com-Thinking Biblically About the day of rest, [23.5.2020].

Kalu, Madeline, "Does COVID-19 Fulfill Biblical Plague Prophecies," www.christianity.com/wiki/bible/does-covid-19-fulfill-biblical-plague-prophecies.html [7.5.2020]

Kumar, Satish, "Slow Sunday: The Simple Solution to Global Warming," *The Guardian*, www.theguardian.com/environment/cif-green/2009/sep/17/low-carbon-Sunday, [17.9.2009].

7. A Biblical Perspective on the Covid-19 Pandemic   141

Manisha, Musona, *The Lockdown Experiences*, Basanti Colony, Odisha: Poets' Pen, 2020.

McGrath, Matt, "Coronavirus: Air Pollution and CO_2 Fall Rapidly as Virus Spreads," www.bbc.com/news/science-environment-51944780, [19.3.2020].

Michael, Valenzuela, philstar global, www.philstar.com, [5.5.2020].

Mounce, D. William, *The Analytical Lexicon to the Greek New Testament*, Grand Rapids: Zondervan, 1993,

Mutharika, Arthur Peter, State President of Malawi, Malawi Broad Casting Television (MBC TV), [27.3.2020].

Naudé, Jackie and R.K. Harrison, *New International Dictionary of Old Testament & Exegesis*, vol. 3, Ed. Willem van Gemeren, Grand Rapids: Zondervan, 1997.

Raimondi, Marcantonio, 'Plague,' *Encyclopaedia of Plague and Pestilence from Ancient Times to Present*, 3rd ed 2008,

Rothstein, Caroline, "We need Shabbat now more than ever in the days of coronavirus," www.jpost.com/diaspora/we-need-shabbat-now-more-than-ever-in-the-days-of-the-coronavirus-623276 [2.4.2020].

Schorsch, Jonathan, "The Sabbath in an Era of Climate Change," www.tabletmag.com/sections/belief/articles/the-sabbath-in-an-era-of-climate-change, [4.2.2020].

Tortelli, Joseph, "If History Rhymes," https://newbostonpost.com/2020/04-/01/if-historyrhymes/, [1.4.2020].

Williams, Paul, "Is Coronavirus the end of the world?" www.youtube.com/watch?v=wQUoS9wQPyQ [10.4.2020].

World Health Organization, Coronavirus disease, www.who.int/emergencies/diseases/novelcoronavirus2019/coronavirusdiseaseanswers..., [15.4.2020].

Chapter 8

Response to Covid-19 by State and Church in Malawi: A Critical Reflection

Stewart Daison Kapinda

Introduction

The spread of infectious diseases which are classified as pandemics causes massive reactions from different sectors of society. In each decade there has been discovery of diseases classified as pandemics which have killed a substantial number of people. Some of these pandemics have affected regions in a continent and in some cases whole continents. In Africa the recent Ebola crisis in regions around DRC Congo caused massive reaction in the surrounding countries. African nations took necessary precautionary measures in order to prevent the disease from spreading among their people. Governments ensured that efforts to fight against such pandemics were funded. However, in Africa there has been massive squandering of financial resources in some quarters. Within Christian circles there has been a tendency to attribute such pandemics to God's judgment towards the sinful world or in some cases as indicating the end of the world (2 Chronicles 7:14, Matthew 24:35). This in many cases has affected how people respond to some of the precautionary measures. Covid-19, a new pandemic which has just emerged, has not been exempted from such type of interpretations.

This chapter investigates the response to Covid-19 by State and Church in Malawi. In order to achieve this, the origins of Covid-19 are highlighted. Of particular importance is how the Church and State responded to the global pandemic and the challenges that have been

8. Response to Covid-19 by State and Church in Malawi

faced. The study also looks at the critical responses which need to be considered in order for the Church to effectively contribute to the fight against the pandemic.

Covid-19 has constituted a serious challenge to the world as a whole and to the Malawian context in particular. For a start, Covid-19 causes respiratory infections ranging from common cold to more severe diseases such as Middle East Respiratory Syndrome (MERS) and Severe Acute Respiratory Syndrome (SARS). Covid-19 is the new disease outbreak caused by one of the strands of coronavirus.[1] It is estimated that Covid-19 transmission is significantly higher than seasonal influenza, MERS and SARS. In terms of transmission the disease is transmitted from person to person through droplets of moisture expelled when coughing or through contacting infected surfaces.[2]

This disease originally started in Wuhan province in China where it was spotted by Chinese scientists. The contagious nature of the disease has led to its rapid spread to major cities in countries like the USA, Italy, Spain and Britain. In Malawi, the first case of Covid-19 was reported on 2 April 2020 and the number rose exponentially until August when the number of cases began to decline.[3] Covid-19 has presented a challenge to the Church as well as to the State. It has affected the day-to-day affairs and operations of these two entities.

Covid-19 has claimed a lot of lives such that many governments have declared it a national disaster or emergency. In response to this threat, various orders have been made which have affected the operations of both the State and the Church. For example, strategies which include lockdown, restrictions of non-essential movements,

---

[1] Lau K.P. Susana and Jaser F.W. Chan, *Corona Viruses: Emerging and Re-Emerging Pathogens in Humans and Animals*, DOI 10.1186/s12985-015-0432-z, [4.5.2020].
[2] John Piper, *Coronavirus and Christ*, Wheaton: Crossway, 2020, 5.
[3] See https://covid19.who.int.

restriction on public gatherings and stay at home orders have been imposed on citizens and on institutions. These strategies have adversely affected people's economic, political and religious rights.

The Church's Public Health Responses

The Church has on the whole been compliant with orders by the State in Malawi.[4] For instance, the Church has adopted public health measures which can help contain the pandemic. In many cases local churches have created task forces to coordinate the Church's response within the congregation and in the community. These task forces have been seen working hand in hand with local health authorities in sensitizing people concerning issues of Covid-19. Furthermore, the Church in Malawi has taken special precautions and public health measures to slowdown or prevent the spread of Covid-19 among its members. For example, these precautionary measures include.

1. Ensuring that ill members stay home.
2. Ensuring social distance during an outbreak.
3. Limiting number of congregants.[5]
4. Providing tissues, masks and small bottles of sanitizer to congregants.[6]
5. Suspending church gatherings in high-risk areas.[7]

It is clear from these guidelines that the Church has accepted and is eager to implement the public health guidelines. This shows that the

---

[4] Gazette Extraordinary, *The Malawi Gazette Supplement*, 9th April, 2020, containing Regulations, Rules, etc. No. 4A, 13.
[5] Ibid.
[6] Jamie Aten and Kent Annan, *Preparing Your Church for Corona Virus (COVID-19): A Step-by-Step, Research-Informed and Faith-Based Planning Manual*, Wheaton: Humanitarian Disaster Institute, 2020.
[7] Ibid.

Church is able to handle issues that pertain to public health in dealing with spread of the virus.

Socio-Political and Religious Challenges

While Covid-19 is a health challenge and a disaster, this virus has also posed a challenge to the socio-political, economical and religious arena. The disturbance that this virus has caused is unimaginable. For instance, political regimes have used force in order to implement strategies which are very strict and sometimes not supported by legal provision. Fundamental rights such as the right to economic activity, rights of assembly, and freedom of the press have been hampered. In Malawi there was a case where the police were involved in chasing people out of the churches in Balaka district.[8] This harsh and unreasonable action was condemned by many in media as violating people's rights. Another development within Malawi's political arena involved the Presidential order which imposed a lockdown. Government ordered a lockdown against the backdrop of containing Covid-19. However, a number of people observed that this order was unreasonable because the process did not take into account the fundamental rights of people.[9] One of concerned civil society groups, the Human Rights Defenders Coalition (HRDC) argued that "they sought the injunction not because they were against the lockdown, but precisely because the government failed to put in place measures to cushion the poor during the lock down."[10]

---

[8] Mary Makhiringa, *Malawi: Police in Balaka Disburse Christians from Congregating.* https://allafrica.com, [13.7.2020].

[9] Hanibal Goitom, *Malawi High Court Temporarily Blocks Covid-19 Lockdown* www.loc.gov>law, [13.7.2020].

[10] Hanibal Goitom, *Malawi High Court Temporarily Blocks Covid-19 Lockdown* accessed [13.7.2020[.

In the United States of America, Kansas State Governor took a similar approach, issuing orders which were unfair and unreasonable. The governor ordered the police to arrest and fine congregants who chose to congregate at the Church Park to listen to sermon while in their cars. The Church challenged this order and was successful in the courts of law on the grounds that this was unfair.[11] Judge John Broome in his statement argued: "Churches and religious activities appear to have been singled out among essential functions for stricter treatment."

Another point worth noting is that Covid-19 emerged in Malawi at a period in which the Supreme Court had just ruled that there should be a fresh Presidential election after the result of the 2019 election was challenged by the opposition parties. Consequently, this scenario proved to be a challenge for Malawi in regard to adherence to public health measures. Political parties were seen campaigning in large crowds without adhering to public health measures. As a result, when the new government came into power people were unwilling to obey its regulations regarding Covid-19. Government officials including the President were seen attending funerals, church services and government functions that exceeded the recommended number of people per gathering as prescribed in Gazette Extraordinary, *The Malawi Gazette Supplement, 9th April, 2020, containing Regulations, Rules.*

In relation to this point, it is important to note that Covid-19 strategies and responses were being leveraged for political gains. In Africa, Covid-19 response funds were sourced from donors and also from tax-payers' money. In some cases, politicians have used organizations proximate to them to produce face masks, conduct

---

[11] Nelson Oliveira, "Federal Judge Halts Kansas Limiting Church Gathering to 10 People Amid Corona Virus," www.nydailynews.com accessed 28/04/2020.

8. Response to Covid-19 by State and Church in Malawi

awareness campaigns and distribute basic necessities.[12] Malawi under the leadership of Professor Peter Mutharika received $4.5 million from the USA and 1.7 billion from the UK in assistance for Malawi to respond to Covid-19.[13] However, it was reported that money intended to counter Covid-19 was being used without transparency. In some instances, cabinet ministers and government officials were reportedly pocketing in excess of K450,000 and K350,000 respectively on trips disguised as coronavirus intervention missions. This was very unfortunate because at this particular time civil servants in the health sector including doctors, nurses and hospital attendants were being denied the necessary risk allocation to help them carry out their duties.[14]

On the religious plane Covid-19 aroused a mixed reaction among various denominations. In some sections, preachers began preaching eschatological messages relating to the emergence of Covid-19. For example, using the imagery found in the book of Revelation, some Christian preachers emphasized that through the coronavirus several prophecies in the book of Revelation were being fulfilled. They focused on the prophecy that government authority would be employed to persecute the Church and also on the restriction on all economic transactions.[15] This was related to the ban on public gatherings, restriction of movement and lockdown. These restrictions were understood in terms of the imagery of Revelation 13:16-17.[16] However, some other Churches rather than alluding to the

---

[12] Hassan Isilow, *South Africa Probing Graft Allegation Over Covid-19 Funds* www.aa.com.tr>africa>safr, [13.7.2020].

[13] Owen Khamula, "Malawi: US Pumps in K3.4bn for Corona virus in Malawi amid Concerns of Fund Abuse," allfrica.com, [13.7.2020].

[14] Charles Pensulo, "Malawi Health Workers Protest Against Lack of Protective Gear," www.aljazeera.com, [13.7.2020].

[15] Ibid.

[16] Ibid.

eschatological message of the Book of Revelation, understood the situation as a crisis which presents a fight between good and evil. They avoided applying the eschatological message to contemporary history. These approaches within eschatological messages preached during this period caused some Christians to live in fear and hence affected their adherence to some of the public health measures. The eschatological messages also affected the way in which congregants accepted the news of coronavirus and also the measures which were being advanced by health officials to prevent the spread of the virus.

Furthermore, Churches remained in dilemma due to the position which was being advanced by the government in banning all gatherings, restricting movement and lockdown. Malawi was considering applying such strict measures following the example of neighbouring countries. However, the Church together with other civil society organizations was highly critical of the manner in which the State was proceeding to impose such measures. Their major concern was that Government was imposing measures without considering the views of other stakeholders like the Church who were to be affected by these restrictions. As one of the key stakeholders of civil society the Church felt excluded by the manner in which the government was handling the issue. Within Christian circles, Church leaders saw the restriction of numbers to 100 people per gathering as being reasonable. However, a problem emerged when the State announced that it is going to allow only 10 congregants per gathering. This announcement sparked massive reaction from the Church. One of the basic reasons was that the Church felt it was doing a great job in adhering to all public health measures, therefore saw no need for the State to impose new regulations. In addition to this, Church leaders thought it unreasonable for the government to effect these additional measures because as far as Malawi was concerned the numbers of infections and deaths were not high as compared to other countries. According to a research done by the Institute of Public

Opinion and Research, it was discovered that 73% of Malawians were ready to practise social distance, 97% were willing to go for testing if showing signs of Covid-19, and 83% feared Covid-19 as serious problem.[17] Perhaps this is why many took seriously Covid-19 measures from the beginning.

The Church's Prophetic Voice and Institutional Approach in Times of Crisis

The Roman Catholic Bishops, in their May 2020 pastoral letter titled *A Further Call for a New Era in Malawi: Leadership at the Service of Citizens*, pointed briefly to a few concerns. The Bishops said, "while appreciating the efforts made so far by the government and the international community in finding resources and setting up committees in response to Covid-19, there is still need for a more inclusive and coordinated approach, more public awareness campaigns and transparent use of resource."[18] What is striking from these sentiments is the fact that the bishops recognized a need for the fight of Covid-19 to be a collective responsibility of all key stakeholders.

Furthermore, in the Malawian context there is a strong folk memory of the time in 1992 when members of the clergy resisted policies and abuses of the government by using institutional and prophetic roles.[19] The Catholic Bishop's Pastoral Letter *Living Our Faith*, popularly

---

[17] Witness Tapani Alfonso, *Social and Economic Effects of Covid-19 in Malawi and Implication for Policy Makers*, Institute of Public Opinion and Research, 11.9.2020.

[18] Episcopal Conference of Malawi, A Further Call for a New Era in Malawi: Leadership at the Service of Citizens. Pastoral Letter 24 May 2020, Balaka: Montfort Media, 2020.

[19] Martin Ott, "The Role of the Christian Churches in Democratic Malawi (1994-1999)," in Martin Ott, Kings M. Phiri and Nandini Patel (eds), *Malawi's Second Democratic Election: Process, Problems and Prospects*, Blantyre: CLAIM, 2000, 122.

known as the Lenten letter of 1992, championed fundamental principles of freedom in society:

> Human persons are honoured – and this honour is due to them – whenever they are allowed to search freely the truth, to voice their opinion and to be heard, to engage in creative service of the community in all liberty within association of their own choice. Nobody should ever have to suffer reprisal for honestly expressing and living up their conviction: intellectual, religious or political.[20]

The above statement affirms the prophetic voice of Clergy in the Roman Catholic Church as regards fundamental principles of freedom in human society. The Catholic Bishops used their prophetic voice to outline these principles. Alister Kee argues that:

> the attempt to separate politics and theology is invariably done out of self-interest: political theology does not arise from opportunism or attempt to win strategic advantage, but a particular understanding of the way we can be true to the fundamental character of Christian faith.[21]

This therefore buttresses the point of engaging Christian faith and mission in matters that affect human society. In this regard, the gospel should not be restricted to spiritual matters. The clergy through this prophetic voice should be willing to stand for truth despite their doctrinal differences and boldly preach against the injustice and oppression which are emanating in this period of Covid-19.

Based on such understanding, it should not be understood that when the Church is preaching against the injustices occurring in this period, this should not be seen as an interference in politics, but rather as a commitment to Christian truth or biblical truth in the political context.[22] The Church should be committed to preach against socio-political injustices and sins in the nation in this period of Covid-19.

---

[20] Ibid.
[21] Alister Kee, *Scope of Political Theology*, London: SCM, 1978, 3.
[22] Ibid.

8. Response to Covid-19 by State and Church in Malawi

If members of the church neglect their prophetic role in a crisis like Covid-19, this can adversely affect the Church and its mission.

Arguably, not only is the prophetic voice necessary, the Church has institutions which are instrumental in governance, development and health.[23] These institutions are departments of church organizations and a vital part of civil society. Church institutions like the Catholic Commission for Justice and Peace (CCJP), Church and Society desks of CCAP Synods, Adventist Development and Relief Agency (ADRA) play critical roles in the socio-political affairs of the state. Therefore, in regard to this period, these institutions need to consolidate their positions and efforts in facing the threat of Covid-19. Therefore, it is important that these civil society institutions are adequately funded so that they engage in the critical of countering Covid-19. What is important here is that the public face of the Church should be directly involved in socio-economic and health affairs of citizens in ensuring people prevent the spread while enjoying their constitutional rights to a good extent. The government by itself alone cannot be victorious against this threat. The victory can only be a product of a collective and consolidated engagement. Therefore, this requires that the resources which are being allocated for Covid-19 should not only be targeted to the government but other institutions like the Church.

The response of the Church goes beyond Church departments and involves influential members of the clergy. Martin Ott in his article on "The Role of the Christian Churches in Democratic Malawi (1994-1999)," rightly observes that in the post one party era members of the clergy became active in the political sphere.[24] Some members of

---

[23] Austin Cheyeka, 'The Church, State and Politics in the Post-Colonial the Case of Zambia,' MA, University of Malawi, 2003, 179.

[24] Martin Ott, "The Role of the Christian Churches in Democratic Malawi (1994-1999)," 127.

the clergy today are incorporated in government functions to serve as ambassadors to other nations, as commissioners, members of boards of directors and chairmen of government parastatals. Consequently, in this period of Covid-19, these members of clergy in leadership positions ought not to find themselves in an ironical situation where, when people are fighting for better service and enjoyment of constitutional rights in the public domain amidst the corona virus pandemic, they find themselves remaining silent as a prophetic voice. The Christian clergy must not conform to the system when dealing with the socio-political sphere. The members of the clergy as part of the kingdom of God and agents therein must act to promote justice, peace and fairness amidst the corona pandemic.

The Church as an Agent of Truth

In view of all this, one can ask the question: should the church compromise its standards because of fear in regard to the virus? The Church must always remember some of the critical scriptures as they serve God in Malawi. These include:

1. You are salt of the earth (Mathew 5:13-16).

2. You are light of the world (Mathew 5:13-16).

3. I send you forth as a sheep among wolves (Mathew 10:16).

These are some of the critical questions in regard to the Church being the voice of the people and the prophetic voice. Micah 6:8 states: "what does the Lord require of you but to do justly, to love kindness, and to walk with your God." In view of Micah's admonishment, the Church and the State should do justly and show love to the people. The Church should not be a spectator in this pandemic. Rather it should be the voice of the voiceless and a prophetic voice to the state. In a period when governments are using the coronavirus pandemic to score political points, the Church ought to speak and condemn such actions. Consequential to this, the Church should defend its voice so that it plays a critical role in safeguarding the rights of the people.

However, speaking as a prophetic voice should not be used a conduit to preach messages that can adversely affect how people respond to Covid-19. Many people including faithful Christians have died in this period. Therefore, while acknowledging that there are various ways in which Covid-19 has been understood using eschatological lenses, preachers should speak the truth to their congregants that Covid-19 is deadly. Hence, they should continue promoting the public health measures. These measures include: social distance during an outbreak, limiting number of congregants, providing tissues, masks and small bottles of sanitizer to congregants, and suspending Church gathering in high risk areas. Preachers should avoid promoting messages which can adversely affect adherence to public health measures.

The State Should Walk the Talk

It is imperative for the State to continue respecting and protecting the rights of its citizens when implementing policies. Though Covid-19 has been very disturbing for government operations, the State still is bound to the constitutional provisions of the Republic. In contrast to the initial period where the Malawi government employed strategies which were very strict and sometimes open to legal challenge, the State should now make proper consultation on the impact of its regulation on the constitutional rights of its people. The State should be reasonable when applying strict measures, considering that many people have lost their jobs, and some are failing to make ends meet. Harsh and unreasonable strategies should be condemned because they violate people's rights.

It is important for the State to be fair and treat all sectors impartially. If the state chooses to implement strategies as those provided in Gazette Extraordinary, *The Malawi Gazette Supplement, 9th April, 2020, containing Regulations, Rules,* the Government should be the first to adhere to such principles. This is in contrast to the unfortunate situation where Government officials, including the President, were seen attending funerals, Church services and government functions where the numbers exceeded the recommended maximum set out in the regulations. The Government should be an example so that people should see how serious it is about containing the virus. Otherwise, if there is no seriousness, the resultant effect will be that people will be unwilling to abide by Covid-19 regulations.

Lastly, the Malawi government has always claimed to be serious about the fight against corruption. However, as seen earlier in this essay, serious amounts of money have been siphoned to organizations which benefit those in government. On the contrary the new government should refrain from abusing Covid-19 funds. In view of the fact that many have lost their jobs and the poor are suffering in the villages, the State should consider the needs of the people. Those who are working day and night as medical practitioners should be fully equipped with necessary equipment so that if Covid-19 spikes again, hospitals should be ready to address the new surge. Covid-19 response funds provided by donors and from taxpayers should not be abused by politicians.

Conclusion

Covid-19 is not a short-term threat; it is a reality that requires long-term strategies. The planning and implementation of strategies requires that the State operate within the confines of its legal mandate and with respect for the rights of the people. Furthermore, the State should not see the Church as an irresponsible organization which does not care about the threat of Covid-19. Rather, the State should recognize the capacity of the Church as an actor in responding to the threat. Furthermore, it crucial for the Church to remain aware that it has a mission to be a voice of the voiceless and the prophetic voice to the State. In cases where the rights of the people are being denied in this period, or at any other time, the Church should be the voice of the people. In addition to this, the Church should be a prophetic voice to the State, offering critical perspectives on policies and strategies being advanced by the State so that the rule of law and the will of the people in this democratic era be respected and protected.

References

Aten, Jamie and Kent Annan, *Preparing Your Church for Corona Virus (COVID-19): A Step-by-Step, Research-Informed and Faith-Based Planning Manual*, Wheaton: Humanitarian Disaster Institute, 2020.

Byamugisha, Gideon (ed), *Church Communities Confronting HIV and AIDS*, London: SPCK, 2010.

Cheyeka, Austin, "The Church, State and Politics in the Post-Colonial the Case of Zambia," PhD, University of Malawi, 2003.

Episcopal Conference of Malawi, "A Further Call for a New Era in Malawi: Leadership at the Service of Citizens," Pastoral Letter, 24 May 2020, Balaka: Montfort Media, 2020.

Goitom, Hanibal, "Malawi High Court Temporarily Blocks Covid-19 Lockdown," www.loc.gov [13.7.2020].

Isilow, Hassan, "South Africa Probing Graft Allegation Over Covid-19 Funds," www.aa.com.tr>africa>safr, [13.7.2020].

Khamula, Owen, "Malawi: US Pumps in K3.4bn for Corona virus in Malawi amid Concerns of Fund Abuse," allfrica.com, [13.7.2020].

Makhiringa, Mary, "Malawi: Police in Balaka Disburse Christians from Congregating," https://allafrica.com, [13.7.2020].

Nosmanga, Julia Molatji and Caroline Tuckey, "Recommendations to Church Leaders and Communities," in Gideon Byamugisha (ed), *Church Communities Confronting HIV and AIDS*, London: SPCK, 2010.

Nelson, Oliveira, "Federal Judge Halts Kansas Limiting Church Gathering to 10 People Amid Corona Virus," www.nydailynews.com, [28.4.2020].

Ott, Martin "The Role of the Christian Churches in Democratic Malawi (1994-1999)," in Martin Ott, Kings M. Phiri and Nandini Patel (eds), *Malawi's Second Democratic Election: Process, Problems and Prospects*, Blantyre: CLAIM-Kachere, 2000.

Pensulo, Charles, "Malawi Health Workers Protest against Lack of Protective Gear," www.aljazeera.com, [13.7.2020].

Piper, John, *Coronavirus and Christ*, Wheaton: Crossway, 2020.

Gazette Extraordinary, *The Malawi Gazette Supplement*, 9th April, 2020, containing Regulations, Rules, etc. No. 4A.

Susana, Lau K.P., and Jaser F.W. Chan, "Corona Viruses: Emerging and Re-Emerging Pathogens in Humans and Animals," DOI 10.1186/s12985-015-0432-z, [4.5.2020].

Ross, Kenneth R., "The Transformation of Power in Malawi 1992-94: The Role of the Christian Churches," in Kenneth R. Ross (ed), *God People and Power in Malawi: Democratization in Theological Perspective*, Blantyre: CLAIM, 1996, 15-40.

Chapter 9

The Abiding Influence of African Traditional Religion among Educated Christian Professionals in Northern Malawi

Joyce Dainess Mlenga

Introduction

African Traditional Religion (ATR) is a designation for the indigenous religious beliefs and practices of Africans.[285] ATR is an inevitable religion among Africans. This is the case because it is not something in which one enrols. Rather one is part of it simply by virtue of being born and raised up in Africa. Those who are born into Christian families are not spared from it; they still get a dosage of elements of African Traditional religion through socialization and other means. This is true even with those who are born in urban settings. This is possible because African Traditional Religion is intertwined with culture, and there is a very thin line between the two. While research shows that education, modernity, and at times, urbanization, play a part in helping individuals to shun elements of African traditional religion,[286] experience has shown that many professionals make use of ATR elements regardless of their exposure to higher education and Christianity. The educated Christian professionals make use of some ATR elements, which are not compatible with Christianity, and this compromises their Christian commitment and

---

[285] Joseph Omosade Awolalu, "What is African Traditional Religion?" *Studies in Comparative Religion* 9.1 (1975).

[286] John Mbiti, *An Introduction to African Religion*, 2nd ed, Oxford: Heinemann, 1991, 192.

living. While at times the professionals appear to reject ATR elements in theory, based on their education or Christian profession, in fact they are much into them in practice and perceptions.

Definitions

The term *professional* in this chapter refers to anyone who earns their living from performing an activity that requires a certain level of education, skill, or training. It refers to someone who does a job that requires special training, education, or skill; someone who is a member of a profession.

Modernity is the state of being current, or up with the times. It is the state or quality of being contemporary.[287] Generally, it refers to adoption of new ideas over and against the traditional or primitive ones. In this chapter, the term has been used to refer to those who have adopted the new (modern) way of thinking, which tends to trivialize the elements of African Traditional Religion. *Urbanization* refers to the process by which more and more people leave the countryside to live in cities.[288]

Education, Modernity, Urbanization and African Traditional Culture

Scholars have written on the effect of education and urbanization on African Traditional culture. Thomas postulates that the need for formal education and urbanization contributes to several people not being attached to their traditional culture. This, therefore, leads to the erosion of traditional culture in Africa.[289] The need for formal

---

[287] Oxford Languages, https://languages.oup.com/google-dictionary-en.
[288] *Cambridge Advanced Learner's Dictionary*, 3rd ed, Cambridge: Cambridge University Press, 2011.
[289] Douglas Thomas, *African Traditional Religion in the Modern World*, Jefferson: McFarland & Company, 2005, 152-153.

9. The Abiding Influence of ATR

education, which is linked to employment, forces many traditional Africans to send their children away from the village to be educated.[290] Apart from children being sent to the cities, some parents live in cities and raise their children there. In traditional society, the village once served as the centre of education and spiritual nutrition.[291] Since the village is no longer central to many who seek formal education, those who live in cities fail to pick up the ATR elements that are generally held and practised in rural areas. Under normal circumstances, this arrangement of staying away from the village would lead to detachment from ATR elements, since it is within the culture that the religious elements are found. However, this appears not to be the case, because the abiding influence of ATR is still very evident in both young and old Christian professionals.

ATR and Educated Christian Professionals

This chapter argues that there is an abiding influence of ATR in educated professionals, something which was expected to be minimized after attaining higher education.[292] A study which I carried out among the Ngonde of Northern Malawi shows that education plays a role in leading Christians to reject some ATR elements.[293] One

---

[290] For parents who send their children to cities for education, the children begin to question, challenge, and ridicule some of the beliefs which parents in the village hold dearly.

[291] Douglas Thomas, *African Traditional Religion*, 152-153.

[292] This is not to say that educated professionals must forsake elements of traditional religion in favour of scientific knowledge, but there are ways in which the illogical things in the traditional religion can easily be spotted by those who have been exposed to higher education. There are times when professionals trivialize certain traditional beliefs and practices, but in the end, they fall into the same wagon of believing in the same things they reject.

[293] Joyce Mlenga, *Dual Religiosity in Northern Malawi: Ngonde Christians and African Traditional Religion*, Mzuzu: Mzuni Press, 2016, 296-297.

of the reasons which the respondents gave for not subscribing to some ATR elements was that they are ashamed to be associated with it because its beliefs do not make sense to someone who has a high critical reasoning capacity. They argued that they failed to see connections between what people believe in and how the beliefs work. The ATR elements appear to be old-fashioned, primitive and illogical as well as irrational. In addition to education, modernity is also bringing in a lot of changes and mixing of cultures which are watering down some of the beliefs and practices.[294] For instance, some educated Christians who go to urban areas and live there for a long time, do not have regard for traditional beliefs when they return to their rural homes. Even when they are in urban places, they do not practise everything their parents taught them when they were growing up in the village, especially those related to ATR. In order to be in line with western thought, the professionals tend to join the western countries in proclaiming ATR as being untrue, shameful, primitive, and pagan.[295] There are also times when some Christian professionals wear a mask in that what they profess is not what they practise. For instance, some claim that witchcraft does not exist, but they are the same people who rush into thinking that they have been bewitched when something goes wrong in their lives. They trivialize some things in public to be seen to be modern while clinging to them dearly in private.

---

[294] Richard Gehman, *African Traditional Religion in Biblical Perspective*, Nairobi: East African Educational Publishers, 1993.

[295] Douglas Thomas, *African Traditional Religion*, 170. Let me add that some reject ATR elements due to their Christian commitment. They do not find them compatible with Christian teachings.

Specific Examples of Involvement in ATR

Many Christian professionals are involved in some way, in the beliefs and practices of ATR, and one of such ways is at the level of perceptions.[296] Perception about causation is one of the major reasons that account for usage of ATR elements by many professionals. These perceptions lead them to behave in a strange way because they become suspicious due to superstition. A good number of those who occupy senior positions in organizations tend to be suspicious that someone might want to take over their positions, through use of witchcraft. It is believed that witchcraft can cause illness in an individual or bring misfortune or even cause someone to be dismissed unceremoniously.

There are several incidents that illustrate the fact that the behaviour of some professionals is motivated by suspicion. I have even witnessed instances where some senior managers do not want to sit in pre-arranged chairs in a meeting.[297] On several occasions, a senior manager with a professorial rank, could change the seating plan before the meeting started. When he was once asked, he indicated that he was not comfortable to use the seats because his perception was that some of his workmates did not wish him well and could therefore harm him through witchcraft. Along the same vein, that same officer could not allow any junior officer to help him carry his bag. When declining the offer, he liked to jokingly say, "*muli nyanga umu*" (meaning there are some charms in this bag). He claimed that it

---

[296] It is important to note that the involvement is sometimes a casual one, but in some cases, what they do reveals what the people really believe in. People normally do what they do because of what they believe. For example, when one gets sick, he may visit a traditional healer, and not the hospital due to perception of causation. But after being educated, we expect such perceptions to change.

[297] Of course, one might argue here that this is also common in political circles, and it is done for security reasons.

was possible for some workmates to place charms in his bag that might harm him. There are also times when some officers move about with office keys, and no one can access their offices if they are away. They are afraid that other professionals can place charms in their offices which can bring bad luck. In some cases, some professionals do not take tea in their offices, and usually prefer soft drinks, which they are sure that no one has administered any herbs into the bottle. There are also occasions where senior officers embark on a journey without informing their colleagues for fear that one may cause accidents through witchcraft. A case in point is one professional who was granted a scholarship to study in the United States of America (USA). He was reluctant to release any information concerning his departure programme. Whenever he was asked about his trip, he lied that his travel schedule had not been confirmed yet and promised to communicate when it would be ready. He only communicated after he had arrived safely in the USA. He hid the information because he did not want people to know that he had left, fearing he would have been involved in an accident that would have made him fail to reach his destination.[298]

Sometimes those who are suspected of practising witchcraft are either sacked or transferred, more especially, junior officers. This is common in the private sector. If they do not have powers to sack or effect transfers, they take steps to defend themselves. To counter the witchcraft attacks, the bosses may visit traditional healers or diviners in order to "protect" themselves from witchcraft attacks.[299] At times, they may seek spiritual interventions from pastors or prophets of

---

[298] It is worth mentioning here that this happens due to fear emanating from their own and other people's experiences.

[299] In a study conducted among the Ngonde, the traditional healers did indicate that they serve a wide range of clients, even those in high positions in institutions. See Joyce Mlenga, *Dual Religiosity in Northern Malawi*. It is not secret that among those who consult diviners or traditional doctors today, Christians are in majority.

9. The Abiding Influence of ATR

different churches. It is usually those occupying managerial positions that become superstitious with every motive of their workmates and are filled with fear thinking that their enemies might bewitch them. The thinking is that others are jealous of their positions. These kinds of demands upon their lives do drive some Christian professionals into practising elements of ATR, a religion not compatible with Christianity.

Besides perception of causation, one of the main reasons why there is an abiding influence of elements of ATR in the minds of Christian professionals is the linkage between religion and culture. It is said that Africans view the world through a religious lens. There is no line of demarcation between the secular and sacred within the traditional African mind. Religion and existence in traditional African society are inseparably linked. Wherever Africans reside, they take their religion with them.[300] Whether they attend a party or religious function, "African peoples do not know how to exist without religion."[301] This explains why some Christian professionals practise ATR elements, whether consciously or unconsciously. For some, they do not practise ATR intentionally, in their mind, they are practising their culture. Being children of culture, human beings assimilate the meanings and values of their culture either consciously or unconsciously, through a process called enculturation. Patterns of culture become second nature to them. Cultural cues are signals that prompt us to behave in a certain way and these cues are assimilated from others in our culture. These cultural cues dictate our behaviour. For instance, perception is one of the cultural cues which define how a person, thing or event is to be perceived. Every person's behaviour would

---

[300] John Mbiti, *African Religions and Philosophy*, New York: Frederic Praeger, 1969, 2.

[301] Douglas Thomas, *African Traditional Religion in the Modern World*, Jefferson: McFarland & Company, 2005, 92.

flow from "implicit norms of perception shared by all in a particular culture."[302] Therefore, even though education plays a part in having people reject ATR elements, it has been argued that cultural practices cannot be changed by education alone.[303] Culture has to do with the assumptions and logic the people use to construct their world.[304] This is therefore what remains in individuals, whether they are educated or not; whether they are Christian or not. It is a fact that ATR elements have survived amidst education and modernity. It is a fact that many of the educated Christian professionals shun some elements, but it is also true that, there are some which still remain in their lives, which are not compatible with Christianity.

Implications for Christian Faith

Definitely, involvement in ATR elements which are not compatible with Christianity, by a Christian, amounts to dual religiosity for a Christian professional. Dual religiosity compromises the Christian faith. Dual religiosity shows that one does not fully trust in God, and therefore thinks of supplementing his faith with something else. It is equivalent to serving two masters, a thing which is discouraged by the Bible.[305] According to Mbiti, the acceptance of Christianity or Islam in Africa means that Africans "come out of African religion but they do not take off their traditional religiosity. They come as they are. They come as people whose world view is shaped according to African Religion."[306] \\\This makes Christian commitment difficult, but the biblical teachings require that commitment. Educated

---

[302] Bruce Malina, *The New Testament World: Insights from Cultural Anthropology*, Atlanta: John Knox Press, 1981, 14.
[303] John Lwanda, *Politics, Culture and Medicine in Malawi*, Zomba: Kachere, 2005, 155.
[304] Paul G. Hiebert, R. Daniel Shaw and Tite Tiénou, *Understanding Folk Religion: A Christian Response to Popular Beliefs and Practices*, Grand Rapids: Baker, 1999, 22.
[305] Matthew 6:24, NIV.
[306] John Mbiti, *African Religions and Philosophy*, New York: F. Praeger, 1969, 11.

Christian professionals must strive to reject those elements, not based on their education and academic qualifications, knowledge or skills, but based on their Christian profession. The Bible is the standard for every Christian, and if some beliefs and practices go against this teaching, those ones should not be encouraged. Hillman rightly states that: "All cultures are presumed to be compatible with Christianity, even though all are defective and always in need of healing grace."[307] Where there is conflict between ATR elements and Christianity, Christianity must always win. It is important to study what God says concerning fear and adopt Christian perceptions, if any, so that if one chooses to subscribe to the Christian faith, he or she must be prepared to live by its standards.

Conclusion

Educated Christian professionals in northern Malawi are humans just like everybody else and are entitled to hold beliefs including those of African Traditional Religion. Education and Christianity play a role in having these professionals reject some ATR elements, especially those which are not compatible with Christianity, but the influence of these continue to persist in their lives, even though they reject them in theory. It is therefore important for the educated Christian professionals to evaluate their Christian commitment using the Bible as a standard for their Christian living. The ATR elements that are compatible with Christianity should be saved, those which are not must be thrown away. The fact that people have embraced Christianity shows that they are not satisfied with the ATR elements, and Christianity is more appealing to them. However, they appear to slip back to the old ways for various reasons, and this compromises their Christian commitment. It is evident that no amount of

---

[307] Eugene Hillman, *Toward an African Christianity: Inculturation Applied*, New York: Paulist Press, 1993, 27.

education can take away ATR elements, but there is need to adopt a new world view, one that avoids dual religiosity.

Bibliography

Awolalu, Joseph Omosade, "What is African Traditional Religion?" *Studies in Comparative Religion* 9/1, (1975).

Gehman, Richard, *African Traditional Religion in Biblical Perspective*, Nairobi: East African Educational Publishers, 1993.

Hiebert, Paul G., R. Daniel Shaw and Tite Tiénou, *Understanding Folk Religion: A Christian Response to Popular Beliefs and Practices*, Grand Rapids: Baker, 1999.

Hillman, Eugene, *Toward an African Christianity: Inculturation Applied*, New York: Paulist, 1993.

Lwanda, John, *Politics, Culture and Medicine in Malawi*, Zomba: Kachere, 2005.

Olowola, Cornelius, *African Traditional Religion and the Christian Faith*, Achimota: African Christian Press, 1993.

Magesa, Laurenti, *African Religion: The Moral Traditions of Abundant Life*, Nairobi: Paulines Publications Africa, 1997.

Mbiti, John, *African Religions and Philosophy*, New York: Frederic A. Praeger, 1969.

Mbiti, John, *An Introduction to African Religion*, 2nd ed, Oxford: Heinemann, 1991.

Mlenga, Joyce, *Dual Religiosity in Northern Malawi: Ngonde Christians and African Traditional Religion*, Mzuzu: Mzuni Press, 2016.

Thomas, Douglas, *African Traditional Religion in the Modern World*, Jefferson: McFarland and Company, 2005.

Chapter 10

Relevance of Theology in the Age of Secular Humanism

Gerard Chigona

Introduction

More than ever before, we seem to be plunging into a sea where theology is regarded with suspicion. This is suspicion of the very basis for theological possibility and certainty. Secular humanism has succeeded in creating a hostile ideological climate that presents itself as a profound theological problematic. It is an age where science and technology are taking centre stage in academic discourse and in the public sphere with the confidence and certainty of religious dogma. A new global society is on the rise built on belief in the omnipotence of science and technology in the face of human predicaments. Simultaneously, in some parts of the world, the religious space is shrinking and blurring, with theology getting more and more confined to the margins of the public discourse.

Could it be that Auguste Comte (1798-1857) was right? Comte advanced what he called laws of three stages in the development of society.[1] Myth and religion, argued Comte, represent efforts of primitive societies to explain reality. For the society of the future, Comte was certain that only science and technology would provide the ultimate response to elusive questions of life. In some quarters, already the language is changing now. There are references to a post-

---

[1] *Reader's Digest Library of Modern Knowledge, Philosophy and Ideas*, London: Reader's Digest, 1978, 649.

Christian era,² with more and more people having no notion of Christianity or any form of religion.³ In recent times, the Covid-19 pandemic with the near closure of places of communal prayer and worship has deepened even more the question of the relevance of religion and theological claims. This chapter addresses the possibility and relevance of theology and theologizing in an increasingly secularizing world.

Secular Humanism

We are familiar with theology, the discourse about God in relation to the world, humanity and history. The expression *in relation* suggests a restricted narrative. It is restricted in that the concern is not so much with God in his abstract immensity, but rather who God is in relation to us women and men. Hence theology could as well be understood as the discourse of the known unknown.⁴ Relations are both constructed and revealed. Constructed relations are founded on shared social nature and human freedom, underpinning all expressions of communal life. On the other hand, revealed relation pertains to the inherent and inalienable condition of dependency on God, beyond human freedom, a gratuitous self-giving of the divine. Thus, John Milbank can write: "theology reserves to itself the knowledge of God as a loving creator who has also redeemed the human race."⁵ For Karl Barth, theology is always a post resurrection

---

² Harvey Kwiyani, *GBN News.Com*
³ An online source: *GBN News.Com*. According to Stephen Bullivant, between 70% and 75% of people in their 30s are not religious, and between 80% and 90% of the population in Europe have no religion.
⁴ Royce Gordon Gruenler, *The Inexhaustible God: Biblical Faith and the Challenge of Process Theism*, Grand Rapids: Baker, 1983.
⁵ John Milbank, Catherine Pickstock and Graham Ward, *Radical Orthodoxy: A New Theology*, London: Routledge, 1998, 21.

phenomenon working within the eschatological horizon.⁶ Theology is a *Theo-centric* world view, a God-centred world view, looking at reality from a revealed perspective, a participation in a received narrative about us, in contrast to all narratives we construct for ourselves. Now this is the basis secular humanism rejects, the very foundation of the revealed narrative, making it baseless and illusory.

The term humanism is traceable to Italian slang centuries back. The first class of people to be called "humanists" were the 15th century teachers in the schools and universities of early Renaissance Italy.⁷ These teachers, or professors, taught what at that time was referred to as *studia humanitatis*, in today's language, humanities, a collection of subjects like literature, philosophy and the arts.⁸ Mark Vernon lists major developments of humanism stretching all the way from the works of ancient Milesian philosophers particularly Thales, Anaximander and Anaximenes. These are considered to be the first generation of thinkers in the development of humanism. Across the ages, the trend is identified with the works of prominent thinkers like Protagoras (5th century BC), Socrates (399 BC), Plato and Aristotle, the Epicurean and Stoic schools (4th century BC), Desiderius Erasmus (1509 CE), Niccolò Machiavelli (1513 CE), Karl Marx (1844 CE), and Jean Paul Sartre (1945 CE).⁹

In the recent past, however, the term humanism first appeared somewhere in the 19th century.¹⁰ It was eventually adopted and redefined by historians to specifically describe the key aspects and features of Renaissance thought. By the 20th century the term had

---

⁶ Graham Ward, "Bodies: The Displaced Body of Jesus Christ," in John Milbank, Catherine Pickstock and Graham Ward, *Radical Orthodoxy*, 163.
⁷ Mark Vernon, *Understand Humanism*, London: John Murray, 2010, xv.
⁸ Ibid.
⁹ Ibid.
¹⁰ Ibid.

come to carry explicit recognition and reference to the belief in the primacy and centrality of the human person in contrast to any belief or view that gives primacy to anything extra human.[11] As a philosophical trend, humanism has evolved over the centuries, without losing its fundamental claim which is the confession in the centrality of the human being as a free, rational and moral agent.[12] This is the cornerstone of humanism. It is about any view that accords primacy to the human being as the centre of the universe other than something else be it God, nature or ideology.

Major Trends and Characteristics of Humanism

There are diverse manifestations of humanism which include Marxist humanism,[13] pragmatic humanism,[14] Christian humanism,[15] Renaissance humanism,[16] and existential humanism. Central to existential humanism is the argument that existence is what is fundamental to the fact of being human, and that this existence is just a series of meaningless disconnected events. Stated differently, so far as it is meaningful to speak of it, ultimate reality is the perspective created by human choice. The world as such is indifferent, utterly

---

[11] Ibid.

[12] Ibid, xvi.

[13] As the name suggest, this trend is firmly rooted in, and draws its inspiration from the philosophy of Karl Marx

[14] This type treats ultimate reality as the general process of experience from which the subject and the object are differentiated as explicit factors. Pragmatic Humanism places primary interest on what works. In inclines more towards practical means and solutions. Leading thinkers in this line of thought include C.S. Pierce, William James and F.C.S Schiller.

[15] Mark Vernon, *Understand Humanism*, xxi.

[16] Ibid.

meaningless and absurd. Freedom is the only possibility of meaningfulness and transcendence, it is argued.[17]

There is also a trend commonly referred to as *atheistic humanism*. This trend is of particular interest to this discussion because of the challenge it presents to theological discourse. Unlike other trends which are largely agnostic,[18] atheistic humanism explicitly refutes and rejects the existence of God. Belief in God is considered a serious obstacle to human progress, growth and maturity.[19] Several grounds are advanced in support of this position. Chief among these is the experience of evil and suffering in the world, and the apparent inconsistencies among and between the very attributes associated with the idea of God.[20] While the problem of evil and suffering gives rise to *metaphysical atheism*,[21] the perceived inconsistencies in the attributes ascribed to the idea of God lead to *logical atheism*.[22] At the heart of logical atheism is the contention that we cannot in any meaningful way talk or say anything about God because the very attributes associated with the idea of God are inherently inconsistent.[23] Now with God dismissed, atheistic humanism resorts to science and technology to respond to questions and experiences of life. In this

---

[17] Central to existential humanism is the argument that existence is what is fundamental to the fact of being human, and that this existence is just a series of meaningless disconnected events. Stated differently, so far as it is meaningful to speak of it, ultimate reality is the perspective created by human choice. The world as such is indifferent, utter meaningless and absurd. But freedom, i.e. human existence itself, is the only possibility of meaningfulness and transcendence.

[18] Meaning they neither affirm nor deny God's existence

[19] Mark Vernon, *Understand Humanism*, xxi.

[20] Ronald Nash, The Concept of God: An Exploration of Contemporary Difficulties with the Attributes of God, Grand Rapids: Zondervan, 1983, 9.

[21] William Hasker, *Metaphysics. Constructing a World View*, Leicester: InterVarsity Press, 1983.

[22] Ronald H. Nash, *The Concept of God*, 9.

[23] Ibid.

regard, theories of evolution are instrumental in trying to explain the origins of life and the universe, with reason and human freedom as the basis of the moral order.[24]

Humanism places emphasis on the common practical human needs and seeks only rational means and approaches in resolving human questions and predicaments. As mentioned earlier, science and technology are, therefore, considered the most and only realizable tools. At the centre of humanism is freedom. Regardless of their preferred school of thought, humanists treat freedom as one of the constitutive ingredients of the very notion of being human. In freedom human beings determine their own actions and shape their fate and identity. For this reason, humanists are suspicious of secular institutions especially governments as well as religious ones like the Church. These pose threats due to their potential to hold people hostage by curtailing individual freedom through laws and doctrines.

Equally critical is the humanists' high esteem of nature simply because human beings are part of the natural world. Humanists have great appreciation of personhood and history. History is considered the most unswerving means of telling the truth, other than the medium of myths or divine revelation which escape verification. This thinking mimics a scientific approach which hinges on verification. Finally, humanists are profoundly sceptical about religion. They are cynical about religious traditions and authorities, thus prompting its rejection altogether. Instead, high value is placed on the unprecedented advances registered by empirical science over the centuries.

The Secular as an Invented Space

For a meaningful engagement, a deeper understanding of secular humanism, particularly atheistic humanism is critical. The reason is that this is the brand of humanism which rejects God's existence

---

[24] Such theories include the Big Bang.

10. Relevance of Theology in the Age of Secular Humanism

based on the experience of evil and suffering in the world. We need to start with the concept of the "secular" itself. The term refers essentially to the worldly realm, marking a sharp distinction and differentiation between the material and the immaterial. In recent times, however, a new development has occurred with an extension to the term *secularism*, thus in turn bringing about new meaning hinging on the rejection of religion. Secular humanism renounces traditional and authoritarian views, particularly those that invoke moral absolutes, established traditions or the will of God. As stated earlier, central to secular humanism is the understanding and belief that science and reason alone are the only reliable tools and authority humanity has at its disposal for empirical and moral knowledge. Beyond these tools, there is nothing reliable. Therefore, although secular humanism is not identical with science, it appropriates scientific theories in arguing for its case.

The term "secular" is a derived from the Latin, *saeculum*. In its original sense and application, the term refers to what today could be called a "generation" or an "age". As a term, "secular" starts to appear in discourse during the medieval times. And at that time the referent was an autonomous space, some sort of an imagined, conceptual and objective space. It is on the basis of this imagined space that we identify the primordial foundations of the modern state. As John Milbank argues, "the conception of society as a human product and therefore 'historical', remains one of the basic assumptions of secular social science."[25] Prior to medieval times, studies show evidence of the existence of a single community of Christendom, with its dual nature of *sacerdotium* and *regnum*.[26] The two institutions constituted the medieval society, and wielded power in determining and regulating

---

[25] John Milbank, *Theology & Social Theory: Beyond Secular Reason*, Oxford: Basil Blackwell, 1990, 11.
[26] Ibid, 9.

both the private and public space. Independent of the two institutions, no space existed for individual freedom and self-determination.

Therefore, "secular" as a term referred primarily to a time, the interval between the *Fall of Man* from grace, and the *eschaton,* i.e. the coming of God's reign. It is this expanse spanning across and in between the two moments of human history to which the term made reference. Again, it is within this interval where coercive justice and private property, begins to appear,[27] hence the emergence of the modern state.[28] Equally worth understanding is that during medieval times, reality in its totality was conceived and expressed in theological terms.

Critique of Secular Humanism

From the foregoing, in its original sense, therefore, the term secular does not in any way suggest or imply the rejection of God and religion. The term secular presupposes the sacred, the very existence of God. Essentially, the term delineates the realm of human freedom and that of the sacred. The affirmation of the sacred, explicitly or otherwise, makes the secular itself possible. Argued differently, for secular humanism to be truly and genuinely secular, it must of necessity affirm or presuppose the realm of the sacred, God. Potentially, the non-existence of the divine renders secular humanism itself empty and meaningless.

In the order of knowledge, three priorities are indispensable as premises. In the first place is the priority of time. When considered in relation to the denial of God's existence, a key characteristic of secular humanism, this can only be subsequent to a priori explicit or

---

[27] Ibid.
[28] Ibid.

implicit affirmation of His existence. Simple logic clearly proves that non-existence is inconceivable without explicit or implicit affirmation of existence. Outside the divine realm, existence never derives from non-existence, but non-existence does. In other words, what is never derives from what is not; but what is not derives from what is.

The second and the third priories are confirmation of the above point, i.e. the priorities of nature and thought process itself. The nature and manner of thought show that negations are always subsequent and not prior to affirmations, explicit or implied. Like a lie which has no independent existence apart from truth, negations have no existence on their own right apart from prior affirmations. If this were not the case, then the negation of the non-existent in either potency or actuality could be mere absurdity. Evidence is to be had of an institution, or indeed set of beliefs exclusively founded on falsehood, and yet has endured the test of time.

Secular humanism faces another monumental challenge in its rejection of God's existence. In every language, the term "God" is a reference to an absolute and necessary being, whether considered in potency or actuality. Now a simple rule is this, concepts relating to absolute or a necessary being or attributes are outside and beyond the realm of negation. As argued earlier, negations belong to the second level of knowledge. They are *extractions or abstractions* from the existent, hence, circumstantial, relative and particular in time and space, and concern accidents of being and not essence.

Theology and the Public Space

So far, we have discussed humanism and its various manifestations, including core arguments and leading trends. Special attention was paid to secular humanism particularly arguments against the existence of God. In this section we would like to proceed by discussing whether secular humanism is right in dismissing God and religion in favour of science and technology; and whether there are still human experiences that escape scientific explanations and only theology can provide the required response.

Beginning with the question of origins, although secular humanism considers scientific theories to be the only and most reliable explanations, it is clear that this does not in any way provide a satisfactory and conclusive response. Secular humanism rejects creation narratives in favour of evolution, but clearly the two respond to different questions of inquiry. Narratives of origins all over the world are deeply preoccupied with the "who" question.[29] For evolution, the concern is strictly on the process, the "how" question. Thus, with two distinct methods of inquiry employed, it is natural to have different conclusions. Nevertheless, difference in conclusions does not necessarily imply mutual exclusion in terms of true or false. In their respects, both could be true. Therefore, God's existence cannot be argued against based on the conclusions of science without, at the same time, falling into categorical error. The tendency among secular humanists to apply conclusions arrived at in one field of inquiry to refute positions advanced in another field, has some merits. But this is with respect to delineating the margins in methods of inquiry, and not in constituting grounds for the dismissal of the substance particular to other fields of inquiry. It is fair to argue that scientific theories of origins are inconclusive as they hardly provide any explanation regarding the origins of the primordial matter.

These shortfalls are not due to the nature of science itself, but rather the manner in which its conclusions are applied by secular humanists. Scientific arguments have validity within their confines. They demonstrate inexorable laws inherent in the universe proving that the

---

[29] Stephen Belcher, *African Myths of Origins*, London: Penguin, 2005. See also Robert E. Wolverton, *An Outline of Classical Mythology*, Totowa: Littlefield, Adams, 1966.

universe is not a haphazard and blind occurrence. For instance, evolution takes place within and not across species. These laws make the universe not only intelligible but also provide the inalienable grounds for the possibility of science itself.[30] It is on the grounds of these inexorable laws that even scientists are prompted to talk about the existence of an intelligent design in the universe.

The Despair of Morality

Questions about right and wrong, the acceptable or unacceptable remain unresolved despite scientific advance. The reason is simple; these questions are outside and beyond the realm of scientific investigation. A renowned ancient Greek philosopher, Socrates, is on record saying, 'the unexamined life is not worth living...'[31] To this day this adage is central to moral inquiries. Rights and wrong presuppose some kind of authority. There are traditions which consider the human person, a rational and free moral agent as he is, to be the primary source of ethics and authority in determining what is right or wrong. This is the ground of autonomous ethics. Scholars like Alfons Auer, Josef Fuchs and Bruno Schuller are among the proponents. Autonomous ethics places emphasis on the human person as discoverer of morality. Moral goodness is a value in itself, and it merits to be realized for the sake of its own dignity and not for the sake of any external authority, it is argued. In contrast is theonomous ethics, also known as revealed morality. Central to this is the understanding that what is considered to be right or wrong is known to be such only by the revealing act of God. Revealed morality serves a prescriptive function by offering authoritative guidance for

---

[30] Andrew G. van Melsen, *The Philosophy of Nature*, Louvain: Duquesne University Press, 1954.
[31] *Apology* 38a.

judgement and behaviour. And as Gustafson observes, revealed morality manifests itself either as law, ideals, or analogies.

There are also scholars who consider the natural law, i.e. *lex naturalis*, to be the source of moral authority. Thomas Aquinas, perhaps the greatest proponent, defines natural law as a reality brought into being, *constitutum*, through reason, a work of human intelligence as ordered to action, *ratio practica*, something humans bring into being by doing, *quod quis agit*. Natural law arises from human nature ordered to its ultimate natural end recognized by the natural light of reason.[32] In other words, the subjective medium of cognition is reason alone.[33] This law is based on the structure of reality itself and is the same for all human beings at all times. The law is naturally knowable as an unchanging rule or pattern which is there for human beings to discover as a guide for their own good. Ockham sees conformity of the natural law to natural reason which is immutable. As a result, there are situations where only natural equity is applicable without recourse to human law or custom. The significance of natural law as a moral authority is twofold. It acts as the basis of a moral order of universal character and constitutes a source of ethical wisdom for it rests on that reality shared by all.[34] Further, natural law serves as safeguard against arbitrary exercise of political and legislative power.

Ethicists also turn to the community as a source and authority of ethics. Generally, it is argued that ethics are expressions of the collective memory, wisdom and shared understanding, hence not inseparable from their founding communities. As Joseph Selling rightly observes, moral rules are always imbedded in a context. The

---

[32] Marcellus Zalba, *Theologiae Moralis Compendium*, Madrid: Biblioteca de Autores Cristianos, 1958, 316.
[33] Karl H. Peschke, *Christian Ethics: Moral Theology in Light of Vatican II*, London: Goodliffe Neale, 1997, 135.
[34] It is on this basis that we can argue for the universality of human rights.

collective social wisdom and historical experiences of a particular community give rise to ethical considerations on right and wrong. This line of thought supports ethical relativism in practice, without rejection of ethical universalism, in theory.

Ethicists lack consensus on the question of sources and authority behind morality. Nonetheless, it can be argued that efforts to identify the ultimate ground of morality on anything other than God create difficulties. Situating morality away from God carries risks of extreme ethical relativism and eventual privatization, thereby undermining the very idea and essence of morality itself. It compromises the shared humanity and the universality of the human rights discourse. Morality seems to make sense only when seen in relation to God as the ground and its intermediate author as implied in theo-nomous and natural law theories.[35] This is clear in Albert Camus who struggles to hold unto morality in a world without God.[36]

Despair of Meaning and Destiny

Meaning and destiny are at the foundation of existentialism, a philosophical tradition grounded in man's state of despair in the face of inevitable death.[37] If there is no reason for morality, then there is no reason or meaning for living. Albert Camus, writing in the *Myth of Sisyphus* says; "the only true significant philosophical issue is that of suicide." Asks Camus; "Why should I not snuff out my life? "Why should I make the effort to go on living?[38] Jean Paul Sartre, another influential existentialist, is equally perturbed with the question of meaning and destiny in the face of death. He asks whether man has

---

[35] Reference to intermediate recognizes the role of human freedom in morality
[36] C. Stephen Evans, *Existentialism: The Philosophy of Despair and the Quest for Hope*, Grand Rapids: Zondervan, 1984, 31.
[37] C. Stephen Evans, *Existentialism*, 31.
[38] Ibid, 46.

essence, a reason for his being, or a purpose for existing. Or is man simply bare existence, a being who first of all just is, and is something only after that? For Sartre, man has no essence, and really, there is no reason why man exists. He just does. On this note, Sartre concludes, life is a meaningless series of disconnected events.[39] The reason is, there is no purpose for man, nothing significant for him to accomplish or to be.[40] He writes:

> I was just thinking," I tell him laughing, "that here we sit, all of us, eating and drinking to preserve our precious existence, and really there is nothing, nothing, absolutely no reason for existing."[41]

Despair for meaning and destiny are not new questions in human history, and neither are Camus and Sartre the only ones ever to have been troubled with the apparent void and meaninglessness of life. The Book of Ecclesiastics expresses the same inherent age-old despair: "Meaningless! Meaningless!" says the Teacher, "Utterly meaningless! Everything is Meaningless."[42] The despair of meaning and destiny in the face of the inevitable death presents yet another dilemma for secular humanism despite its faith and trust in the presumed omnipotence of science and technology.

True Nature of Meaning and Destiny

Man instinctively knows his end. He can even foresee it, not in the manner of occurrence, but as a matter of fact. Soon or later, the flame of life will extinguish. This instinctive knowledge creates the anxiety and urgency for response and certainty to this question, perhaps the only question that qualifies as truly fundamental, as it concerns the very foundation of our being This not a question about daily needs

---

[39] Ibid.
[40] Ibid, 47.
[41] Jean Paul Sartre, *Nausea*, New York: New Direction, 1959, 151.
[42] Ecclesiastes 1:2ff.

10. Relevance of Theology in the Age of Secular Humanism

of life for physical survival. Science has answers for that, or at least will continue to search and provide answers. The question is fundamental due to its concern with the very being of our existence, its meaning and destiny. This instinctive knowledge of man's definite and definitive coming to an end suggests that man is on the journey and is himself that journey. Man's being on the journey is an act that happens to him outside his control, a product of facticity and accident independent of his freedom and choice.[43] From this perspective, human existence could be seen as nothing but fate subject to the mercy of the blind laws of determinism. Born at a particular point in time and space, man is not free to be otherwise than on this journey towards his coming to a definite and definitive end.

On the other hand, man himself as the journey introduces a new and radical dimension, a dimension that brings uniqueness and distinction to his being in the world. It is this act of man, as himself a journey on the journey that makes him not only historical but also historic. It is precisely at this level that freedom is located. To understand man as on the journey, a critical understanding and appreciation of his nature is pivotal. If the ends that man seeks escape the material, hence beyond the comprehension of science, then this is the realm of the spiritual. As an inherent quality, it is evident in his yearning for meaning, a deeper realization of the impotence of the material to provide response that quenches the thirst for meaning.

This yearning reveals man as an open being, and not a closed one, an openness only satisfied by transcendence. The search for meaning acts like a natural seed of protest against the temptation to reduce and equate the being of man to the material order contrary to secular humanism. Meaning is not something that man creates and imparts to himself as he does for his material existence. Meaning and destiny,

---

[43] Jean Paul Sartre, *Being and Nothingness*, New York: The Philosophical Library, 1992.

are given from outside the material order, for ultimately man is not meant for that order, hence cannot find satisfaction and meaning in that material realm. Here we find another space for theology, helping man to understand and establish his true self. Augustine of Hippo puts it very well when he says; "We are made for Thee, Oh God, and our hearts are restless until they rest in Thee."[44] Man is made and meant for God in an inherent relationship of love and freedom. It is only this inherent relationship which possibilizes man's satisfaction, and nothing else.

Man is born with thirst for God, the thirst that cannot be quenched by anything less than God. The inherent thirst is in itself a pointer to something beyond. In searching for the beyond, there is tendency to resort to sensory tools. This reduces the objective of his search to the level below himself. The use of the sensory to establish the objective of the search is something particular and applicable to realities only equal to, or below man. While these can confirm, they do not establish traces of the eternal. It is only through revelation that traces of the eternal are known. Revelation is an act of God towards man. It is not an act of man towards God. If that were to be the case, then that would have been a reduction of the eternal to any object equal or less man.

An encounter with traces of the eternal in history always entails mission. This is the mission of love, compassion, the mission of truth and justice, the mission of life, the very footprints of God's revelation (Mt 25: 31-38). These are the footprints of the eternal, the footprints in which humans are invited to walk.

---

[44] Cit. John K. Ryan, *The Confessions of St. Augustine*, New York: Image Books, 1960.

The Mystery of Evil and Suffering

Secular humanists reject the existence of God based on the experience of evil and suffering. This becomes more complex when considered in light of the suffering of the innocent and those forms of evil that cannot be explained on the grounds of human freedom. For generations arguments and counter arguments have been advanced in search for a convincing and lasting response, but all demonstrate immeasurable limitations. The problem of evil and suffering when raised in relation to God takes a totally different dimension. It ceases to belong to the realm of empirical science or philosophy. Instead, when God is brought into the equation, the question turns theological. And like any other field of knowledge, theological investigation departs from and proceeds on specific method using tools particular to this field. Theology is fundamentally built and proceeds on this conviction alone that God reveals himself through the universe as his creative act, and through history as a dramatic instance of his encounter with humanity, a nexus of interface between divine and human freedom. Theological investigation proceeds from this understanding and conviction that God reveals the world to humanity and through the universe and history humanity begins to get the glimpses of the divine.

Now from a Christian perspective, the full revelation of God has occurred in the historical person, a poor man called Jesus.[45] In his life, suffering, death and resurrection, God has revealed his own nature, the identity and meaning of time and history. Therefore, the full response to the problem of evil and suffering is not an empirical scientific or abstract philosophical proposition. Instead, the response is the concrete person, Jesus Christ, God incarnate. As the Nicene

---

[45] José Cardenas Pallares, *A Poor Man Called Jesus: Reflections on the Gospel of Mark*, Maryknoll: Orbis Books, 1986.

Creed confesses, "...For us men and for our salvation, he came down from heaven: by the power of the Holy Spirit he was born of the Virgin Mary, and became man."

In Christ Jesus God has experienced what it means to be human and this experience includes suffering and death. In the person of Jesus we encounter God's concrete response to the problem of evil and suffering.[46] This encounter constitutes an invitation for a personal and existential identification with Jesus and that in him, with and through him alone; one experiences this response in the face of suffering and evil.[47]

What is also critical here is that God's response is not so much about dealing with evil and suffering in its isolated occurrences and in a manner that is technical. Rather the response deals with the ultimate root of evil, and this is sin.[48] At the heart of sin is not so much about the material act, but the spirit of disobedience, what other theological traditions discuss in relation to the fundamental option theory. From Eden to Gethsemane, we are confronted with the history of man's failure to do God's will. Only in Jesus is perfect obedience to God, and only in him is the reversal to Adam's disobedience (Genesis): "Father, if you are willing, take this cup from me. Yet not my will, but Yours be done" (Luke 22; 42). Both scripture and tradition are unambiguously very clear that it is Jesus alone who takes away the sin of the world.

In the Gospel of John we read, "Look, the Lamb of God, who takes away the sin of the world." The Apostle Paul writing to the Philippians says, "And being found in appearance as a man, He

---

[46] Joseph Kimu, *The Theology of Suffering in the Teaching of John Paul II*, Balaka: Montfort Media, 2013.

[47] Joseph Kimu, *The Theology of Suffering in the Teaching of John Paul II*.

[48] Romans 5:12ff.

humbled Himself and became obedient to death-even death on a cross" (Philippians 2:8). The Letter to the Hebrews also carries the same confession, "Although He was a Son, He learned obedience from what He suffered..." (Heb. 5:8). And in the Great Prayer, before anything else, we are called upon to pray for God's will to be done on earth (Matthew 6:10). Both the Anglican and Lutheran liturgical traditions have this confession, "Lamb of God, you take away the sin of the world, have mercy on us". The same is also part of the Gloria in Excelsis, an ancient prayer, and central the Catholic liturgy: "Lord, Lamb of God, Son of the Father who take away the sin of the world, have mercy on us". Thus sin, the root of veil and suffering, is nothing else but disobedience to God.

In the resurrection of Jesus Christ is seen the ultimate defeat and the end of the reign of sin, evil and suffering. In Christ Jesus a new creation is born free from sin, evil and suffering. In his resurrection, there is no return to the ordinary space and time. His history is over and has moved into a final and definitive state of existence. Thus, Richard McBrien can write: "by the resurrection, Jesus entered a completely new universe of being, the end-time of history, beyond the control of history and beyond the reach of historians." For N.T. Wright, resurrection is the reversal of death, its cancellation, the destruction of its power.[49] Arguing on the same point, Marcus Borg says, resurrection has little or nothing to do with a corpse and the resumption of one's previous life, but with entry into a different kind of existence.[50]

Christ, the new creation, is the ultimate response to the problem of evil and suffering. The response transcends the realm and imagination of empirical scientists and philosophers, including

---

[49] Bishop John Shelby Spong, First Congregational United Church of Christ, Eugene, Oregon: Online publication.
[50] Ibid.

secular humanists. What this means, at least from the Christian point of view, is that the denial of God's existence as is the case with secular humanists is implicitly a rejection of the only definitive response to the problem of evil and suffering.

Conclusion

Science and technology have indeed registered immense progress in responding to human predicaments including suffering. Secular humanism is right in recognizing this tremendous progress. However, there are human experiences which science is unable to adequately explain. These are questions revolving around origins, morality and its relationship to meaning and destiny, evil and suffering. Dismissing God on scientific grounds, as secular humanism does, fails to do justice to methods of academic inquiry. Similarly, the value and credibility of theology rest on its ability to concentrate and convincingly respond to these perennial questions that fall outside the domain of science.

We hold the view that secular humanism need not be considered an ideological adversary. Rather, it is an opportunity for theological developments especially in university and theological colleges in response to the changing context. Theology as a discourse of the known unknown is ever open-ended. Yes, indeed, as long as history is never over, theology and theologizing are never over. At the heart of theology is the space of the possible, what Richard Kearney calls the divine "perhaps." Kearney writes:

> For it is the divine "perhaps", hovering over every just decision or action that ensures history is never over and our duty never done. The posse keeps us on our toes and reminds us there is nowhere to lay our heads for long. God depends on us to be. Without us no Word can be made fresh. If Moses, for example, had not listened to the voice of the burning bush, there would have been no Exodic liberation. If the Shunamite woman had refused Solomon's advances, there would have

been no theo-erotic song of songs. If a young maid from Nazareth had not said yes to the annunciating angel, there would have been no Christ. And if we say no to the kingdom, the kingdom will not come.[51]

The relevance of theology rests on the extent to which it responds to changing contexts, and not so much on strict adherence to classical positions in the name of doctrinal orthodoxy. Doctrines remain important as both an end and the starting point with each generation in search for response. Theologizing, however, calls for engagement with contemporary questions such as climate change, globalization, the international refugee Crisis, population, gender and self-identification, global inequality, genetically modified organisms, and cloning. Engagement with such issues will enhance the relevance and credibility of theology in public space.

---

[51] Richard Kearney, *The God Who May Be: A Hermeneutics of Religion*, Bloomington: Indiana University Press, 2001, 4.

Chapter 11

Towards Retaining Young People in the 21st Century African Christian Church: Selected Sociological Factors

Frank Barden Chirwa

Introduction

The influence of some sociological factors and how they affect the relationship between young people and older people in church as far as modernity is concerned can be a very comprehensive discourse. I restrict this study to factors like standpoint, bifurcation of consciousness, and obscurantism, since I believe these factors contribute to disharmony between the young people and older people in church as far as culture is concerned. A critical explication of these factors can reduce the clash and help in returning the youth to the church. It may appear that modernity is a rival to culture and religion due to the fact of paradigm change. The opposite is true, however, since modernity also comes with vast progressive advantages to benefit the church. But, that is not my main focus in this chapter. I limit my study to the fact that due to differences between youth culture in modernity and indigenous culture, youth are labeled deviants who must always submit to the dominating elderly people and their dictates. This disturbs the young people and, as a result, they abandon the faith. This chapter discusses some selected sociological factors relating to modernity and the church in Africa can retain the youth in the 21St century.

Modernity and Paradigm Change

Modernity is a culture that has been formed during the historical period termed the modern era. It is a collection of particular socio-cultural norms, attitudes and practices that arose during the "Age of Reason" – the 17th-century and 18th-century Enlightenment. It embraces existential experiences and conditions which have impact on human culture, institutions, and politics.[1] The modernization process is dated from the pre-modern social organization of the 14th to the early 16th centuries. The period from the 16th to the 19th century saw a transition from pre-modern to modern society, and the 20th century is seen as the period when modernity emerged in its fullest expression.[2]

Modernity and Postmodernity

There exists a broad consensus as to the pre-modern-modern-postmodern division of history.[3] I adopt the theory of "modernity" in general recognizing the parallels that exists between the pre-modern, modern, and postmodernism.[4] Issues raised by the emergence of modernity and postmodernity are closely linked to the factors that influence the clash between the young and older people in church. The discreet analysis and synthesis of such factors, in the context of a "paradigm change," can enhance interdependence of

---

[1] Marshall Berman, *All That is Solid Melts into Air: The Experience of Modernity*, Brooklyn: Verso, 2010.
[2] M.P. Hornsby-Smith, J. Fulton and M. Norris, *The Politics of Spirituality: A Study of a Renewal Process in An English Diocese*, Oxford: Clarendon Press, 1995.
[3] M. King, *Postsecularism: The Hidden Challenge of Extremism*, Cambridge: James Clark & Co, 2009, 46.
[4] Antony Giddens, *Modernity and Self Identity*, Cambridge: Polity Press, 1991; R. Geaves, and G.D. Chryssides, *The Study of Religion: An Introduction to Key Ideas and Methods*, London: Continuum, 2007, 60.

both the young and older people in the church instead of having a situation of clashes between them.

By the nature of "paradigm" or "frame of reference,", I affirm the fact that worldviews, as paradigms, change over long periods of time. When paradigm change occurs, the model of interpretation clash as a discomfort around the old model and a new one increase.[5] Thus, due to holding on to different paradigms, people respond to reality as if they live in different worlds.[6] But, evidently, change brings about progress since new paradigms appear to resolve problems better than previous paradigms.[7] Generally, due to modernity, young people tend to be more progressive than older people. They accept change of paradigm faster than older people.[8] This can create clashes between them ending up in the decline of young people attending church.

Categorization of Modernity

Modernity is categorized by, the rejection of tradition, prioritization of individualism, freedom and formal equality, rationalization, secularization and representative democracy.[9] Rationality is the core since each person reasons and decides as an individual. Unbelief is paramount since man has overcome the irrationality of belief due to modernity.[10] It is perceived that humankind has evolved from being

---

[5] T.S. Kuhn, *The Structure of Scientific Revolutions*, Chicago: The University of Chicago Press, 1962, 110; David J. Bosch, *Transforming Mission: Paradigm Shifts in Theology of Mission*, New York: Orbis Books. 1991, 185.
[6] Bosch, *Transforming Mission*, 184.
[7] Ibid, 152.
[8] Kuhn, *The Structure of Scientific Revolutions*, 169.
[9] Michel Foucault, *Discipline and Punish: The Birth of the Prison*, translated by Alan Sheridan, London: Penguin Books, 1977, 170-177.
[10] J. Casanova, "The Secular, Secularizations, Secularisms," in C. Calhoun, M. Juergensmeyer & J. van Antwerpen, (eds.), *Rethinking Secularism*, Oxford: Oxford University Press, 2011, 54-74 [59].

11. Retaining Young People

primitive to being modern. Being "primitive" is equated to the religious notion of man and being modern to the secular notion of man.[11] Religion is thus regarded as intolerant and responsible for creating conflict.[12]

Modernity also includes public, legal and nominal perversions in society including collective political protests that challenge autocratic authoritarian structures.[13] Some describe it as a "culture without faith." Religious leaders have no more authority over the morality of their individual members since religiosity and spirituality become private matters.[14] Hence, young people in modernity tend to rationalize religious traditions and beliefs. Tradition is viewed as archaic while the youth prefer progressiveness; the elderly people are mostly conservative; hence, clashes with young people.[15]

The categorization of modernity continues in postmodernism. In conflict with religion, postmodern mindset is embroiled with suspicion and skepticism while religion depends on a "hermeneutic of trust."[16] With the postmodern paradigm, any rigidity and fixed

---

[11] Ibid, 58.
[12] Ibid, 69.
[13] Antonio L. Rappa, *Modernity and Consumption*, Singapore: World Scientific, 2002.
[14] K. Dobbelaere, "The Meaning and Scope of Secularization," in P.B. Clarke (ed), *The Oxford Handbook of the Sociology of Religion*, Oxford: Oxford University Press, 2011, 606-07; Charles Taylor, *A Secular Age*, Cambridge: Harvard University Press, 2007, 535.
[15] For most of the information from this section I am indebted to Jaco Bayer's article, "The Church and the Secular: The Effect of the Post-secular on Christianity", Department of Science of Religion and Missiology, University of Pretoria, South Africa, http://www.scielo.org.za/scielo.php?script=sci_arttext&-pid=S0259-94222014000100025 Correspondence/ [3.10.2019].
[16] M. King, *Postsecularism: The Hidden Challenge of Extremism*, Cambridge: James Clark & Co., 2009, 23.

dogmatism is suspiciously questioned. This is because, postmodernism abandons any fact that is based on a single truth claim since truth is relational; hence, transforming into secularization opposed to religious tradition.[17] In lieu of this, the challenge that complicates such modernity categorization is effected by contextual sociological factors that demands a critical explication.

The Challenge of Contextual Sociological Factors Standpoint Perspective

In order to harmonize the relationship between young and old people in the church, understanding the standpoint sociological perspective is appropriate. It stresses that what one knows is largely affected by where one actually stands in a particular society.[18] What we know about others is conditional since one cannot look at the world in any way other than one's given standpoint.[19] I situate the standpoint of the young people and older people on culture since older people use it as a tool for judging lifestyle in modernity and youth culture even in the church. This breeds clashes. Bifurcation of consciousness and obscurantism worsens the conflict.

---

[17] Ibid, 202-03.

[18] Dorothy E. Smith, *From the Margins: Women's Standpoint as a Method of Inquiry in the Social Sciences*, Online: www. doi.org/10.1177/097185249700100106. Article information, Volume: 1 issue: 1: 113-135, March 1, 1997, [6.3.2020].

[19] Ibid; I restrict the theory of "standpoint" to its historical usage relating to identity and consciousness in relation to the struggles of the oppressed groups due to the dominance of the powerful group. I also recognize its original usage in its historic Marxian tradition. Several groups used the standpoint theory such as on Race, ethnicity-based, anti-imperial, and social justice movements. (See: Michel Foucault, *Power/Knowledge: Selected Interviews and Other Writings, 1972-77*, trans. Colin Gordon, Leo Marshall, John Mepham, and Kate Soper, New York: Random House, 1980); Hill P. Collins, *Fighting Words: Black Women and the Search for Justice*, Minneapolis, MN.: University of Minnesota Press, 1998.

Bifurcation of Consciousness

This relates to a separation between the world as you actually experience it and the dominant view to which you must adapt.[20] The older people tend to dominate on the subordinate group (young people). They at times remain unconscious and unmindful of the worldview of the subordinate group (young people) who are expected to abide by the culture and the tradition of the older people.[21] When this happens, conflict is inevitable.

Obscurantism

Deliberately presenting information in an imprecise and concealed manner in order to prevent further inquiry and understanding entails obscurantism.[22] It is the denial of empirical truth because of the disagreeable moral consequences that might arise from acceptance of fact.[23] Obscurantists tend to modify or reject verifiability and logic to subdue necessary information.[24] In a church setting, some authorities prevent young people to seek further clarification and answers relating to some facts. The youth are thus manipulated since culturally they must be subordinate to elderly people who must not be questioned both culturally and religiously.

---

[20] Dorothy E. Smith, *Institutional Ethnography: A Sociology for People*, Walnut Creek, CA: AltaMira Press, 2005, 82.

[21] Ibid.

[22] *Oxford English Dictionary*, (3rd ed.). Oxford: University Press, 2004. Opposition to Inquiry, Enlightenment, or Reform.

[23] Friedrich August von Hayek, 2018, www.amedleyofpotpourri.blogspot.com-/2018/10/obscurantism.html, [23.3.2020].

[24] Richard Rorty, *Contingency, Irony, and Solidarity*, Cambridge: Cambridge University Press, 1989; See also, Seymour, M. Hersh, "Selective Intelligence," *The New Yorker*, 12 May 2003.

Culture and its Implication on Modernity

Culture is handed to generations through words, gestures and actions. It expresses our identity in comparison with others. It is what a group of the same locality or community have in common. It makes communication possible.[25] Culture relates to worldview, a lens through which people in a given culture read and interpret the world around them. It is a construct that provides a point of departure, sense of direction, and a strategy of unity for human thought, life, and action.[26] It has a shaping power because it unifies the African's mindset, the good life to pursue and guides the thinking, choices, and actions.[27] The information implicit in culture relates to the well-being and behaviour of individuals that is acquired through teaching, imitation, and other symbolic forms of social transmission. With this, people communicate, perpetuate, and develop their knowledge and attitudes toward life.[28] In an African Malawian context, there are a few symbolic forms like bowing, kneeling, eye contact, language tone, approach, dressing, just to mention a few. In modernity, this affects the relation between the young and older people in church.

Challenges of Culture in Modernity

There are many challenges relating to culture but I take only two. First, there are a diversity of cultures on the basis of ethnic or

---

[25] J. Prinz, "Culture and Cognitive Science." *The Stanford Encyclopedia of Philosophy*, E.N. Zalt, 2016, https://plato.stanford.edu/archives/fall2016/entries/culture-cogsci. [6.3.2020].

[26] John Fowler, "World Views," A paper presented at the Faith and Learning Seminar UEAB, Kenya, 1998.

[27] Zacchaeus Mathema, "Towards an Understanding of the African Worldview," in Kwabena Donkor, ed., *The Church, Culture and Spirits: Adventism in Africa*, Hagerstown: Review and Herald, 2011, 37.

[28] D. Sperber, *Explaining Culture*, Oxford: Blackwell, 1996.

religious differences. Secondly, there is a developing international culture rooted in a transnational modernity characterized by "multiculturalism."[29] This strongly causes clashes between the young people and older people. Young people in modernity are influenced by their peers internationally and acquire a multicultural attitude.[30] Such a bearing can be challenging to the relationship between young people and older people due to fact that older people are judgmental towards that intercultural "youth culture."

Youth Culture: The Need of Competent Leadership[31]

Youth culture designates the way young people live; the norms, values, and practices they share. It differs from the culture of the older generation.[32] Distinctly, it puts emphasis on clothes, popular music, sports, ever-changing vocabulary, and dating rather than beliefs and behaviors.[33] Fads and leisure activities are also part of youth culture.[34] It can be noticeable through the language young people use to create meanings distinct to them. For example, in a

---

[29] B. Wilkerson (ed), *Multicultural Religious Education*, Birmingham: Religious Education Press, 1997, 2.

[30] J. Sorber, "Multicultural Student Ministry," in D.A. Anderson and M.R. Cabellon (eds), *Multicultural Ministry Connecting Creatively to a Diverse World*, Downers Grove: IVP, 2010, 133; D. Parks, *Multicultural Youth Ministry on The Rise: Safe and Accepting Place*, 1999, Online: www.bpnews.net/412/multicultural-youth-ministry-on-the-rise-8216safe-and-accepting-place, [19.12.2019].

[31] For most of the insights and information given in this section, I am indebted to the summarized article of a recently completed Masters in Theology (MTh) Thesis entitled "A Practical Theological Study of Multicultural Youth Work in Pretoria, South Africa" by Alexander Strecker at the University of South Africa.

[32] F. Rice, *The Adolescent: Development, Relationships and Culture* (7th ed.), Boston: Allyn & Bacon, 1996.

[33] Frank A. Fasick, "Parents, Peers, Youth Culture and Autonomy in Adolescence", *Adolescence*, 19(73), 1984, 143-157.

[34] Lawrence O. Richards, *Youth Ministry: Its Renewal in the Local Church*, Grand Rapids: Zondervan, 1985, 28.

Malawian context, the youth use terms like *Masiten* to designate mother, *madala* for father, *chick* for girl, *den* for a home, *chilling* for chatting, *kufila*, satisfied, *battrey*, for testicles and so forth. Some of such terms can be offensive to older people.

Dressing style like pants-down, *kumphwefula* (wearing of jeans with under-pants visible), the dressing of caps with the front flip to the back are offensive to older people. On the girls, body revealing fads like mini-skirts, tight pants, torn jeans and shorts, bare backs and bare breasts, are also offensive to the older people. This leads adults to overemphasize the differences between youth and other age groups. It also reflects a breakaway from traditional cultural values; hence a clash with older people. Competent youth leaders need to understand the "youth culture" in modernity and accommodate it for the sake of strategizing their leadership style insightfully in order to retain the young people in church and leading them to maturity in faith.

Application of the Malawian African Cultural Perspective

The indigenous culture of respect for elderly people in an African Malawian context is critical in as far as peaceful co-existence between the young and older people is concerned. In an African cultural setting, the elderly people get involved in various forms of cultural scrutiny relating to custom and discipline. Growing-up among such elders demands a lot of cultural humility and discipline. In context, elderly people never err or blunder, young people are expected to render absolute respect to the elderly.

Appropriation of Elderly People's Mistakes

One custom I learned was to appropriate the mistakes the elderly commit. One extreme example is farting. When one of my elderly uncles "puffed," there was a very pungent smell. One person in the group then queried, *"Ndani wanya chiphwisi?"* meaning, "Who has farted?" I knew it was an elderly person who sat close to me; but, as a well cultured African young person, I answered, "I am sorry, it's me." By so doing I followed the custom of saving the face of the elderly person. He respected me as well. Such is rare among the young people in modernity.

Relieving Katundu from Elderly People

It is expected of young people to relieve the elderly people carrying *katundu* (luggage) and humbly escorting them home as a matter of due respect. This is rare among the modern young people.

Surrendering a Seat

It is expected of a younger person to surrender a seat to an elderly person in bus, house, or in church. This also is rare among the youth in modernity. Elderly people resent this as deviant. But when I interviewed Dexter Maseko, he observed that in Botswana, younger people observe this culture. He contended that in Malawi the situation is worse because he once saw a pregnant woman standing in the bus without a seat and beside her was a young man who was seated and he did not venture to surrender his seat to the woman.[35]

Elderly People Counsel

Counsel of the elderly is to be obeyed without queries regardless of irrationality. This is enforced through such proverbs as, *Mau a Akulu akoma akagonera*, meaning, "the words of the elderly people are helpful especially after a long time passes." Also, *Galu wamkota sakandila pa chabe*, meaning "An old dog does not dig for nothing." This means a point of discipline ear-marked by the elders as being of the very great importance; experience is a better judge.[36] The acceptance of such

---

[35] Int. Dexter Mndala Maseko – Frank Chirwa, Malawi Adventist University, Lakeview, 23 November 2020.
[36] J.C. Chakanza, *Wisdom of the People: 2000 Chinyanja Proverbs*, Blantyre: Kachere-CLAIM, 2000, 33.

wisdom claims by elderly people for rationality's sake is rare among the youth in modernity who believe in individualism, rationalism, skepticism and multiculturalism.

Eating Custom and Habits

Where food is served on the same dish, tradition dictates that young people must wait for the elderly to wash hands first. Also, young people are not allowed to finish eating and washing hands before the elderly people. Where relish like chicken is served, culture dictates that a younger person does not take the gizzard or the back-piece of a chicken, *chinyophilo*. These parts are strictly reserved for elderly people. A young person who does that is seriously rebuked as disrespectful and a glutton. Among the youth in modernity, this is rare due to the fact that "modernity" is characterized by the rejection of tradition.

Respect for Older People

The mode and quality of the language and its accent shows the respect of the young ones in addressing elderly people. For example, in an African cultural context, it is disrespectful to call the elderly person by his/her first name, by the second person singular *iwe* (you), but by the third person plural *Imwe* (them). Girls are supposed to bow their knees when giving something or greeting the elderly people. The young men are supposed to bow. Such is rare among the youth in modernity, hence a clash with the elderly people.

Synthesis and Missiological Implications

Since there must be harmony of relationship between the young and older people in the church that is complicated by the categories of modernity, the missiological concept of paradigm change or frame of reference must be managed very wisely. Church leaders need to realize that worldviews, as paradigms, change over a long period of time. As a result, the models of interpretation clash due to the discomfort between the old and the new model. This is what happens between the young and the older people in church because they respond to reality as if they live in different worlds.[37] It appears that young people embrace paradigm change faster than older people.[38] It is thus of vital importance that the elderly people who are more experienced and mature in culture, mission, and religion, need to understand the standpoint of the young people and thus manage well bifurcation of consciousness and completely avoid the attitude of obscurantism.

Traditionally, the elderly and young people are integrated in their identity through entrenched African Cultural tradition and values that originate from the African heritage handed down from one generation to the other. The elderly people dominate in propagating such beliefs and values, be they cultural or religious. All young people in that cultural context are subordinate to whatever the elderly people dictate regardless of the question; hence, leading to the bifurcation of consciousness. Young people in modernity engrossed in their standpoint and paradigm, characterized by democracy, protest, rationality, and rejection of tradition, resent such type of dictatorial behavior. Challenging the standpoint of the young people in modernity by the Bible as a lashing tool only leads to resentment and decline of young people in church attendance. Obscurantism worsens the decline. When young people question the rigid traditional orders, the older people turn to the Bible and use it to obscure reality, logic, and rationality, young people protest such unfair use of the Scriptures. They are thus labeled as rebellious with censure.

---

[37] T.S. Kuhn, *The Structure of Scientific Revolutions*, 110; David J. Bosch, *Transforming Mission*, 185.
[38] Kuhn, *The Structure of Scientific Revolutions*, 169.

There is need to learn how to handle conflicting worldviews in the church as this causes clashes between the young people in modernity and older people who hold on to "orders" of tradition. Paul Hiebert observes that the central issue in Christianity should not be "order" but "right relationships." It is to create shalom, dignity, equality, justice, love, peace, and concern for others.[39] The greatest value in such a mission is willing to live with ambiguity, unpredictability, flexibility, avoiding rigidity in tradition in order to shape genuine human relationships. It is vital to empower young people as well as permitting them to make mistakes just as the older people also commit and learning from them. But, building relationship is paramount because it is the heart of effective evangelism.[40]

I think the Apostle Paul used this strategy effectively in his own right as missionary *par excellence*. He addressed the minors in faith not as spiritual giants but as "worldly" and mere infants in Christ. Since they were still young and not yet mature, he gave them milk and not solid food. The purpose was to dismantle divisions among them and bring harmony and maturity in Faith (1 Cor. 3:1, 2). In Hebrews, "milk for infants" is metaphorically the teaching of elementary truths of God's Word. "Solid food" is for mature people who by experience and much training are able to distinguish good from evil (Heb. 5: 11-14). The Apostle Peter advocates the same for the sake of avoiding malice, deceit, hypocrisy, and slander. Like new-born babies, young people in church must partake of pure spiritual milk in order to grow up in salvation (1 Pet. 2:1,2). This overrules rigidity in tradition, bifurcation of consciousness, and obscurantism. It demands mature leadership to utilize the best that paradigm change in modernity can provide for the sake of relevancy and managing altruistically and astutely the

---

[39] Paul G. Hiebert, *Anthropological Reflections on Missiological Issues*, Grand Rapids: Baker Books, 2001, 142-146.
[40] Ibid.

negatives thereof. The purpose is to retain younger members in church and bring them to maturity in faith.

Conclusion

Hypothetically, this study asserts that there is need for both young and older people to intentionally agree to exist together in harmony as parts of the "Body of Christ" though amidst the challenges of modernity and youth culture. I establish the rationale for this mutual relationship in its biblical basis of Romans 12:14-15; Eph. 1:22-23, and 1 Cor. 12:12-23. The modernity discomforts that influence clashes between the young and older people in the church must be wisely managed in order to edify the church. This is possible by building effective interpersonal relationships through functional interdependence between the young and older people within the use of diversity of spiritual gifts. In the church, interdependence, even with those parts deemed weaker, is indispensable (1 Cor. 12: 24-26).

Finally, to be effective, there is need to employ youth ministry competence approaches such as the "preparatory approach." This relates to a specialized ministry to young people that is able to prepare them to participate as leaders in church.[41] Also, the "missional approach" which advocates that youth culture must be taken seriously in order to provide the young people with both the sociological and theological bridge from the secularized world of the youth into a broad and loving community of faith.[42] With such a competency in Youth Leadership, young people can be retained in church until maturity in faith. Only when this is prioritized can the

---

[41] M.H. Senter, W. Black, C. Clark, & M. Nel, *Four Views of Youth Ministry and the Church: Inclusive Congregational, Preparatory, Missional, Strategic*, Grand Rapids: Zondervan, 2001, 40.

[42] Ibid, 87.

negatives of sociological factors be controlled and the negatives of secularization in modernity be tamed.

References

Arieli, Yehoshua, "The Theory of Human Rights its Origin and its Impact on Modern Society," in *mishpat ve-historyah*, [Law and History] 25 (Daniel Gutwein & Menachem Mautner (eds), Merkaz Zalman Shazar le-todot Yisra'el, (in Hebrew), 1999.

Barclay, J. M. G., *Paul and the Gift*, Grand Rapids: Eerdmans, 2015.

Berman, Marshall, *All That is Solid Melts into Air: The Experience of Modernity*, London and Brooklyn: Verso, 2010.

Bosch, David J., *Transforming Mission: Paradigm Shifts in Theology of Mission*, New York: Orbis Books, 1991.

Burlingame, W.V., "The Youth Culture." In E.D. Evans (ed), *Adolescents: Readings in Behavior and Development*, Hinsdale: Dryden Press, 1970.

Casanova, J., *Public Religions in the Modern World*, Chicago: University of Chicago Press, 1994.

Casanova, J., "The Secular, Secularizations, Secularisms", in C. Calhoun, M. Juergensmeyer & J. van Antwerpen (eds), *Rethinking Secularism*, Oxford: Oxford University Press, 2011, 54-74.

Chakanza, J.C., *Wisdom of the People: 2000 Chinyanja Proverbs*, Blantyre: Kachere-CLAIM, 2000.

Clark, C. "Abandonment - The Defining Issue for Contemporary Adolescents" in Chap Clark, *Hurt 2.0: Inside the World of Today's Teenagers*, Grand Rapids: Baker, 2011.

Clark, C. "View Three - The Adoption View of Youth Ministry" in C. Clark (ed), *Youth Ministry in the 21st Century*, Grand Rapids: Baker, 2015.

Collins, P.H., *Fighting Words: Black Women and the Search for Justice*, Minneapolis: University of Minnesota Press, 1998.

Collins, P.H., *Black Feminist Women and Standpoint Theory*, Hub Pages, 2016.

11. Retaining Young People

Dobbelaere, K., "The Meaning and Scope of Secularization," in P.B. Clarke (ed), *The Oxford Handbook of the Sociology of Religion*, Oxford: Oxford University Press, 2011.

Erikson, E.H., "Identity and The Life Cycle," *Psychological Issues* Vol 1(1), New York: International Universities Press, 1959.

Fasick, Frank A., "Parents, Peers, Youth Culture and Autonomy in Adolescence," *Adolescence*, 19(73), 1984.

Feldman, Christine, *"We Are the Mods:" A Transnational History of a Youth Subculture*, New York: Peter Lang, 2009.

Fields, D., *Purpose Driven Youth Ministry*, Grand Rapids: Zondervan, 1998.

Fowler, John, "World Views," A paper presented at the Faith and Learning Seminar UEAB, Kenya, 1998.

Foucault, Michel, *Discipline and Punish: The Birth of the Prison*, translated by Alan Sheridan. London: Penguin, 1977.

Friedrich August von Hayek, Online: www.amedleyofpotpourri.blogspot.com/-2018/10/obscurantism.html.

Fulton, J., "Young Adult Catholics: Contemporary Culture and Religious Orientation," paper presented at the British Sociological Association, Sociology of Religion Study Group, Religion, Culture and Ideology Conference, St Mary's University College, 3 April, 1996.

Geaves, R. and G.D. Chryssides, *The Study of Religion: An Introduction to Key Ideas and Methods*, London: Continuum Books, 2007.

Giddens, Anthony, *The Consequences of Modernity*, Cambridge: Polity Press, 1990.

Giddens, A., *Modernity and Self-Identity*, Cambridge: Polity Press, 1991.

Gelder, Craig van, *The Essence of the Church: A Community Created by the Spirit*, Grand Rapids: Baker Book House, 2000.

Harper, Steve, "Theological Obscurantism," 2018. Online: www.oboedire.com/-2018/11/20/editorial-theological-obscurantism/

Hiebert, Paul G., *Anthropological Reflections on Missiological Issues*, Grand Rapids: Baker, 1994.

Hornsby-Smith, M.P., J. Fulton and M. Norris, *The Politics of Spirituality: A Study of a Renewal Process in an English Diocese*, Oxford: Clarendon Press, 1995.

Inglehart, R. and C. Welzel, *Modernization, Cultural Change and Democracy: The Human Development Sequence*, Cambridge: Cambridge University Press, 2005.

King, M., *Post secularism: The Hidden Challenge of Extremism*, Cambridge: James Clark & Co, 2009.

Kuhn, T.S., *The Structure of Scientific Revolutions*, Chicago: The University of Chicago Press, 1962.

Latham, Angela, *Posing A Threat: Flappers, Chorus Girls, and Other Brazen Performers of the American 1920s*, Hanover: University Press of New England, 2000.

Luckmann, T., *The Invisible Religion*, London: Collier-Macmillan, 1967.

Luckmann, T., "Shrinking Transcendence, Expanding Religion?" *Sociological Analysis*, 50(2), 1990.

MacIntyre, A., *God, Philosophy, Universities: A Selective History of the Catholic Philosophical Tradition*, Lanham: Rowman and Littlefield, 2009.

Mathema, Zacchaeus, "Towards an Understanding of the African Worldview," in Kwabena Donkor, (ed), T*he Church, Culture and Spirits: Adventism in Africa*, Hagerstown: Review and Herald, 2011.

O'Callaghan, P., "The Eclipse of Worship: Theological Reflections on Charles Taylor's A Secular Age," *Euntes Docete*, 62/2, 2009, 89–123.

Parks, D., *Multicultural Youth Ministry on The Rise: Safe and Accepting Place*, 1999, Online, www.bpnews.net/412/multicultural-youth-ministry-on-the-rise-8216-safe-and-accepting-place.

Parrett, G., "Ministering in the Real World: A Multicultural Perspective on Youth Ministry," *Christian Education Journal*, 3, 2, 1999.

Parsons, Talcott, "On the Concept of Influence", *27 Pub. Opinion Q 37*, 1963.

Prinz, J., "Culture and Cognitive Science., *The Stanford Encyclopedia of Philosophy*, E.N. Zalta (ed), 2016, https://plato.stanford.edu/archives/fall2016/entries/-culture-cogsci/.

Rappa, Antonio L., *Modernity and Consumption*, Singapore: World Scientific, 2002.

Rice, F., *The Adolescent: Development, Relationships and Culture*, 7th ed, Boston: Allyn & Bacon, 1996.

Richards, Lawrence O., *Youth Ministry: Its Renewal in the Local Church*, Grand Rapids, Zondervan, 1985.

11. Retaining Young People

Ritzer, George, *The McDonaldization of Society*, 4th ed., Thousand Oaks: Pine Forge., 2004.

Rorty, Richard, *Contingency, Irony, and Solidarity*, Cambridge: Cambridge University Press, 998.

Sally, Engel, "Merry, Constructing a Global Law? Violence against Women and the Human Rights System," *Law and Social Inquiry* 28 (2003).

Schellebach, C., *Developmental Stages*, Blackwell Reference, 2007. Online: www.sociologyencyclopedia.com.oasis.unisa.ac.za/subscriber/tocnode.

Senter, M.H., W. Black, C. Clark and M. Nel, *Four Views of Youth Ministry and the Church: Inclusive Congregational, Preparatory, Missional, Strategic*, Grand Rapids: Zondervan, 2001.

Steinberg, L. and A.S. Morris, *Adolescent Development*, 2001, www.colorado.edu/-ibs/jessor/psych7536-805/readings.

Schwartz, G. and D. Merten, "The Language of Adolescence: An Anthropological Approach to the Youth Culture," *The American Journal of Sociology*, 72(5), 1997.

Smith, Dorothy E., *Institutional Ethnography: A Sociology for People*, Walnut Creek: AltaMira Press, 2005.

Smith, Dorothy E., "From the Margins: Women's Standpoint as a Method of Inquiry in the Social Sciences," www. doi.org/10.1177/097185249700100106. Article information, vol. 1/1 (1997), 113-135.

Sorber, J., "Multicultural Student Ministry," in D.A. Anderson and M.R. Cabellon (eds), *Multicultural Ministry Connecting Creatively to a Diverse World*, Downers Grove: IVP, 2010.

Sperber, D., *Explaining Culture*, Oxford: Blackwell, 1996.

Seymour, M. Hersh, "Selective Intelligence," *The New Yorker*, 12 May 2003.

Talcott, Parsons, "On the Concept of Influence," *27 Pub. Opinion Q 37*, 1963.

Taylor, Charles, *A Secular Age*, Cambridge: Harvard University Press, 2007.

Wilkerson, B. (ed), *Multicultural Religious Education*, Birmingham: Religious Education Press, 1997.

Chapter 12

Pain and Trauma: The Experience of Widowhood

Gertrude Aopesyaga Kapuma

Introduction

"I had lost my husband, my child and my dad, and now I was sent away by the church. The recent experiences made me reflect on the situation of widows even more, especially the humiliation they go through both in the church and society. You may think people sympathize with you till the end."[1]

Death of a husband brings many emotions and challenges. Widows go through painful experiences when such happens. They say its pain is like that of thorn in the flesh. This experience is common in many African countries including Malawi. The widow goes through a period of pain and trauma. Kabonde says: "with the loss of a husband the widow is already in great pain. She may not know what to do with the breadwinner of the family gone."[2] There are several challenges that take place in her life within a short period of time and these may continue for a longer period. The community and the Church take it for granted that she is going through her grieving period in a normal way, little do they know the actual pain she is going through at that time that will need attention. The shock of losing a beloved one and beginning a new life and the trauma that follows because of the

---

[1] M. Mwingi, "My Life can be Meaningful," in Esther Mombo and Hellen Josiasse (eds), *If you have no Voice just Sing! Narratives of Women's Lives and Theological Education at St Paul's University*, Limuru: Zapf Chancery, 2011, 78.

[2] Peggy Mulambya Kabonde, "Widowhood in Zambia: The Effects of Rituals," in Musimbi Kanyoro and Nyambura Njoroge (eds.), *Groaning in Faith: African Women in the Household of God*, Nairobi: Acton, 1996, 196.

traditional rituals that she must go through is a challenge to the Church today.

The Church's presence should be felt in all the stages of grieving and giving a helping hand. With Mwingi's case above, she lost three close relations and a job that could sustain her to look after her mother and the siblings. The Church did not see the need to be with her and help her go through this difficult time of loss. Instead of providing her with a caring and listening ear, the Church chose to distance itself from her problems and even created another problem. She further says that: "I was left as a nobody in the Church and in the society. It was not easy to cope with this."[3] How did they expect her to heal? How could she see Jesus' love in the midst of all the traumatic problems? This experience is not exclusive to Mwingi who is Kenyan, but also a problem across Africa. There are many women who have gone through similar experiences of suffering as widows, the Church did not help them at a critical time when they needed care. Below are some of the experiences that widows go through.

Trauma

Death comes in as a shock to many people because of the loss of a beloved one. Trauma is a difficult experience that many women have experienced through the loss of a dear one and or through abuse. This kind of experience has been left unattended to, by the church or family members which result in serious psychological emotions thereafter. According to Collins, "The immediate effects of a trauma or other stress inducing event are well known – along with emotional

---

[3] M. Mwingi, "My Life can be Meaningful," 77-79.

responses such as fear, uncertainty, anger, or confusion."[4] These symptoms go unnoticed because of lack of care.

News of the death of a husband will come as a shock to many women, particularly if it is through a tragic accident and or at a young age. One young widow shared her traumatic experience on how she could not believe the news broken to her by the police officer of the car accident that killed her husband. She thought for a moment and said that it could not be her husband, "you have taken my husband alive to the mortuary. I will not believe you unless I feel him." The way the news is broken to many women is very insensitive and leaves them in a state of shock without someone close to turn to for support. Sometimes people are not sensitive enough as to how much this can affect the person's life. At the time of breaking such difficult news, it is important to make sure that there is someone near to assist with anything that may come as a reaction to the shocking news. Our African communities are supposed to be supportive but are confronted with some "cultural practices" which often leave the widow a victim. Many people no longer live in family units or clans that can support them at a time like this. Death may happen whilst you are away from home working in the urban area and your immediate family members are far away.

Anagama who I have known for some years now, was involved in a car accident with her husband. The husband was severely injured and was taken to a hospital. She saw her husband struggling for life and eventually he died. It was a traumatic experience for her. Her blood pressure went up and she was admitted in the same hospital for observation whilst the family came to take the remains for burial. Cultural practices demanded that he be buried immediately. In this culture it is believed that a person who died in a car accident may not

---

[4] Gary Collins, *Christian Counselling: A Comprehensive Guide*, 3rd ed, Nashville: Thomas Nelson, 2007, 766.

12. Pain and Trauma: Experience of Widowhood

have his body lie in state because it is believed that if the dead body goes in the house and lies in state as normally happens, misfortunes will affect the entire family, that is, people will die of accidents. This cultural practice made Anagama not to attend the funeral of her husband. A few years later when I began to talk to her about it, she was highly emotional. She talked of the shock she had on that fateful evening and that she has found it difficult to bring closure to it because she was not there when the husband was buried. To make it worse she was discharged later that very day, only to find people coming back from the graveyard. The fact that she was not at the grave to experience closure by seeing the body of her husband being lowered into the ground was difficult. It is difficult for someone to know that this was her problem and has been suffering silently until I engaged her to speak out. Because of lack of pastoral care many women continue to suffer in silence like her. At the same time some of these cultural practices have to be challenged.

Maluleke and Nadar agree with Racoczy that: "while cultural norms and values are very important in our lives, they are not absolute. Cultures are not static but undergo change over both short and long periods of time."[5] The family members and the community should be able to understand and use *Ubuntu* in dealing with sensitive issues like death.

The woman is seen at this time not to be able to make concrete decisions. Decisions are imposed on her. She cannot decide on how her husband's funeral should be conducted. Of course, as Collins puts it, "grief usually involves intense sorrow, pain, loneliness, anger, depression, physical symptoms and changes in interpersonal relationships."[6] But this should not make the family of the deceased

---

[5] Tinyiko Maluleke and Sarojini Nadar, "Breaking the Covenant of Violence Against Women," *Journal of Theology for Southern Africa* 114, 14.

[6] Gary Collins, *Christian Counselling*, 347.

husband to take things for granted that the widow is not in a position to make her own decisions. In some families, they discuss all the funeral arrangements behind her back, even deciding on who has to inherit the property without her consent. She is made vulnerable and expected to go through all the customs/traditions and rituals without question.

Pain

The experience of widowhood is painful. A widow comments that: "The pain of loss was unbearable. One moment he was here with me and the next he was gone."[7] "Becoming widowed, and the choice of words is deliberate, is possibly the most painful difficult thing one can ever have to undertake in life. First, it is never a choice one makes… It is a situation that is forcefully imposed on one."[8] Many women are left to keep their experiences of pain to themselves without someone to share with. Sometimes it is because there is no one in the community she can trust and confide in. On the other hand, the community expects the widow to adhere to all death rituals without questioning and in some of these rituals, she has to distant herself from people because she is seen to be unclean. During this time, the widow has so many things going through her mind. She is not given a chance to talk about what she went through during and after burial of her husband.

A widow I chatted with in South Africa, was widowed for more than 20 years and still hopes that one day her husband will return. She is afraid to sleep alone in the bedroom because of all the nightmares she has. She would sleep with the door open thinking that the

---

[7] Isabella Matheka, *Reflection of a Widow: My Journey of Marriage to Widowhood*. Nairobi: Publishing Institute of Africa, 2013, 46.
[8] T. Rowland, *Becoming Widowed: The Last Stage of Marriage*, Randburg: Marfam Publications, 2006, 4.

husband will come whilst she is asleep and should not miss the door that led to his former bedroom. Matheka further comments that: "Many have experienced waiting for him to come home, while others pick up the phone to call him only to remember you cannot talk to him."[9] This is a reality in the experience of widowhood. After such a long period of time, this widow was still in pain, with nobody to share with her experiences. The widow is marginalized with no one to turn to for support. In some cultural practices, she is required to wear black as a symbol of mourning. It is a painful experience when she is not accepted by the community but seen as someone bringing misfortunes. In South Africa when a widow goes to use public transport, she is not allowed to queue with other people but must stand aside and wait for a sympathetic taxi or bus driver to allow her in. Even then, there may be other passengers who do not want to sit next to her, and she may be forced to sit at the back of the taxi or find herself sitting on her own in the bus.[10] The pain of loss, loneliness, cruel rituals and cultural expectations can make the widow live in pain for a long time. When she looks to the church for refuge, she finds she is treated as an outcast. She is not expected to celebrate communion with others in some churches. She sits at the back and is the last one to be served. The church which is the body of Christ forgets at this moment that when one part of the body is in pain, the whole body should feel the pain, according to Paul's teaching.

Widowhood Inheritance

Property of the deceased is one of the issues that families have problems with. A widow may be inherited by her in-laws so that they

---

[9] Isabella Matheka, *Reflection of a Widow*, 57.
[10] Puseletso Masebolao Dlukulu, "Black Urban Widows: Their Experiences and Coping Bereavement in a Transitional Society," PhD, University of Pretoria, 2010, 68.

can control the property and children. The understanding is that she is already married to the family and can only be looked after by them. Others believe that the dead husband would put an eye on her so that other men should not have a chance to see her. Where there is no inheritance, the in-laws make sure that all property is taken away from her and she is left with nothing and she must continue raising the children on her own without support.

The widow suffers after many years of working in the home and having acquired property together with her husband, all is taken away and she is left with children without money to survive on. Moyo narrates an experience of a widow she interviewed:

> My husband was a retail shop businessman…After his death his brother locked up the shop and he could not allow me to access money from it. After six months, I went to confront him. He told me that if I am interested in the benefits of the shop then I should cooperate with him. I said I was willing to work with him. He told me he would come to my house later on after closing the shop. He came and that is when I realized what he meant by cooperating with him. He allows me to have cash whenever I cooperate with him.[11]

The woman is a victim after years of working together with her husband. She does not just lose a husband, she loses the property, she is sexually abused for her to access the money she worked for with her deceased husband, the money that belongs to her. When this happens, the woman will cease to be an active member of the church because she has committed adultery.

So many things come her way because of the inheritance custom. Kirwen narrates his conversation with a widow who was a strong

---

[11] Fulata Moyo, "A Quest for Women's Sexual Empowerment Through Education in an HIV and AIDS Context: The Case Study of Kukonzekera Chinkhoswe Chachikhristu (KCC) among Amang'anja and Ayao Christians of T/A Mwambo in Rural Zomba, Malawi," PhD, University of KwaZulu Natal, 2009, 255.

church member, on how the custom of inheritance had brainwashed some women who thought that it was better for them to be inherited than to lose the children and everything. "The only decent way for her to live and support her children, despite the opposition of the Church, was in a leviratic union with her brother in-law."[12] Women agree to be in this situation for the sake of the children.

Nyangweso further says that: "The transfer of the deceased property to the levier associated with widow inheritance has led to the misuse of some of the widow's property, especially during funeral rites, often widows are left in a state of economic hardship. At death, a widow may lose literally everything, from her husband's clothes to property, including that which was acquired in marriage and children."[13] This happens in a community which has church members but do nothing to protect her. Some of the perpetrators could be members of the church and nothing is done to them.

The widow is not given a breather to concentrate on the loss, but she goes through another tragedy, this time of losing all the property. White et al tell a story of how one widow has suffered from this practice after the death of her husband; "The couple invested in a block of four houses for leasing to tenants, and a grocery shop, which Sara the wife managed... Sara's brother in-law ordered her not to return to her matrimonial home. Instead, they took over the home and all the investments. They did not even give her a share in the property. Sara complained to the Chief who distributed the property. Sara and her children were given two houses. Her in-laws were given the other two houses and the grocery shop. After this, Sara was still

---

[12] Michael Kirwen, *African Widows*. Maryknoll: Orbis, 1979, 9.
[13] Mary Nyangweso, "Religion, Human Rights and the African Widow," *Peace Human Rights Governance*, 1/3 (2017), 371.

advised by her in-laws to return to the village."[14] The in-laws inherited everything that Sara had worked for leaving her and the children with nothing. There are many widows who have experienced such treatment from the in-laws. Thus, it makes the widow lose everything with no consideration for the work she was doing and the children that she has.

This suggests that women are only honoured and respected by the in-laws when the husband is alive. When he dies, anything can happen to her. She does not just lose a husband, she loses the property, she becomes a sexual object and is abused, for her to access the money she worked with her deceased husband, the money that belongs to her. Kabonde articulates what is involved in this practice: "a woman is more like a spectator who is told do this and that without the power to refuse what she does not like…in many cases women remain with the children while the relatives take all the money and property. Sometimes, this is accompanied by insults, for a widow is not regarded as part of the family anymore."[15]

In situations where the woman is a bread winner, the property is labelled male. The family does not even care to understand who was doing what in the family, and how they accumulated what they have. In so doing their interest is to distribute the property even if it means to distant relations. Women who have higher paying jobs than their husbands are at a disadvantage, because anything accumulated in the home is seen to be achieved by the man. Some women have been robbed of property that belongs to them and still have to pay the loan they took to obtain that property because of in-laws who are greedy. This happened to a friend that at the death of her husband, his family

---

[14] Seodi White, Dorothy Kamanga, Tinyade Kachika, Asiyati Chiweza and Flossie Gomile-Chidyaonga, *Dispossessing the Widow: Gender Based Violence in Malawi*, Blantyre: CLAIM-Kachere, 2002, 56.
[15] Peggy Mulambya Kabonde, "Widowhood in Zambia," 197.

12. Pain and Trauma: Experience of Widowhood 215

came from all over and even outside Malawi. After the funeral, they proceeded to share amongst themselves all the property, including a car stolen by the in-laws and it was registered in her name. The police returned her car as it was about to cross the borders of Malawi.[16]

Widowhood Cleansing

The concept of ritual cleansing is rooted in many traditional societies in Africa. Rituals are performed after the death to cleanse or purify the affected person and in this case the widow. They do this in fear of evil spirits that are regarded as agents of death. A widow in this case is regarded as being ritually unclean because of her husband's death. She goes through many hazardous experiences. Even though Malawi as a country is trying to educate communities through their Traditional Authorities the dangers of practising such rituals because of HIV/AIDS, some families continue to practise cleansing rituals. These are members that belong to our churches, hence the need for churches to take a leading role in helping to raise awareness on the dangers of these practices. Those who still practise feel that mourning the deceased is complete when the wife performs the required rituals. The most common cleansing ritual is what they call *kupita kufa* or *kuchotsa fumbi* (literally, taking away dust after death). In this practice a man is identified in the community to perform the ritual of cleansing and is paid. His responsibility is to have sexual intercourse with the widow. In doing this the family believes that they are cleansed from evil spirits that cause death. But this raises many questions. What has sexual intercourse got to do with cleansing of the whole family clan? Why should it be the widow who is already devastated by the death, experiencing loss and vulnerable in most

---

[16] Gertrude Kapuma, "A Story of Pain, a Need for Healing," in Jurgens Hendriks, Elna Mouton, Len Hansen and Elisabeth le Roux (eds), *Men in the Pulpit, Women in the Pew? African Perspectives of Gender Equality*, Stellenbosch: Sun Press, 2012, 65.

cases? Two examples of such experiences from women I interacted with:

> Widow A's husband died when she was fully pregnant.[17] He was killed by a crocodile. After giving birth to her child, she was asked by the family to go through the ritual of cleansing. She refused, and four years later the child died of cerebral malaria. The family made her to believe that the child died because she refused to be cleansed. Because of fear that she will lose her children, she accepted to go through the ritual. Since there were two deaths, that of her husband and her child she was to be cleansed twice.
>
> The cleanser came four times skipping days in between. Unfortunately, she became pregnant out of this ritual. Because this happened outside marriage she was disciplined at church. The family still asked her to go for another cleansing ritual to protect the child that was born from the ritual so that she is made strong from calamities. The relationship between her children and this child is very sour. It pains her all the time.
>
> Widow B had a different experience, the cleanser was HIV positive and she contracted HIV.[18]

There is no respect for this woman who once was the wife of their son, they cannot give her the dignity she requires and deserves. She does not just lose a husband, she also loses her integrity, identity, dignity and her property which could sustain her and the children. She is seen as someone without a right to be heard. The family and community are supposed to show respect and apply *Ubuntu*, making sure that her rights are not violated. Metz in explaining *Ubuntu* says that: "communal relationships are well understood in the sub-Saharan tradition as a combination of what I call 'identity' and 'solidarity'. Part of what it is to enter into community with others is to

---

[17] Widow A is not real name. She is one of the women I interacted with to help me understand the traditional practice of widowhood cleansing.

[18] Widow B is another woman that I interacted with. She had a different experience from Widow A.

identify with them, or share a way of life with them by which is meant roughly enjoying a sense of togetherness."[19] If this is applied, it means that the widow can be protected by the community by not allowing harmful practices to be imposed on her.

The fact that the practice of *Ubuntu* is declining, the widow is not consulted on what the in-laws intend do for them to perform the final death rituals so that she can give consent. This experience occurs not only in Malawi. Reggy-Mano gives the example that, in Kenya a young widow received advice from an older widow who claimed to be a born–again Christian saying:

> Don't follow Christianity blindly. When it comes to Luo tradition make sure that you put your house in order. When she asked what she meant by that, the old widow said, 'you pull down your pants. It is the way things are done. It will only be for one night and your family will be taken care of. In the morning, you can repent, and go on with your Christianity.[20]

Women have suffered this silently and other women have forced them to go through the experiences they had when they were in a similar situation, saying that it is the best way of respecting the in-laws. Her rights and dignity are not taken into consideration. What may happen to her is not important but the ritual.

Impact on Children

Death of a father has made many children suffer without a good future. As a widow the mother does not just fight her loneliness and other problems, she has to fight for her children's future. She has to help the children find a place in the society that can welcome them as they are, and also help them understand and accept the new status

---

[19] Thaddeus Metz, "African Values and Human Rights as a Two sides of a Coin: A Reply to Oyowe," *AHRLJ* 24/2 (2014), 309.

[20] M. Regg-Mano, *Widows: The Challenges and Choices*, Nairobi, Salamta, 1999, 49.

in their life. Helping children adjust and go on with life without their father is one of the biggest challenges a widow goes through. In unfortunate situations when all property is taken away from them the children find it difficult to adjust to the new situation and environment. They have many questions and do not understand why they are in that situation. "When is dad coming back home?" is one of the difficult questions the mother has to answer. They may ask why they have moved from town to the village where there is no running water. She may not explain well to what is happening and that their dad will not come again, because she is also in pain and full of emotions. Mlowoka shares his experience: "My mother went through a sad experience after the death of my father in 1980. In fact, she was forced to be inherited by the elder brother of my father in the name of *chihalo*. (This means inheritance by a brother to take over responsibility over the family which means being in control of all the deceased property). We were badly treated and insulted by both our uncle and his wife to the point that my uncle went to the surrounding schools, ordering them not to allow us to go to school. This really made the whole family to live a miserable life compared to what we were used to. Our father did not only die but his death took away everything that we had. Unfortunately, both of my sisters prematurely got married and my two elder bothers dropped from school. This situation affected our family severely."[21] In this case, the family had no one to go to for support and or counselling. Instead of her concentrating on and nursing her grief, she had to assist the children to cope with life through the difficult times. The pain will stay much longer, and it will be difficult for her to move on with life. In another situation, a woman was married to a man whom she met at work.

---

[21] Mlowooka Mhango was a student at Zomba Theological College and I interacted with him on how the death of his father affected his family.

They had one child together and invested in a house together. The man went to work in another country and left the family behind.

Unfortunately, he died whilst there and the remains were brought to Malawi. What shocked the wife is that the funeral was at his brother's place instead of their house. The family took all the property from his work and left the wife and child with nothing. The child was going to a good private school and now the mother cannot afford. This has affected the child; her performance at school has dropped and is psychologically not right, she got depressed. She does not want to see people; she wants to be alone in her room. She feels embarrassed to see her friends having everything at school when she cannot afford them. Therefore, dispossession does not just affect the widow, it also affects the children and their future.

Facilities to help such people are not available. The nearest available institution is the church. Some of the mothers in their own state of grieving may find it difficult to help the children and will end up in losing them to other forces. Because she does not have the strength and capacity at this time to help her children, who are also grieving, pastoral care for her and the children will help to solve the situation. A caring church can save many lives of children who lose hope after the death of their father. Such kind of care can help the widow not to lose her children.

Role of the Church

A widow is human being and has to be treated with dignity. God created male and female in His image, this means that the widow is in the image of God. We need to look at our theology and see what we can do to address the issue. What does God say about widows? How can dignity be restored to these women when they read scriptures? Will they find affirmation? What is the role of the Christian church on issues of violence? These are some of the questions that we need to look at and address them so that dignity is restored, and healing is achieved.

As I have written elsewhere, "We need our theology to be able to address the realities and problems of these widows... Our theology and our Churches should give recognition to and address the experiences and realities of widows."[22] This is an issue of pastoral care and leaders have to be equipped in holistic counselling so that widows can be liberated from all kinds of problems they face.

Many women become widows at an early stage, a difficult time of uncertainty and reproach. This needs some mechanisms or special facilities that would help and assist them to heal and liberate themselves from unfortunate and negative widowhood experiences. The widow is expected to go through all mourning rites in order to be accepted again in the community. As Oduyoye puts it: "It is assumed that a husband's soul will not rest until the widow has completed elaborate mourning rites and has been purified."[23] How can such a woman be helped to understand death and to go through the grieving stages which will help her accept it at the end? A process that can maintain her dignity. What mechanisms or systems are there in the Church to help and assist widows in their experience of pain as well as their healing? How do widows understand the liberation wrought by a God who was so particular about widows and their problems?

The Church is called to listen to the stories being told by women, of their experiences of abuse and pain, of the struggles they go through and how these can be tabled to bring positive change. Through the

---

[22] Gertrude Kapuma, "A Story of Pain," 68.
[23] Mercy Amba Oduyoye, "Women and Rituals in Africa," in Mercy Oduyoye and Musimbi Kanyoro (eds.), *The Will to Arise: Women, Tradition and the Church in Africa*, Maryknoll: Orbis, 1992, 15.

12. Pain and Trauma: Experience of Widowhood

Truth and Reconciliation Commission of South Africa, Finca says that listening to the stories that were being told or uncovered by different people was not easy it was painful experience to both the listener and the victim. He observed that through the process of telling the story helped many to begin to heal or reconcile with the past. He says: "Telling your story of obedience to a higher goal is a liberating act. You bless your memories of pain and struggle as you fit together in one picture the act of liberation."[24] It is the church's responsibility to liberate women from the unjust experiences they go through in the community so that their dignity could prevail. "Liberation must be viewed as men and women walking together on the journey home, with the church as the umbrella of faith, hope and love." Through some practical pastoral care models, the church may achieve wholeness, healing and liberation for widows and become an instrument of justice to widows and those who are marginalized. "The Church is asked to be in solidarity with women because in the body of Christ the women members (widows) are in pain."[25] The church should empower both men and women to understand issues of death and dying. It should help couples prepare well for such a situation. Women in the women's groups should be helped to discuss such topics and helped to support other women.

Conclusion

This raises many challenges to the African church. The Church should know its community and its cultural practices in order to help and give proper guidance when need arises. There are a number of such practices that affect women and the girl child. Wadesango,

---

[24] Bongani Finca, "Learning to Bless our Memories," in Philippe Denis (ed), *Orality, Memory and the Past*, Pietermaritzburg: Cluster, 2000, 15.
[25] Mercy Oduyoye, *Who will Roll the Stone Away? Ecumenical Decade of the Churches in Solidarity with Women*, Geneva: WCC, 1990, 44.

Rembe and Chabaya further comments that: "Harmful traditional and cultural practices maintain the subordination of women in society and legitimize and perpetuate gender-based violence."[26] With this knowledge the church should have proper organized counselling sessions in which the widow is helped to appraise herself in her new situation realistically. She should be equipped with new skills to avoid disappointments. She will need help to acquire strategies for handling grief without getting hopelessly broken. She should be helped on how to handle loneliness, how to make decisions and how to cope with her new responsibility as a bread winner. The church and its theology should provide refuge and emotional support acknowledging that the Christian widow is a person created in the image of God. There should be room to allow the widow to tell her stories that can help her in the healing process, as Oduyoye rightly says:

> The stories we tell of our hurts and joys are sacred. Telling them makes us vulnerable, but without sharing we cannot build community and solidarity. Our stories are precious paths on which we have walked with God and struggled for a passage to full humanity. They are events through which we have received the blessings of life from the hand of God. [27]

Many Churches have in place disciplinary actions for members who do not follow the rules, practices and procedures of the given church. Can the church today think of putting a disciplinary action to all their members who go and illegally inherit the property of their deceased relatives making the family left behind to suffer? Those members of the church who force widows to go through hazardous rituals. Is this possible? Could this be a good way forward?

---

[26] Newman Wadesango, Symphorosa Rembe and Owence Chabaya, "Violation of Human Rights by Harmful Practices," *Anthropologist* 13/2 (2011), 121.
[27] Mercy Oduyoye, *Introducing African Women's Theology*, Sheffield: Sheffield Academic Press, 2001, 21.

References

Collins, Gary, *Christian Counselling: A Comprehensive Guide*. 3rd ed, Nashville: Thomas Nelson, 2007.

Dlukulu, Puseletso Masebolao, "Black Urban Widows: Their Experience of Coping with Bereavement in a Transitional Society," PhD, University of Pretoria, 2010.

Finca, Bongani, "Learning to Bless Our Memories," in Philippe Denis (ed), *Orality, Memory & the Past*, Pietermaritzburg: Cluster, 2000, 11 19.

Kabonde, Peggy Mulambya, "Widowhood in Zambia: The Effects of Rituals," in Musimbi R.A. Kanyoro & Nyambura J. Njoroge (eds), *Groaning in Faith: African Women in the Household of God*, Nairobi: Acton, 1996, 195-203.

Kapuma, Gertrude A., "A Story of Pain, a Need for Healing," in Jurgens Hendriks, Elna Mouton, Lens Hansen and Elisabeth le Roux, eds, *Men in the Pulpit, Women in the Pew? African Perspectives of Gender Equality*, Stellenbosch, Sun Press, 2012.

Kirwen, Michael, 1979. *African Widows*, Maryknoll: Orbis.

Maluleke, Tinyiko S. and Sarojini Nadar, "Breaking the Covenant of Violence Against Women," *Journal of Theology for Southern Africa*, 114 (2002), 5-17.

Matheka, Isabella G., *Reflection of a Widow: My Journey in Marriage and Widowhood*, Nairobi: Publishing Institute of Africa, 2013.

Metz, Thaddeus, "African Values and Human Rights as Two Sides of the Same Coin: A Reply to Oyowe," *African Human Rights Law Journal*, 14 (2014), 306-321.

Moyo, Fulata L., "A Quest for Women's Sexual Empowerment Through Education in an HIV and AIDS Context: The Case Study of Kukonzekera Chinkhoswe Chachikhristu (KCC) among Amang'anja and Ayao Christians of T/A Mwambo in Rural Zomba, Malawi," PhD, University of KwaZulu Natal, 2009.

Mwangi, M., "My Life can be Meaningful," in Esther. Mombo and Hellen Joziasse (eds), *If you have no Voice Just Sing! Narratives of Women's Lives and Theological Education at St. Paul's University*, Limuru: Zapf Chancery, 2011, 77-79.

Nyangweso Mary, "Religion, Human Rights and the African Widow," *Peace Human Rights Governance*, 1/3 (2017), 371.

Oduyoye, Mercy Amba, *Who Will Roll the Stone Away? The Ecumenical Decade of the Churches in Solidarity with Women.* Geneva: WCC, 1990.

Oduyoye, Mercy Amba, "Women and Rituals in Africa," in Mercy Amba Oduyoye and Musimbi R.A. Kanyoro (eds), *The Will to Arise: Women, Tradition, and the Church in Africa*, Maryknoll: Orbis, 1992, 9-24.

Oduyoye, Mercy Amba, *Introducing African Women's Theology*, Sheffield: Sheffield Academic Press, 2001.

Reggy-Mamo, M.A., *Widows: The Challenges and Choices*, Nairobi: Salamta, 1999.

Rowland, T., *Becoming Widowed*, Randburg: MARFAM Publications, 2016.

Wadesango, Newman, Symphorosa Rembe and Owence Chabaya, "Violation of Human Rights by Harmful Practices," *Anthropologist*, 13/2 (2011), 121-129.

Chapter 13

Cold War between Reverends and Ruling Elders in CCAP, Synod of Livingstonia: From Ruling to Assistant Elders

Moses Mlenga

Introduction

The silent war between Reverends and Church Elders in the Church of Central Africa Presbyterian (CCAP) Synods in general and Livingstonia Synod in particular, is real. Ruling elders appear to sing joyfully in their white uniforms while they have unresolved issues with men and women in Presbyterian gowns and collars. CCAP Synod of Livingstonia operates from a premise that Teaching and Ruling Elders are equal with different functions. Ruling Elders give false respect to pastors when they actually have issues with them. There are numerous cases of gossiping that takes place over administrative issues between men and women in white clerical collars and those in white jackets and white blouses. While the majority of Teaching Elders do not see any problem, many Ruling Elders are of the opinion that pastors have encroached into the power zone and are using them as mere figureheads.

Presbyterianism was born as a reaction against a church system that was controlled by a Pope and his team of high-ranking clergy like Cardinals and Bishops. The protesters opted for a system of church government that distributes equal powers with separate functions to both the clergy and lay leadership. The clergy are referred to as "Teaching Elders," popularly addressed as "Reverends" while "Ruling Elders," are referred to simply as Elders.

The study issue arises from the scenario that while the Presbyterian leadership model espoused by John Calvin and other reformers give equal powers to the two sets of elders,[1] the Teaching Elders (Reverends) appear to have systematically taken the administrative powers from Ruling Elders. This study uses the term "cold war" because it describes a power struggle between reverends and elders within the power structures of the CCAP Synod of Livingstonia. What is happening is like a cheating husband who goes out with other women while assuring his wife that she is the only one who is legally married to him. The unfaithful husband assures the wife that she can ignore the other women because they are not appearing on their marriage certificate. In theory, reverends and elders are equal. In practice, Teaching Elders have systematically usurped powers of the Ruling Elders and have reduced them to the level of "Church Assistants." While some elders have opted to observe and suffer in silence, this study brings this power encroachment into the public domain for discussion.

This research investigates the causes and impact of the conflict between the two sets of elders within the context of Presbyterianism and explores possible ways to remedy the disappointments brought about by the power encroachments. The term "conflict" is defined in this chapter as a sharp disagreement that takes place as a result of a clash of ideas or interests. The chapter adopts Webster's New World Dictionary definition of "cold war," as being a sharp conflict that originates from economic disagreements between nations. Crucial in times of disagreements is the ability to resolve religious controversy

---

[1] R.E.H Uprichard, *What Presbyterians Believe*, Ahoghill: The Oaks, 2011, 83.

13. Cold War between Reverends and Ruling Elders in CCAP 227

amicably because failure to do so, even if it means agreeing to disagree, ultimately leads to the disintegration of the church.[2]

As a researcher, I ventured into this enquiry as an insider having served in various official offices of the Synod. These include the position of Vestry Chairperson, Session Clerk, Executive Member of the Presbytery and Board Member of Synod Boards. In addition, I taught and served for many years as College Principal in several of the campuses of the University of Livingstonia.

Historical Background

The power politics between the clergy and the laity has a long history. After the death of Christ, his disciples carried the baton of ministry and handed it over to prominent Apostolic Church Fathers like Clement of Rome, Tertullian, Jerome and others.[3] Thereafter, various factors led to the birth of the Roman Catholic Church in AD 200, led by Bishops. With passage of time, the clergy began to abuse their ecclesiastical power far beyond what was expected of them as men of God. The laity observed with amazement that the clergy were misusing church funds, engaging themselves in immoral activities and usurping absolute powers. The leadership of then medieval Roman Catholic Church around 1500 refused to take on board suggestions from some of the sincere reformers like Wycliffe and Hus. This left members of the sixteenth century church with no option but to rebel against clerical arrogance.[4] The laity organized protests against clerical arrogance, resulting in the disintegration of the old Roman Catholic

---

[2] Kerry Patterson, Joseph Grenny, Ron McMillan and Al Switzler, *Crucial Confrontations: Tools for Resolving Broken Promises, Violated Expectations, and Bad Behavior*, New York: McGraw-Hill, 2005, 5.
[3] Earle E. Cairns, *Christianity through the Centuries: A History of the Christian Church*, Grand Rapids: Zondervan, 1981, 72.
[4] Earle E. Cairns, *Christianity Through the Centuries*, 273-284.

Church and the birth of splinter churches. Presbyterianism started at this time.

The man behind the Presbyterian model of Church government was John Calvin.[5] His goal was to bridge the gap between the clergy and the laity. Thereafter, John Knox gave impetus to the new model by urging Christians to resist not only the compromised old Roman Catholic clergy, but also civil governments that oppress God's people.[6] In the mind of Calvin, Ruling Elders exist to govern and administer discipline while Teaching Elders are concentrating on their prophetic role. Ruling Elders are not assistants to pastors but partners in the ministry as outlined in the core beliefs of the Presbyterians, defined in the Westminster Confession of Faith.[7]

Biblical Light on Power Dynamics between Teaching and Ruling Elders

The Presbyterian notion of Teaching and Ruling Eldership is derived from two terms: *episkopos* - translated as "pastor" and Πρεσβύτερος (presbuteros - translated as "elder"). The two Greek words denote the same idea of a religious leader in a community. No distinction is made to differentiate the two sets of elders. It should also be noted that Scripture was written from two different backgrounds. The Greek Community used the term "pastor" while the Jewish one used the word "elder." Scripture depicts elders, generally as being

---

[5] Steven Paas, *Ministers and Elders – The Birth of Presbyterianism*, Zomba: Kachere, 2007, 54.
[6] H. Griffith, in the *Evangelical Dictionary of Theology*, ed. Walter A. Elwell, Grand Rapids: Baker Book House, 1987, 615.
[7] *The Westminster Confession of Faith*, 3rd ed, Atlanta: Committee for Christian Education & Publications, 1990, xv.

responsible for preaching, teaching and leading the affairs of the church.[8] Various texts in the Bible allude to the same.[9]

It is like having various names to refer to or describe the same person or office. One example is that of the word "mother." The Chewa community refer to a mother as *"a mayi"*, the Tumbuka as *"a Mama"* and colloquial *Chibulazi* as *"masiteni."* In the language of the New Testament Greek, the terms "pastor" and "overseer" are used interchangeably to depict the same notion. The context determines which word should be used. The early reformers avoided the terms "Reverend" or "Pastor" but opted for "Teaching" and "Ruling" Elders instead for a reason. They were of the opinion that both Teaching and Ruling Elders use delegated powers from God for the spiritual benefit of God's people.

The New Testament model of putting pastors and elders on the same level with different responsibilities is benchmarked by Jethro's advice to his son-in-law, Moses (Ex 18:19-23). Being a man of God who spoke directly with God and knew His word, it was very easy for Moses to judge his people. However, the work was cumbersome. It is not that Moses was unfit to settle disputes. Moses was faulted for spending his time unwisely and wasting the time of his followers unnecessarily. Jethro advised "elder" Moses to stick to his prophetic calling of being the people's representative before God while empowering other "elders" to take care of administrative and

---

[8] Solomon Andria, in the *Africa Bible Commentary*, ed. Adeyemo Tokunboh, Zondervan: WordAlive, 1469-1476.

[9] Elders exist to teach and preach the Word of God (2 Timothy 4:2; I Timothy 3:2); provide leadership to the Church (I Peter 5:1-2; I Tim. 5:17); safeguard the church from false teachers (Acts 20:28-31); carry out pastoral duties to the sick (James 5:14) and encourage and reprimand church members in all matters of sound doctrine (2 Timothy 3:13-17).

disciplinary issues.[10] After delegating, Moses had to concentrate his energies on teaching the Word of God.[11] It is particularly difficult to delegate when many are looking at yourself as a star performer. There is a high likelihood that the chosen judges did not perform at the level of Moses. The gist of Jethro's advice was that Moses could not do everything on his own. In God's vineyard, it is important to share the load. Grooming new leaders does not mean abandoning responsibility. Church leaders must learn to listen to others, equip those selected and promote others to become effective leaders.[12]

A Reverend is supposed to be first among equals. The "first among equals" model protects the anointed servant of God from overworking. The same was the case during the early years of the Christian Church when the apostles had to delegate selected "elders" so that they would not *leave the word of God and serve tables* (Acts 6:2-4). It appears that many reverends are more comfortable doing the work of serving tables than their primary calling because of material and monetary benefits. The Presbyterian system has already put in place a system of identifying capable Elders to serve the tables while Reverends are preaching. Those whom God has called are always in danger of trying to do more than what they are able to do.

Reverends are specifically called to a holy ministry and are not supposed to be entangled with too many administrative issues. Too much involvement in administrative issues can distract Ministers from the original goal of their calling. Such an approach often results in Reverends failing to find quality time to receive from God what they are supposed to share with their flock.

---

[10] Abel Ndjerareou, "Exodus" in the *Africa Bible Commentary*, 108.
[11] https://bible.org/article/who-should-run-church-case-plurality-elders.
[12] https://digitalcommons.andrews.edu/cgi/viewcontent.cgi?article=1548&-context=dmin.

Synod's Deviation from Original Presbyterianism

Synods are assemblies of overseers and other appointed church officers. They exist to create a forum where Teaching and Ruling Elders can meet to deliberate on issues crucial to the growth and improvement of the church.[13] While Synods play a crucial role in Presbyterian government, they are sometimes used to pass resolutions that conform neither to the Scriptures nor to the Presbyterian *ethos*. It should be noted that throughout the history of the church, Synods or Councils have sometimes made serious theological errors that ended up ruining the church. This being the case, not all Synod decisions should be regarded as gospel truths that can act as a basis for the rule of faith or practice.[14]

The term "synodicalism" refers to the way in which the Synod arrives at resolutions and Synod officers implement such resolutions. In its leadership model the Synod of Livingstonia has inherited practices from Scottish Presbyterianism, a type of Presbyterianism that is heavily saturated with Anglicanism - a church controlled by Bishops.[15] Through Synod meetings which Teaching Elders control,

---

[13] The Confession of Faith, together with the Larger Catechism and the Shorter Catechism with the Scripture Proofs, 3rd ed, Century Saite: Committee for Christian Education & Publications, 1990, 95.

[14] Ibid, 96.

[15] J.J. Van Wyk writes, "The Scottish Reformers followed the Geneva model, but they had to act in the context of an Episcopalian State Church. Attention for the local congregation was replaced by attention for the Church as an institution. Consequently, the clericalist approach of the office of minister and the conception of the other offices as assistants to the higher office, have made it impossible for the offices of elder and deacon to develop in their own rights. ... Scottish Presbyterianism reflects the consequences of replacement of the government by Christ by a government by man and the consequential idea of office-bearers as servants of an institution." J.J. Van Wyk, *The Historical Development of the Offices according to the Presbyterian Tradition of Scotland*, Zomba: Kachere, 2004.

Ruling Elders have silently been "downgraded" to a "lower administrative scale."

Firstly, some Teaching Elders sponsored a measure that requires that all Synod Departments should be headed by a Teaching Elder. At one of its Synod Meetings, held at Phwezi, it was resolved that all Synod Departments, including campuses of the University of Livingstonia, should be headed by Reverends. At the time of research, the clergy were occupying the key positions of Vice-Chancellor, Campus Principals in the University of Livingstonia, College Registrars and Deans of Student. Before the Synod Garage became bankrupt, it was headed by a Reverend with a technical background. There was a case where the Synod appointed a Reverend as Hospital Administrator of a Mission Hospital, but the government licensing body, Medical Council of Malawi, refused to assent to the appointment.

These positions were formerly occupied by professional Teaching Elders who trained in those specific fields. Because of what some people perceive to be material benefits attached to those prestigious positions, the Synod agreed to have those positions occupied by Reverends only. Unfortunately, the majority of the appointed Reverends trained in the field of theology only. While the Synod has legal documents like Constitution, Practice and Procedures and Synod Minutes for guidance, senior Reverends often use synod resolutions to usurp power from Ruling Elders.

Secondly, there is a departure from Presbyterian tradition in terms of composition of the top five officials in the hierarchy of the Synod of Livingstonia. The "one Reverend – one Elder" Presbyterian arrangement has been seriously compromised. The Secretariat comprises four Reverends and one Elder, an arrangement which is different from Presbyterian tradition.[16] It should not be surprising, therefore, that the Synod Secretariat has wielded a lot of power, with Synod General Secretaries operating more like Catholic Bishops, the very model the early Reformers protested against during the Reformation Era.

Thirdly, Reverends prefer to work in Synod Departments where they get a competitive salary than serve in a congregation. While Teaching Elders receive a monthly stipend, many of those who have obtained a Bachelors or Masters or PhD in Theology prefer to work in Synod Departments. While some Teaching Elders remain role models to many in their ministerial calling, the majority prefer serving God in administrative positions because of monetary benefits. The fact remains that too much involvement in administrative issues compromises a Reverend's original calling, making it hard for men and women of God to find quality time to receive from God what they are supposed to share with the flock.

Selected Issues Causing Tension Between the two Sets of Elders

Reverends are undermining Session Clerks, who are top lay leaders

A Ruling Elder, who has served in the office of Session Clerk for 29 years, argued strongly that Teaching Elders have given themselves too much authority over Ruling Elders. Being a Session Clerk, graduate teacher and a politician (Ward Counsellor), he had been engaging boldly the Reverends he worked with for three decades in various congregations. According to him and the experiences his

---

[16] The four include the Moderator; Moderator–Elect; General Secretary; Deputy General Secretary and General Treasurer (only elder). Presbyteries are arranged in a similar manner.

colleagues from various congregations, Reverends make crucial decisions in the area of administration and ask Ruling elders to simply rubber-stamp such decisions. Teaching Elders strive to control finances by imposing their decisions when allocating monthly funds after the Deacons Court meetings. More so, Reverends have a tendency to reverse decisions made by lay leaders during their absence and yet they hardly stay at their duty stations due to various administrative issues. Furthermore, elders abhor Reverends' tendency to influence elections of Session Executive members and chairpersons of Session Committees, to ensure that their preferred candidates win. As if this is not enough, the lay leaders resent especially young Church Ministers, who join the ministry on the pretext of a "holy calling" while their hidden actual goal is to plunder church resources. They abuse their privileged position by creating unnecessary financial demands for the congregations to meet. In addition, Ruling Elders bear a grudge against the deteriorating moral standards of Reverends. Elders cite both the officially reported and unreported shameful and immoral acts. Elders also dislike Reverend's tendency of instituting major changes in a congregation without consulting relevant stakeholders or by using the "divide and rule" approach. Lastly, Ruling Elders are not comfortable with the claim that Reverends are answerable to God only and not any individual at congregation level.

Reverends Belittling "Local Evangelists" (Lay Preachers)

Most evangelists are good preachers and tend to win more souls than Reverends. A story is told of a local evangelist who preached during the first service during the evangelistic rally where many responded in an altar call and gave their lives to Christ. During the second service, a Reverend preached but no one responded to his altar call. This enraged the Reverend to extent that he refused to offer a lift in his car, forcing the evangelist to walk back to the Mission Station.

13. Cold War between Reverends and Ruling Elders in CCAP   235

They two had travelled together when going to the evangelistic rally. The Reverend's open display of jealousy of lay people who are endowed with various spiritual gifts, not evident in some pastors themselves, create unnecessary tensions. The Synod has for a long time been employing full time lay preachers to work in new founded congregations. Their assignment was to build the pastor's house as well as the church building before a Reverend can be assigned to that place. Evangelists were used like caterpillar machines that clear the road to pave way for other vehicles to use the road properly.

However, due to perceived jealousy, some Reverends successfully sponsored a motion to the Synod Conference to have the office of local evangelist abolished. They argued that the Synod has enough ordained Ministers and the need to recruit lay leaders is no longer there. The fact remains that abolition of the office of an evangelist that created employment to lay people has fuelled the already existing tension. Lay preachers enjoyed serving the Synod while living in an official Church house (Manse) and getting a small monthly stipend.

Reverends Aggrieved by Ruling Elder's Encroachments into their Power Domain

While the study has established that Church Elders are victims due to Teaching Elders' power encroachment, there are cases where Reverends too are victimized by Ruling Elders. Ruling Elders tend to exploit the fact that they are more conversant with the customs and traditions of Church than the new Reverends. While some elders are respectful to their Church ministers, others are not. Those who know more about the traditions and practices than the young Church Ministers tend to sometimes belittle Teaching Elders. There have been times when a young Minister has made a technical mistake through omission or additions in church liturgy. Experienced elders have often treated such incidents unprofessionally by publicly embarrassing their new Reverends.[17]

Proposed Way Forward to Ease the Tension between the Two Sets of Elders

It is imperative that the Synod should go back to the drawing board with an open mind. The process requires that the church should raise real and soul-searching questions if CCAP is to go back to the original Presbyterian model. The study has listed below some suggestions that can assist in going back to the original model.

1. The Synod should ensure that only the offices of the Synod Moderator and Moderator-elect are occupied by Teaching Elders (Reverends), while the offices of the Synod General Secretary and the Deputy are occupied by God fearing and professionally trained Ruling Elders, carefully selected. The General Secretary should be a God-fearing and respected Ruling Elder who possesses an advanced degree in Church or Public Administration, Business Administration or any other related field. The Synod Deputy General Secretary, who functions as Personnel Manager, should be a God-fearing Elder who possesses an advanced degree in Human Resource Management or any other related field.

2. Reverends should focus on the higher calling of teaching God's word to the people and administering sacraments while Ruling Elders are serving tables in the Synod departments.

3. Teaching Elders should learn to respect and treat Ruling Elders on the basis that the two sets of elders are equal with different responsibilities.

---

[17] Lapani Nkhonjera (Rev), Campus Registrar, University of Livingstonia, 22 June 2020.

4. Evangelists, who are lay preachers, should be recalled and incorporated into the ministry because they have a unique role to play.

5. There is need to expose Ruling Elders to basic theological studies through TEEM or other training Institutions because these people are already offering pastoral services at vestry level. Such training sessions should be done at vestry, session or presbytery level.

6. Matters of administration and finances should be left in the hands of competent and God-fearing Ruling Elders. The Synod should encourage Church ministers to control their appetite for church finances in congregations.

Conclusion

The cold war between Teaching and Ruling Elders in CCAP, Synod of Livingstonia is real. The main cause is temptation, on the part of some Church Ministers, to operate like Presbyterian "bishops" and view Ruling Elders as their assistants. Reverends want to preach the gospel, administer sacraments and serve the table at the same time. In the language of Scripture, both the Teaching and Ruling Elder refer to the same office. The difference comes in when it comes to the functions. This being the case, there is no need for one form of eldership to belittle the other form. Even in secular governments, a Minister of Finance is at the same level with the Minister of Youth and Culture. The two cabinet ministers are on same level with same privileges, but different functions. Despite their exposure to theological training, a Teaching Elder should always remember that he/she is first among the equals.

References

Personal Interviews

Harawa, Jane, elder and Primary School Adviser, Luwuchi, Rumphi, 16.6.2020.

Malongo, Isaac (Rev), Synod Moderator-Elect, Mzuzu, 21.6.2020.

Mazunda, Overtoun (Rev Dr), Former Synod General Secretary, Mzuzu, 23.6.2020.

Mfune, Mbezuma, (Rev), Retired General Secretary, Betania House, Mwazisi, Rumphi, 25.6.2020.

Msiska, Gezamchere, Retired Session Clerk, Livingstonia, 5.6.2020.

Msukwa, Bellings, Serving Session Clerk for 29 years, Mlare, Karonga, 3.6.2020.

Nkhonjera, Lapani (Rev), Campus Registrar, University of Livingstonia, 10.6.2020.

Minutes

Minutes of the General Administrative Committee held at Livingstonia from 21st to 26th August 1968.

Minute No. 1066/92 of the Synod Meeting held at Bandawe Mission Station from 10th to 23rd August 1992.

Minutes of the Synod held at Karonga Teachers' Training College from 12th to 17th November 2020.

Secondary Sources

Bolman, Lee G., *Leading with a Soul: An Uncommon Journey of Spirit*, San Francisco: Jossey-Bass, 2001.

Cairns, Earle E., *Christianity through the Centuries: A History of the Christian Church*, Zondervan: Grand Rapids, 1981.

Gifford, Paul, *African Christianity: Its Public Role*, Bloomington: Indiana University Press, 1998.

Noll, Mark A., "Puritanism," in the *Evangelical Dictionary of Theology*, ed. Walter A. Elwell, Grand Rapids: Baker Book House, 1984.

Paas, Steven, *Ministers and Elders - The Birth of Presbyterianism*, Zomba: Kachere, 2007.

Patterson, Kerry, Joseph Grenny, Ron McMillan, and Al Switzler, *Crucial Confrontations: Tools for Resolving Broken Promises, Violated Expectations, and Bad Behavior*, New York: McGraw-Hill, 2005.

13. Cold War between Reverends and Ruling Elders in CCAP   239

The Westminster Confession of Faith, 3rd edition, Atlanta: Committee for Christian Education & Publications, 1990.

Uprichard, R.E.H., *What Presbyterians Believe*, Ahoghill: The Oaks, 2011.

van Wyk, J.J., *The Historical Development of the Offices according to the Presbyterian Tradition of Scotland*, Zomba: Kachere, 2004.

Chapter 14

The Bible and the Concept of Separation of Powers: Could the Bible Constitute the Foundation for Malawi's Good Governance?

Mzee Hermann Y. Mvula

Introduction

At a popular glance, it would seem that the Bible has nothing to do with governance and the political processes. However, critical reading and reflection on the Bible shows that it teaches much about these issues. Biblically, good governance is based on the principles of justice, righteousness and compassion, defending the rights of the poor and marginalized and protecting the people from conflict. Although it is hard to hold on to the idea that the Bible could constitute the foundation of politics, political processes and good governance at popular level, the concept of separation of powers, could essentially be argued as founded on biblical principles. It is therefore the aim of this chapter to demonstrate that the Bible contains the principles for good governance, in particular the question of the separation of powers within the government. Special attention is given to the book of Isaiah that directly, albeit implicitly at the popular level, speaks of the threefold nature of the government. And this helps us argue that the Bible could constitute the foundation of the concept of separation of powers and consequently an important basis for good governance in Malawi.

Separation of powers and reciprocal checks and balances incorporated throughout the US Constitution has been heralded as one of the most important features of American government, enabling it not

14. The Bible and the Concept of Separation of Powers 241

only to survive but to thrive for over two centuries. History was filled with examples showing that when government power was centralized in one body or leader, that government always became a danger to the rights of individuals. It is important to know that the Founding Fathers had not only the examples of history to guide them but also the teachings of the Bible.

This chapter first discusses the biblical precursor to the concept of separation of powers, therefore alluding to its biblical origin. This is followed by an analysis of Isaiah 33:22 which forms the implied theological foundations of separation of powers. Then the implications of a divided government emphasizing on the necessity of the Judiciary to matters of good governance. Thereafter, a conclusion follows.

Biblical Precursors to the Principle of Separation of Powers

The first five books of the Bible are commonly referred to as the "Books of the Law," "Pentateuch" and the "Decalogue." These books contain legal codes that governed the every-day life of the ancient nation of Israel, ranging from personal hygiene to how to prosecute law breakers. Implicitly and explicitly, ethical principles and moral values for entrenching good governance are found in the Pentateuch. Furthermore, the Hebrew prophets railed against the kings of their day for making "unjust laws" and "oppressive decrees" (Isaiah 10:1), implying that there are an unjust laws—and woe to the legislators who write them, woe to the judges who bend them; and woe to the king who enforces them.

Afrifa Gitonga states that "democracy as a system of governance has its foundations in principles of goodness, fairness and justice."[1] Consequently, these ideals which could be said to have theological overtones on which democracy depends must be promoted. Political leaders must be accountable on these ideals and values, and must uphold them if democracy is to be entrenched. Such a posture and upholding of biblical ethical principles and moral values may help repudiate the bad elements that perpetuate hegemonic demagoguery among some political leaders. Apparently, most political leaders in Malawi go contrary to the will of God for themselves as leaders as leaders and for the people.[2] The history of Malawi since independence is replete with examples of bad governance tendencies and behaviours. However, the Bible shows that good governance can among others come through entrenchment of the concept of separation of powers of government as presented in the Pentateuch and reinforced by the prophet Isaiah and his contemporaries.[3]

Therefore, some biblical scholars and ethicists postulate that the biblical-historic pattern for a separated judicial power had evolved as an instrument to satisfy the public hunger for justice. The Bible constitutes one of the ancient origins of separation of powers with its ardent focus on justice which must be upheld by all. Exodus narratives demonstrate the principles laid down for good governance through separate statuses of offices. For instance, Moses' selection of men of truth, hating covetousness, into a separate category of people authorized to settle the disputes signified the birth of the judiciary as

---

[1] Afrifa Gitonga, "The Meaning of and Foundations of Democracy," in W.O Oyugi and Afrifa Gitonga (eds), *Democratic Theory and Practice in Africa*, Nairobi: East African Educational Publishers, 1987, 2.

[2] This is in spite of the popular sentiments that Malawi is a God-fearing nation.

[3] This doesn't mean having the Bible as the constitution of the nations. But it means upholding the principles of good governance as laid down in the Bible, which reveals God's will for harmonious living among the people.

an independent institution.[4] It is significant to observe the dramatic relationship between Judge Samuel and King Saul of Israel long before John Locke and Montesquieu's postulation of political frameworks for governance. Such a relationship assumes that the idea of an independent judge as the guardian of the "rule of law" and ultimately of justice existed long time ago. Consequently, there is a correlation between the biblical roots of judicial systems and their administration on one hand and kingly administrative operations on the other. In fact, we can confidently speak of separation of powers only in a situation where the judiciary is separated, fully or partially, from the executive and legislative branches of government and enjoys sufficient independence.[5]

Critical reading of the Pentateuch (for instance, Deuteronomy 4:6-8) shows that Israel would be shaped and characterized by the laws and institutions of the Sinai covenant, and she would be a highly visible exemplary to the nations both as to the nature of the God they worshipped and as to the quality of social justice embodied in their community.[6] Christopher Wright argues that this was a deliberate link of Israel's role among the nations to the socio-ethical structure of their corporate life: mission and ethics combined. Israel's mission was to be a model to the nations.[7] Wright continues stating, "Mission was not a matter of going but being; to be what they were, to live as people of Yahweh their God in the sight of the nations."[8] Wright argues that "hermeneutically this perspective also offers a potentially more

---

[4] See Exodus 18.

[5] Another criterion of separation of powers is whether the actions of the executive branch of government fall within the jurisdiction of the courts. See "The Judiciary" in *Government and Politics in Malawi*, Zomba: Kachere, 2007.

[6] See S.D. McBride, "Polity of the Covenant People: The Book of Deuteronomy," *Interpretation* 41 (1987), 229-244.

[7] Christopher Wright, *Deuteronomy*, Grand Rapids: Baker Books, 1996, 13.

[8] Ibid, 13.

fruitful way of handling the law as regards contemporary ethical relevance."⁹ The issue of the applicability of Old Testament law in the contemporary social context is crucial. Therefore, according to Wright "the purpose of the law must be set in the light of the universal significance of Israel for the nations as a presupposition of any extended application."¹⁰ Indeed, for Wright, to answer the question, 'Why the law?' we need to ask 'Why Israel?' in the first place."¹¹ Theologically, Wright states:

> The law was designed to mould and shape Israel in certain clearly defined directions, within their own historico-cultural context. That overall shape... thus becomes the model of paradigm intended to have a relevance and application beyond the geographical, historical and cultural borders of Israel itself.... The point is that this paradigmatic nature of Israel is not just a hermeneutical tool devised by us retrospectively, but theologically speaking, was part of God's design in creating and shaping Israel as he did in the first place.¹²

It is in this manner that the missiological significance of Israel and its law will be given practical and context-specific ethical expression in a way that is faithful to the dynamic pattern of the Old Testament law and the prophets.¹³

The theological background for the concept of separation of powers could be said to be found in Deuteronomy chapters 16 and 17 which set four offices of authority in Israel side by side: judge, king, priest, and prophet. Christopher Wright argues that the fact that these are placed side by side gives us an insight into its "constitutional" intentions.¹⁴ Ideally, the clear distinction of the different kinds of

---

⁹ Ibid.
¹⁰ Ibid.
¹¹ Ibid, 13.
¹² Ibid, 14.
¹³ Ibid.
¹⁴ Ibid, 203.

14. The Bible and the Concept of Separation of Powers

authority can be seen as a significant precursor of some of the principles of democratic government, especially the separation of powers.[15] Theologically and indeed practically, no single person could hold all four offices. None of the authorities is given supreme authority over the others. Certainly, the king (who doesn't even come first) does not appoint the others, and though executive in the political sphere, has very explicit limitations set on his power.[16] Consequently, Wright argues

> If any priority is evident, it would be in the first and last of the list: the judge (who administers the law of God) and the prophet (who speaks for God). The supreme authority is thus Yahweh himself, whose theocratic focus of power and authority in a vertical sense effectively flattens and disperses power at the horizontal level. The constitutional aspects of human authority are thus set firmly in the context of God's transcendent authority and revealed will and word.[17]

It is interesting to note that God's vertical transcendent power flattens and is dispersed at the horizontal level so as to have separated constitutional powers for good governance to be manifested.[18] Wright is correct when he states that "apart from the dimension of covenant theocracy, the principles enshrined here still have political and constitutional relevance."[19] The separation of powers is an important bulwark against tyranny. Therefore, "there is no doubt that there will be a greater commitment to justice in society when there is

---

[15] Ibid.
[16] See Deuteronomy 17:14-20.
[17] Wright, *Deuteronomy*, 203.
[18] Ibid. Unfortunately, at popular level we often think of theocracy as God running affairs of the earthly governments. In reality, theocracy means God's vertical transcendent power (reign) flattening, thereby dispersing and distributing governance power horizontally to different authorities: Judges and Kings—Judiciary, Executive and Legislature.
[19] Wright, *Deuteronomy*, 204.

some consensual submission to a *transcendent norm*, however articulated, that stand above all participants in the socio-political processes."[20]

Indeed, the Bible is a source of inspiration for law and justice, the independence of the judiciary whose separation from the Executive power was established by Moses (Exodus 18). This means that the Bible has something which can be regarded as a precursor of a modern constitution, and constitutionalism with its intricate principles or concepts or theories of "rule of law," "transparency and accountability," "limited government," "respect for human rights," and "the supremacy principle." Consequently, the origin of the principle of separation of powers as a philosophical, political and most important constitutional principle has deep theological roots. While its authorship is usually ascribed to John Locke and Charles de Montesquieu, other scholars go further back in time, referring to the wise men of antiquity, such as Aristotle, Plato, Epicurus and Polibius; this chapter goes further to the time of biblical prophets and other characters.

Accordingly, the Bible shows the divine origin of the judiciary and the basis of its independence from the king. For instance, in Exodus 18, Deuteronomy 16:18-20; 17:1-13, the book of Judges, the narratives of Judge Samuel, and the prophetic books. In Israel the main judicial role initially belonged to judges who had distinguished themselves: ethically, morally, wisely, and experientially. As for the monarchy, it was not established until several centuries later, with limitations stipulated by Judge Samuel who used Judge Moses' ideals about the duties of kings. The judges administered the laws, and they were independent from tribal chief or the king.

---

[20] Ibid, 204. Italics mine.

14. The Bible and the Concept of Separation of Powers

Biblically, the functions of the judicature are set within the Bible which shows that the judiciary was God's will prior to the power of kings, and was of itself divine in origin. Evidently, in the mind of God who reveals his governance ideals in the Bible, the king was subject to the *Torah*.[21] This was Samuel's passionate homily against unlimited royal power as a state institution.[22] Therefore, the text of the Old Testament—the Pentateuch (Exodus and Deuteronomy) and Historical books (1 and 2 Samuel), and Prophetic books—exemplify and formulate the most important theses of the concept of separation of powers. Mention must be made that the Bible is not a systematic book presenting its theories and theses systematically. Rather, it is a book with historical facts and ethical principles that are relevant for human affairs in all ages. Hence, the principles set in it are eternal and consequently applicable to all peoples in all generations everywhere. Consequently, honest theological scholars, legal experts, political scientists, humanists, and development strategists cannot fail to observe these biblical trajectories for our modern governance principles.

Isaiah 33:22: Analysis and Reflection on the Theological Basis of Separation of Powers

Although some maintain that the Bible is not a public policy manual, others hold it in high esteem as a public policy manual. For example, America's fourth President James Madison, at the Constitutional Convention in 1787, proposed to set up the three branches of the U.S. government: Judicial, Legislative, Executive. He discovered this as the model, reading Isaiah 33:22 "For the LORD is our Judge, the

---

[21] This is a precursor for our modern presidents and other government officials who swear by oath to uphold the constitution.

[22] See 1 Samuel 8:10-18.

LORD is our Lawgiver, the LORD is our King; He will save us."[23] Therefore, while reflectively searching and researching scriptures, I learned something new. It really seems that the three branches of government in our modern democratic constitutions and arrangements are set out in scripture: "For the LORD is our Judge, the LORD is our Lawgiver, the LORD is our King; He will save us."[24] Salvation comes from God. It is God who can absolutely offer salvation to people, in all ages—past, present and future. Therefore, as a Judge, God will not judge with partiality. As a Lawgiver, God will not frame and give laws that are inhumane. As a King, God will not enforce illegal, unethical and immoral laws. God wants this posture of His to be modelled in the world by all public officials. Indeed, Madison's observation on Isaiah 33:22 as regards the separate statuses of the government could rightly constitute the basis of the concept of separation of powers.[25]

Thus, in the separation of powers, there is not only a unity of power vested in each civil government, but also a diversity of power within each civil government. The experience of history teaches that man governs best when each of these types of civil power is vested in a different body of persons. Therefore, the principle of horizontal unity and diversity among civil powers, or the separation of powers,[26] was pointed out by Prophet Isaiah. We have already noted what Christopher Wright states concerning these as placed side by side

---

[23] "Separation of Powers," www.conservapedia.com/Separation_of_Powers, [12.3.2020].
[24] Isaiah 33:22.
[25] "Separation of Powers," www.conservapedia.com/Separation_of_Powers, [12.3.2020].
[26] Herbert W. Titus and Gerald R. Thompson, *America's Heritage: Constitutional Liberty: Separation of Civil Powers,* https://lonang.com/commentaries/conlaw/americas-heritage-constitutional-liberty/separation-of-civil-powers/ 12.3.2020].

which gives us an insight into its "constitutional" intentions.[27] Ideally, the clear distinction of the different kinds of authority can be seen as a significant precursor of some of the principles of democratic government, especially the separation of powers.

Therefore, Isaiah 33:22 is very pertinent as it depicts the Bible's posture and portrayal of the nature of governance through the concept of separation of powers. This means that the threefold nature of government is theological in origin as depicted in Isaiah 33:22 demonstrating that no man can be trusted with all three functions of government. However, despots seek to exercise all the three functions of the government. Consequently, good governance is based on the separation of powers. Edouard Nsiku argues that "Quite apart from its value as a means to obviating tyranny and despotism, no person should be accuser, judge and executioner all in one. This device is also a matter of practicalities and is based on the need to share out work for greater operational efficiency for good governance consolidation everywhere in the world."[28]

However, besides the practical efficacy, the threefold nature of government is a theological category, i.e., it has its foundations in the Bible's ethical principles and moral values. Commenting on this verse, Edouard Nsiku argues, "To communicate a global idea of what the Lord does for Israel, Isaiah shows how God combines in himself judicial power (our Judge), legislative power (our Lawgiver), and executive power (our King)...."[29] These are powers that our modern democratic governments have. Raymond Ortlund, states,

> Three different functions that are generally carried out by human governments are here attributed to the Lord: Judge (for deciding proper

---

[27] Wright, *Deuteronomy*, 203.
[28] Edouard Kitoko Nsiku, "Isaiah," in *Africa Bible Commentary*, Tokunboh Adeyemo (ed), Nairobi: Word Alive Publishers, 2006, 833.
[29] Ibid.

interpretations and applications of the laws); Lawgiver (for making the laws); and King (for enforcing the laws and defending the nation). This shows that government rightly fulfils its role only when it is carried out in submission to the will and purpose and laws of God.[30]

Indeed, the government fulfils its role when it carries out its functions of administering justice and restraining evil in submission to God's will and purpose as instructed in His laws in the Bible. Herbert W. Titus and Gerald R. Thompson argue that:

> Isaiah 33:22 indicates that all civil authority is not of the same nature. "The Lord is our judge" refers to judicial power, "the Lord is our lawgiver" refers to legislative power, and "the Lord is our king" refers to executive power. This scripture is not merely a descriptive statement, but a normative one as well, stating a legal distinction between kinds of civil power. It also contains a promise that God, the supreme judicial, legislative and executive authority, will exercise His power lawfully, for the verse concludes with "He will save us...."[31]

The antecedent of the triune God shows this very principle: God is One, but in three persons. Each individual person is distinct from another, but they all co-operate in everything that each one person does. Consequently, what God does, he wants it to be exemplified in this world. Through this pattern, God desires for man to exercise judicial, legislative and executive powers in accordance with law. God has established the threefold nature of power in the civil realm as He has in His own realm but He has dispersed His vertical power horizontally.[32]

---

[30] Raymond Ortlund (ed), *ESV Bible Study*, Wheaton: Crossway, 2008, 1299.
[31] Herbert W. Titus and Gerald R. Thompson, *America's Heritage: Constitutional Liberty: Separation of Civil Powers*, https://lonang.com/commentaries/conlaw/americas-heritage-constitutional-liberty/separation-of-civil-powers/ 12.3.2020].
[32] Romans 13:1-7 specifies that the civil ruler is a "minister of God, an avenger who brings wrath upon the one who practices evil." Thus, all civil officers are ministers of God, and bound by the law of God respecting civil power.

14. The Bible and the Concept of Separation of Powers

The above discussion on Isaiah 33:22 shows that quite contrary to some views, God is the originator of civil government and He desires good governance and democratic ethos to reign in our governance affairs. Malawi's political leaders and the people would do better to know this "not-so-much discernible biblical ethical truth" about the Bible and the separation of powers. There is therefore no doubt that there will be a greater commitment to justice in society when there are checks and balances and eventual submission to transcendent norm that stands above all participants in governance and socio-political processes. Isaiah 33:22 therefore shows that no man can be trusted with all three functions of government, i.e., government functions must be separated in their tasks. This demonstrates that the modern concept of separation of powers is principally and perpetually based on biblical revelation as in Isaiah 33:22, which constitutes the origin, theological foundation and ethical bedrock of good governance.

In summary, critical reading of the Bible shows that it calls the government to administer justice. This is an attempt to ensure that justice is seen to exist and being upheld by all especially those in leadership positions: Judges, Members of Parliament and the President. The giving of the law was God's pointing out the correct way for the Israelites to follow; in so doing exemplifying what it means to be the light to the nations. It is therefore the duty of all citizens to follow that path and ensure that they "hate what it evil, love what is good/right, and ensure that justice flows like a river."[33] History shows that "more than 2,500 years, long before Baron de Montesquieu and John Locke, the biblical prophets Isaiah, Jeremiah, Amos, Zechariah, and Hosea advocated for good governance by among others proclaiming equality of all humanity in the eyes of

---

[33] See Amos 5:15, 24.

heaven—and the fact that leaders, too, will be held accountable by God."[34]

The Implications of a Divided Government:[35] Judiciary, Legislature, Executive - the Necessity of the Judiciary

Apparently, at the popular level, the Bible does not offer an expanded theory of separation of powers. Such a theory was formulated in sufficiently complete form in the 17th and 18th centuries and was largely practically implemented at the end of the 18th century in the United States. However, the Biblical roots of the Judiciary and its independence from influence by the other branches of government was a convincing argument in favour of the practical implementation of the principle of the separation of powers. A king under the tutelage of law has its roots in the Bible.[36] Therefore, the following is a brief summary on the specific duties of the three branches of government and its implications in most of the contemporary nations.[37]

---

[34] Robert Hutchison, *The Politically Incorrect Guide to the Bible*, Washington DC: Regnery, 2008, 183-184.

[35] The term "Divided Government" is used interchangeably with the term "separation of powers."

[36] See Wright, "Deuteronomy," 201-221. In his discussion, he focuses on chapters 16-17 of Deuteronomy: "Leadership in Israel: Judges and Kings" and Deut. 18: 1-22: "Leadership in Israel: Priests and Prophets."

[37] Some people argue that the threefold nature of government was a Christian formulation, hence, it has biblical basis. John Calvin contributed something on how a civil government must function. His "Ecclesiastical Ordinances" were adopted by Genevan government as the constitution. See his *Institutes of Christian Religion*, trans., Henry Beveridge, Peabody: Hendrickson, 2008. For more information on the theological foundations of the threefold nature of government, see Hermann Mvula, *The Theory, Praxis and Pursuit of Constitutionalism in Democratic Malawi: An Old Testament Ethical Perspective*, Zomba: Kachere, 2020.

14. The Bible and the Concept of Separation of Powers

The Executive

1. Execution of laws and government policies
2. Maintenance of public order through its various arms and agencies
3. Management of State corporations and parastatals
4. Administration of foreign policies
5. Provision of public services
6. Making and allocation of government budgets

The Legislature

1. Framing of laws
2. National representation
3. Budget approvals
4. Checks and balances

The Judiciary

1. Interpretation of laws
2. Arbitration
3. Checks and balances on Executive and Legislative branches

The three branches exist collectively to administer justice. The independence of the judiciary recorded in the Bible, directly impacted the American concept of separation of powers. It is interesting to also note that this majority rule principle had antecedents in the biblical prescriptions of majority rule among the judges. A leading constitutional law scholar, Professor Henkin argues that "the separation of powers, just as the principle of checks and balances, are the basic principles of American constitutionalism that correlate, without any particular strain, with the biblical separation of the powers of the king from those of prophet or judge, which in the final analysis served as an important curb on earthly political power."[38] The Bible therefore shows the nature of true governance through God's revealed ideals.

Conclusion

This chapter has demonstrated that good governance principles have their antecedents in the Bible. The principle of separation of powers has antecedents in the biblical narratives: Pentateuchal, Historical books and the prophetic books. In Exodus 18 and Deuteronomy 16:18-20, Moses laid down the judicial procedures and the functions of its officers. In the history of Israel, Samuel stands out as an epitome of judiciary whose functions must be to check on the executive's excesses, arrogance and all conducts of impunity.[39] However, it has been argued that the principle of separation of powers is candidly based on Isaiah 33:22 which speaks of Yahweh as our Judge, Lawgiver and King, the antecedent of our contemporary government branches of Judiciary, Legislature and Executive. Paradoxically and remarkably, the Bible begins with the Judiciary, Legislature and then Executive in that order perhaps as point of departure on the importance of the three branches of the government respectively.[40]

---

[38] L. Henkin, "The Constitution and Other Holy Writ: Human Rights and Divine Commands. The Judeo-Christian Tradition and the US Constitution," Proceedings of a Conference at Anneberg Research Institute, 1987, 61, 62.

[39] Other latter prophets/judges in the history of Israel did like Moses and Samuel. For example, prophets Nathan and Gad to King David.

[40] In our political and governance history in Malawi, we cannot overemphasize the importance of the Judiciary. Recently, we observed how the Malawi judiciary (the Constitutional Court) independently handled the presidential election dispute of May 2019. Its verdict of 3 February 2020 was upheld by the Supreme Court of Appeals on 8 May 2020. That was a reminiscent of Samuel-Saul tale in the Bible.

14. The Bible and the Concept of Separation of Powers

Therefore, since the Bible still remains the most widely distributed, read, and studied book by Christian and non-Christian alike, one cannot deny its influence on the formation of the fundamental principles of Law and Justice. While the Bible speaks of eternal values, it intrinsically inspires the modern ideas of governance, justice, human rights and dignity. Against all this background, the following conclusion can be reached.

First, that some biblical passages implicitly contain constitutional ideals in which the judiciary is created and placed on a footing equal to the legislative and executive functions. At times it is even placed higher, above these other two. The verse in Isaiah could demonstrate this as the chronology of the branches begins with the judicial system. Second, the necessity for such ideals can be seen in the Exodus, which was a massive movement of people, and one that required a complex method of both administration and arbitration of disputes. Third, is the notion of an independent judiciary, fulfilling a divinely ordained function, as can be seen in Moses' appointment of judges (Exodus 18), as well as his instruction for judges in Deuteronomy 16:18-20. Fourth, is the equal standing of the judiciary as a separate power evident from the fact that Judge Samuel did not give an administration of justice to the first king, though in subsequent years, Israel's kings pre-empted the constitutional powers of the judges. Lastly, is one which clearly sees these ideals in the Bible, if the biblical text is allowed to speak for itself and is not treated as something lacking consistency or completeness.

Therefore, public leaders must acknowledge and uphold these biblical truths and principles and know that they are accountable to a higher authority. Hence, for good governance to be entrenched in Malawi, the Judiciary, Legislature, and Executive must dialogue,

---

Such a relationship assumes the idea of an independent judge as the guardian of the rule of law. Law must reign supreme.

interact and work together. None should control or overshadow the other. None should usurp the power that belongs to another. The three should know that and practise the notion that no one should be above the law. Someone rightly put it: "It is religion [biblical morality] in one way or the other, which can make, not the world good for democracy, but democracy good for the world."

References

Assman J., *Moses the Egyptian: The Memory of Egypt in Western Monotheism*, Cambridge: Harvard University Press, 1997.

Barton, David W., *Original Intent: The Courts, the Constitution, and Religion*, Wallbuilder Press, 1996.

Carson D.A., R.T. France, J.A. Motyer and G.J. Wenham (eds), *New Bible Commentary*, 21st Century Edition, Downers Grove: Intervarsity Press, 1994.

Henkin L., "The Constitution and Other Holy Writ: Human Rights and Divine Commands. The Judeo-Christian Tradition and the US Constitution," Proceedings of a Conference at Anneberg Research Institute, 1987.

Hutchinson, Robert, *The Politically Incorrect Guide to the Bible*, Washington, DC: Regnery, 2008.

Kitoko, Nsiku E., "Isaiah," in Tokunboh Adeyemo (ed), *Africa Bible Commentary: A Commentary Written by 70 African Scholars*, Nairobi: Word Alive Publishers, 2006.

Montet, P., *Everyday Life in Egypt in the Days of Rameses the Great*, Philadelphia, 1981.

Norton, Mary, et al, *A People and a Nation: A History of the United States*, New York: Houghton Mifflin Company, 1986.

Ortlund, Raymond (ed), "Isaiah," *ESV Bible Study*, Wheaton: Crossway, 2008.

Scheel, I.B., *Egyptian Metalworking and Tools*, Aylesbury, UK, 1989.

Siri, Gloppen and Fidelis Kanyongolo, "The Judiciary," in *Government and Politics in Malawi*, Zomba: Kachere Series, 2007.

Wright, Christopher J.H., *Deuteronomy*, Grand Rapids: Baker Books, 1996.

14. The Bible and the Concept of Separation of Powers   257

Documents

The Constitution of Malawi, Lilongwe: Ministry of Justice, 2004.

Outline of US Government., US State Department: Bureau of International Information Programs, 2013.

Internet Sources

Herbert W. Titus and Gerald R. Thompson, "America's Heritage: Constitutional Liberty: Separation of Civil Powers," https://lonang.com/commentaries/-conlaw/americas-heritage-constitutional-liberty/separation-of-civil-powers/ 12.3.2020]

John Farmer, 2006, https://votesmart.org/public-statement/191389/isaiah-3322-our-form-of-government#.Xmno06NKjcs, [12.3.2020].

Biography.com Editors, https://sites.google.com/site/floresworldhistory7/the-enlightenment/montesquieu-separation-of-powers, [8.8.2017].

Separation of Powers, www.conservapedia.com/Separation_of_Powers [12.3.2020].

Chapter 15

The Church in a New Era of Democracy: A Call for Non-Partisan Prophetic and Pastoral Functions

Timothy Kabulunga Nyasulu

Introduction

The influence of Christian churches in building a stable and war-free Malawi before and after multiparty democracy has been massively appreciated. The churches' non-partisan approach to political matters brought positive impact. However, observations have been made that the churches' behaviour between May 2019 and June 2020 in response to political issues was partisan which, if we are not careful, might create fertile ground for violence and civil war. During this period, many churches and faith institutions identified themselves with political parties. When organizing prayers, churches or political parties engaged those leaders that would speak in support of them, thereby creating more tensions between political groupings.[1]

The role of Christian churches in the early 1990s will always be remembered. They played a significant role in Malawi's transition from one party dictatorship to multiparty democracy and did so in a non-partisan manner.[2] The churches spoke with one voice. They tried

---

[1] During Synod meetings and political campaign rallies, Synods and political parties chose who to invite.
[2] Kenneth Ross reports that between 1992 and 1994 it is the church that facilitated the transition from dictatorship to democracy. The Roman Catholic Church through their Bishops wrote a pastoral letter in 1992, they were later joined by the CCAP Livingstonia and Blantyre Synods, Anglican Council of Malawi, Muslim Association of Malawi (MAM) etc. They ended up making what is now called Public

15. The Church in a New Era of Democracy

their best to amicably assist to bring about peace and reconciliation during the transition, although there was resistance from the incumbent MCP government at that time. There were no serious issues of violence reported. Operation Bwezani, which was actioned by the Malawi Army, was only meant to disarm and disperse the Malawi Young Pioneers.[3]

This time around, the opposite is true. There were different voices from faith groups, contradicting each other. However, some studies show that the situation was different and have categorized this approach by the churches as a prophetic role as opposed to the identificational model which applied when all Malawians had one common enemy to deal with, i.e., one party dictatorship rule under Dr Kamuzu Banda.[4] However, one would still expect their continued one-voice noble task of giving proper guidance in a more non-partisan manner especially given that the current situation is characterized by political pluralism.[5] It seems that this time around, faith institutions had not unanimously taken a deliberate move to seriously reflect on their role in the actual operationalization of multiparty democracy, especially to promote peace, justice, tolerance and reconciliation. Kenneth Ross has referred to the important

---

Affairs Committee (PAC). See Kenneth R. Ross, "The Transformation of Power in Malawi 1992-94: The Role of the Christian Churches," in Kenneth R. Ross (ed), *God, People and Power in Malawi: Democratization in Theological Perspective*, Blantyre: CLAIM-Kachere, 1996, 15-40.

[3] For further details see James Tengatenga, "Operation Bwezani: A Theological Response," in Matembo S. Nzunda and Kenneth R. Ross (eds), *Church, Law and Political Transition in Malawi 1992-94*, Gweru: Mambo-Kachere, 1995, 103.

[4] Billy Gama, *The Role of the Church in Politics in Malawi*, AcadSA, 2011, 147-154.

[5] While there might be voices from religious bodies, the question has been whether these voices take a non-partisan stance.

"midwifery" role of the church.[6] There is high expectation that it will guide the citizenry in the right direction. Borrowing from Francis of Assisi, the church is supposed to be an instrument of peace and stability.[7]

This chapter evaluates the ministry of the church focusing on the period from May 2019 to June 2020, when the fresh Presidential election took place. It considers the role of the church in such a volatile situation. It contributes to the debate on the role of the church in a multiparty democracy. The chapter gives Malawian churches food for thought in terms of preparing for future similar situations. The aim is that the churches may not repeat the same mistakes. It argues that non-partisan prophetic and pastoral roles need to be employed as the church deals with political tensions.

The first section starts with an introduction. The second is concerned with the role of the church amidst political turbulence during the May 2019 to June 2020 period. The third is a reflection on the involvement of the church in politics. The fourth concerns the biblical portrayal of the pastoral and prophetic role of the church. The fifth presents a panorama of the importance of pastoral and prophetic roles in the history of the church over the centuries. Last comes the conclusion.

The Church Amidst Political Turbulence in Malawi: May 2019 to June 2020

There was political turbulence between May 2019 and June 2020 in Malawi. However, it did not turn into a war; otherwise Malawians were going to accuse churches of betraying them through the mistakes they made. For the future, we can learn from mistakes made

---

[6] Kenneth R. Ross., "A Practical Theology of Power for the New Malawi," in Kenneth R. Ross (ed), *God, People and Power in Malawi*, 225-67.
[7] www.azquotes.com/author/616-Francis of Assisi.

15. The Church in a New Era of Democracy 261

by the Catholic Church in Rwanda in the 1990s. Their partisan politics resulted in a serious genocide that killed over 800,000 people. As Timothy Long has observed:

> Christian churches were deeply implicated in the 1994 genocide of ethnic Tutsi in Rwanda. Churches were a major site for massacres, and many Christians participated in the slaughter, including church personnel and lay leaders. Church involvement in the genocide can be explained in part because of the historic link between church and state and the acceptance of ethnic discrimination among church officials. In addition, just as political officials chose genocide as a means of reasserting their authority in the face of challenges from a democracy movement and civil war, struggles over power within Rwanda's Christian churches led some church leaders to accept the genocide as a means of eliminating challenges to their own authority within the churches.[8]

In Malawi, prior to the elections some churches displayed political inclinations. They endorsed presidential candidates according to their faith, regional and political affiliations. This was done during political campaign rallies, in homilies at worship services, church announcements, pastoral letters etc. This trend continued up to the time of elections. The declaration of the incumbent President Arthur Peter Mutharika as winner was contentious. While some churches accepted the results, others rejected them. The Malawi Congress Party (MCP), United Transformation Movement (UTM), Human Rights Defenders Coalition (HRDC) - all of them with their supporters rejected the results. They mobilized people to conduct demonstrations against the declaration by Malawi Electoral Commission. At the same time the grievances were taken to the Constitutional Court in order to challenge the results, accusing the Malawi Electoral Commission

---

[8] Timothy Long, "Church Politics and Genocide in Rwanda," *Journal of Religion in Africa* 31/2 (2001), 163.

(MEC) of mismanaging the elections, particularly the Presidential election.

The Constitutional Court's judgment was that the elections process was indeed full of irregularities and illegalities. This was later upheld by the Supreme Court of Appeal after the Democratic Progressive Party appealed against the ruling. For over twelve months there was conspicuous destabilization of many activities. The demonstrations that were meant to be peaceful, advocated by the HRDC and endorsed by many institutions including churches, ended up creating an uncontrolled and volatile situation. There was damage to property, a few killings, sexual assaults and abuses and persecutions of some individuals of the society. The economy, security and personal relationships were negatively affected. Finger pointing, demeaning, obscene and bad language dominated the speeches of many Malawians in social media and groupings including religious institutions and demonstrators.[9] The situation became very scary and most business transactions came to a standstill.

What went wrong? Some commentators noted that religious bodies took a partisan role. Those who claimed to be playing a prophetic role were those criticizing government. However, they were being partisan in the sense that some were seen to have been sent by the opposition. Those that showed allegiance to the state were suspected of supporting the status quo and were accused of having been corrupted by the government. When it came to prayers, the government chose people who would pray to their favour. The same applied to the opposition party: they also invited church people who

---

[9] A *Nyasa Times* article of 19 July 2019 reported that some protesters in Mzuzu actually dressed a dog with DPP cloth. The dog was dressed in DPP cloth not only as part of the protests, but also the dog was running in front of the demonstrators referring to DPP as a party that has lost its value and can be likened to a dog. This was a way of demeaning the party.

15. The Church in a New Era of Democracy

would pray and counsel them to their favour. In short, partisan politics affected churches' prophetic and pastoral services.[10]

What is happening in politics in Malawi now does not have impact only on the current situation. It also affects future generations. As a church, we need to be already thinking about our role during the next election year. The violent behaviours that dominated the scene during demonstrations are to be critically analyzed and if possible controlled so that we don't fall into a situation like Rwanda's. Malawi, poor as it is, cannot afford to bear the effect of demonstrations and vandalism. Church leaders must be concerned. The issue jeopardizes the mission of the church (*Missio Ecclesia*). I argue that some church leaders claimed to be playing a prophetic role by even lobbying and joining demonstration,[11] while others claimed to be playing a pastoral role by maintaining the already existing peace in spite of accusations that Malawi Electoral Commission messed up the May 2019 elections. However, while the matter was in court, each side needed to avoid the extremes of their inclination to become assimilated and aligned to a political party.

The Involvement of the Church in Politics

Although there are diverse views on how the church should relate to politics,[12] the Calvinistic stand is very clear. The church should be involved in politics, but in a non-partisan manner. With the current

---

[10] Democratic Progressive Party officials accused Public Affairs Committee of supporting the opposition, Tonse Alliance supporters accused Interfaith Forum for Peace Justice and Dialogue of supporting DPP. Humphrey Mvula, *Nyasa Times*, 31 July 2019.

[11] There were several times when PAC openly endorsed demonstrations. Livingstonia Synod too endorsed demonstrations including the one that aimed to close airports in the country.

[12] For details see James Tengatenga, *Church, State and Society in Malawi: The Anglican Case*, Zomba: Kachere, 2006.

situation when relationships between different political parties are not healthy, many people will look to churches as sources of hope. What has been at stake in the one-year experience is how churches have behaved. A Pastoral Letter written by Blantyre Synod in 1993 has an important lesson to teach us:

> We must emphasize that the Church is indeed involved in politics but not partisan politics. If we look at our own history as the CCAP during the time of the struggle for Independence, we will see that Blantyre Synod was very much in support of the Nyasaland African Congress (later called the MCP). Because of this very verbal stance on the side of the MCP, after Independence, the CCAP was aligned closely with the government and become so assimilated with the government's activities that the Synod was often invited to pray and participate as a Church at various government functions. However, because of this assimilation and alignment with the MCP, the Church gradually lost its ability to admonish or speak pastorally to the government. We do not want to make the same mistake at this time in order to ensure that the Church retains its prophetic voice throughout the coming years of our country's history. We must remember that the Church is the Church, and as the Church must remain neutral with respect to party politics.[13]

The churches are encouraged to be involved in politics.[14] Blantyre Synod of the CCAP guided its faithfuls to be involved in politics but in a non-partisan way. They did not want to repeat the same mistake of playing a role of partisan politics. Billy Gama likens this approach to the transformational model of prophetic theology,[15] which guides the churches on matters of social and political importance, but in a balanced manner. It is both caring and critical towards the person in the wrong; bearing in mind God is the ultimate judge of all situations.

---

[13] For the full text of the Letter see Kenneth R. Ross (ed), *Christianity in Malawi: A Source Book*, Mzuzu: Mzuni Press, 2020, 274-79.
[14] Billy Gama, *The Role of the Church in Politics in Malawi*, 93.
[15] Ibid, 148-159.

15. The Church in a New Era of Democracy 265

Concerning the revolutionary approach to political matters Billy Gama writes:

> But Calvin did not teach a radical revolutionary stance. He did not believe that it is right to disturb the social order. What Calvin did advocate is a prophetic witness that takes a firm stand for truth and justice but does not seek to take matters into its own hands. God himself will sooner or later deal with the evil rulers.[16]

For Calvin, the "social order" was paramount when dealing with political matters. It is a spiritual matter in family, institution, community, business, etc. When the social order is disturbed, all things come to standstill. While a society will never be perfect, nonetheless a certain degree of order will be a fertile ground for transformation and development. Calvin's trust in God was stronger than trusting human effort in politics. In his section on Faith and Politics, Kenneth Ross writes:

> The Calvinists have been moved by the conviction that not only are personal and church life to be subject to the demands of the Gospel, but equally public and political life. They have recognized that there is much that is wrong with this world but have believed that it belongs rightly to God and can be transformed in a godly direction...[17]

Calvin's doctrine of "total depravity" teaches that no human being is perfect. Every leader who is put in position is susceptible to falling short. Of course, when leaders are just ushered into a position, they will appear as angels, but later they change colour. Kamuzu Banda started as a liberator and was even called Messiah. He later turned into a dictator. Bakili Muluzi started as a true democrat. Later he wanted to change the constitution so that he would be given a third term. It is also alleged that he swindled 1.7 billion Kwacha. Bingu wa

---

[16] Ibid, 157.
[17] Kenneth R. Ross, *Gospel Ferment in Malawi: Theological Essays*, Gweru: Mambo-Kachere, 1995, 33 (Mzuzu: Luviri Press, 2018, 33).

Mutharika also started very well in the first five years of his term. Later he became notorious for his dictatorship. Joyce Banda started well. She was later entangled in the notorious Cashgate scandal. Arthur Peter Mutharika too promised paradise. But when he got into government, there was looting of funds by many of the DPP officials. People are still skeptical about whether Lazarus Chakwera will deliver. Ross has argued that the political situation wants God's grace to be reflected in the external, temporary dealings of the political community.[18] However, this does not mean that we stop correcting each other when one has gone wrong. There are many methods the church can employ to correct the situation.

As followers of Christ, churches are what Christ is to the world. They have been seasoned with heavenly doctrine. In Matthew 5:13 they exist to give flavour to the earth because the earth without God's doctrine is tasteless.[19] For John Stott, "If the beatitudes describe the essential character of the disciples of Jesus, the salt metaphor indicates their influence for good in the world."[20] Christians are supposed to be moral disinfectants in the world where moral standards are low. But when it loses its saltiness, it becomes useless. The saltiness of salt can be lost if it dilutes. If church leaders enter into politics with the whole head, they will not stand the pressure of politics' demands. They must be careful of how they operate to avoid compromise lest they lose their saltiness. Salt was also connected with purity, preservation and flavour.[21]

---

[18] Ibid, 33.

[19] *Calvin's Commentaries*, Matthew 5 in StudyLight.Org, www.studylight.org-/commentaries/cal/matthew-5.html.

[20] John Stott, *The Message of the Sermon on the Mount: The Bible Speaks Today* (BTS), Leicester: InterVarsity Press, 1978, 57.

[21] William Barclay, *The Daily Study Bible, The Gospel of Matthew*, Revised edition by William Barclay, Edinburgh: St Andrew Press, 1975, 118-124.

Light in Matthew 5:14 is connected to visibility. The light shines to the world and seen by the world. The light is also connected with guidance. A Christian must make the way clear to others. A light is also connected with warning. So, a light can be a warning light to halt when there is danger. In 1 Peter 2:9-13, the church is known for its sacredness. It is an alien, chosen people, a royal priesthood and a holy nation. Some churches have misunderstood "alien" to mean "not to be involved" in politics. To some of us, it means our permanent citizenship is in heaven. Although our citizenship is in heaven, we are ambassadors on earth. On earth the church should display good life; holy in nature among both Christians and non-Christians so that when they see good deeds, pagans will be able glorify God because of such good living displayed by them. Thus, the church should be in the world but carrying out its holistic God-given role.[22] The involvement starts right away from the church itself where the liturgy includes prayers for rulers and those in authority.[23]

While God has ordained civil authorities to be answerable to him on all physical needs and social welfare of his people, God has also put in place religious institutions to primarily check if the will of God is followed. However, churches are not only looking into spiritual affairs of humanity. They are also involved in socio-political matters. God has armed civil authorities with the power of the sword to defend and encourage those who are good and punish evil doers.[24] The churches have been armed with spiritual weapons to stamp out sin and lead people to a better earthly life and salvation.

---

[22] James Tengatenga, *Church Sate and Society in Malawi*, 190.
[23] See W.H.K. Jele and R.F. Ndolo, *Ndondomeko ya Visopo: CCAP Synod of Livingstonia*, 1968, 30. See also Anglican Council of Malawi, *Mapemphero ndi Nyimbo za Eklesia*, 1980, 40.
[24] For details see Rowland S. Ward, *The Westminster Confession: A Study Guide*, Melbourne: New Melbourne Press, 1996.

A Biblical Portrayal of the Prophetic and Pastoral Functions of the Church

Those that claim to be playing a prophetic role of the church take their justification from both Old and New Testaments. However Old Testament prophets were more confrontational and retributive. Of course, a critical study of the New Testament also shows that to some great extent there were some confrontations like when Jesus confronted Pilate and Herod. He also confronted the Sadducees who were the political gurus of the nation. He did likewise to the lawyer – the judicial leader of that time. This posture also characterized John the Baptist. However, there is not much of such Old Testament behaviour. Jesus Christ who is believed to be the fulfilment of all prophets emphasized his teaching on dialogue, forgiveness and love for enemies. While in the Old Testament confrontations and vengeance were common, the New Testament instead promotes unity, peace, dialogue and love for your enemies.

During the prophetic era the holy nation of Israel was characterized by playing both pastoral and prophetic roles. In the chosen nation of Israel there arose pastors and prophets. A leader of the nation was playing both roles of king and pastor. So, he would lead worship and prayers and rebuke their evil doing.[25] Nathan's approach to rebuke king David for committing adultery with Bathsheba was highly diplomatic (2 Samuel 12:1-14). Such approaches are more effective to people of authority in society. It has been submitted that in certain periods prophets were there to criticize the status quo if they had performed contrary to the will of God. At a certain point they were also there to energize the status quo if they performed according to

---

[25] In the time of Abraham up to Moses, religious leaders were also political leaders. They would lead the people in wars and also in political affairs of the nation. In 2 Samuel 8 we read David is dedicating the house of God and all the material meant to finish up the construction.

15. The Church in a New Era of Democracy

the will of God. They also played an advisory role to the kings.[26] So, prophets were not only waiting to see the wrong thing to criticize. But they also appreciated the good features of existing reality.[27]

Violence was strictly controlled except in very few cases of war against enemies (Ex 20:13; 21:12-27; Deut 19:1-13).[28] The life and the safety of the chosen people and those who sojourned among them was respected. There were rules designed to control violence and war. The prophets would go and challenge the status quo for the political, social and moral decay the society was facing.[29] They warned the people when they practised idolatry, embraced immorality and social injustice. During the monarchy, they counselled the kings, either encouraging them to walk in the way of Yahweh or, more often, rebuking them for failing to do so, thus misleading the people.[30] During the Exile and post-exilic period prophets played a role of encouraging energizing because people needed some comfort in a foreign land.

In the New Testament Jesus is the Prophet and the chief high priest playing both prophetic and pastoral roles. The stress is on the love of God. Jesus hates religious hypocrisy as displayed by religious leaders. He even taught his disciples to love and care for their enemies.[31] In John 20, Jesus commands Peter to tend his sheep. He underscored the importance of tending his sheep. After regressing it was

---

[26] William Sanford La Sor, David Allan Hubbard and Frederic William Bush, *Old Testament Survey: The Message, Form, and Background of the Old Testament*, Grand Rapids: Eerdmans, 1996, 303.
[27] During this period the confrontational approach was rarely employed.
[28] Michaela Davy, *Mastering Theology*, London: MacMillan, 2001, 266.
[29] John E. Schwarz, *The Compact Guide to Christian Faith*, Minneapolis: Bethany House Publishers, 1999, 133.
[30] During this period there were more prophesies that were confrontational towards the status quo.
[31] Michaela Davy, *Mastering Theology*, 272.

worthwhile to remind Peter about his role as a church leader to *"tend."* In Tumbuka, *liskanga* and *lelanga*, mean to take care. They are inclusive terms. When you keep a child, you also make sure that that child is growing in the way you want, so that the child does not put you to shame as a parent. A parent makes sure to put the child right if he/she is going wrong. The act of collecting, criticizing, admonition, and any form of advice is being prophetic.

A Panorama of the Implications of Prophetic and Pastoral Functions in Church History

From the Early Church, prophetic and pastoral roles of the church have been recognized as very important components of the ministry to ensure the membership is sustained and above all that members are not lost to eternal damnation. In his work Taylor describes the writings of John Chrysostom in the 4th century CE. He writes:

> A pastor must be able to mingle with people from all walks of life. He must not confine himself to the work of the sacraments and preaching. He must move among the people and preside over all the great moments of human life. He must be present and involved so as to bring the resources of the Christian faith to people at every stage and every crisis of their lives.[32]

In short, according to Taylor, Chrysostom's analysis of the work of the pastor is that it must in particular include "the cure of the souls." St Augustine of Hippo is reported to have said:

> The pastor must be ready to help all sorts of people in the following ways: the *disturbers* are to be rebuked, the *low spirited* are to be encouraged. He also said *the infirm* are to be supported. The *objectors* are to be confuted. These were those that probably opposed true teaching. Those *eager* to serve Christ but unskilled are to be taught properly, those lazy in service of the church are to be aroused and awakened, those

---

[32] Harold Taylor, *Tend my Sheep: Applied Theology* 2, London: SPCK, 1989, 2.

15. The Church in a New Era of Democracy 271

who are *contentious* are to be treated with patience. Such people are usually those that want to argue all the time. The *proud* are to be shown the path of humble service, the *oppressed* are to be set free, the *good* are to be improved and encouraged. The *evil people* are to be "borne with," and treated with patience and care. Finally, *all people*, whoever and whatever they are, are to be loved. It suffices to argue that pastoral function of the church is holistic and inclusive of all aspects of church's ministerial work.[33]

Augustine was concerned with violence. He taught that war can be justified if it is for defence, but it should be the last resort after all efforts to bring peace have been exhausted.[34]

Between 500 and 1500 CE onwards the functions of the church as stipulated by Chrysostom and Augustine were upheld. While some of them are being emphasized, some had been added and developed such as business function, acquisition of land, wider administrative functions as a number of congregations increased. Some civil and political functions related to government and commerce were also added.[35] During this period, there was prohibition against individual violence. Both Protestants and Catholics held that violence was a legitimate tool in the hands of the secular authorities and not religious authorities. For the secular authorities, their attempt must mainly be to keep peace and eradicate lawlessness.[36]

The churches extended their work to all people. Richard Baxter emphasized not only the need for a ministry to individual people and family groups but also to a congregation as a whole. He also taught that those who are not Christians are not to be neglected. While those strong in the faith are to be further strengthened and encouraged,

---

[33] Harold Taylor, *Tend my Sheep*, 20.
[34] Michaela Davy, *Mastering Theology*, 276.
[35] Harold Taylor, *Tend my Sheep*, 2, 21.
[36] Michaela Davy, *Mastering Theology*, 278.

those who are not Christians should also be considered to have access to good news so that they can leave their sinful ways and follow what God requires of them. The similar inclusive pastoral function of the church was echoed by Dietrich Bonhoeffer in the middle of twentieth century. He said, "The Church has an unconditional obligation to the victims of any ordering society, even if they do not belong to Christian community."[37] He would even go further by encouraging Christian disobedience by resisting the unjust laws as part of obedience to God.[38] He has also stated that the church can act towards the state by asking it whether its actions are legitimate and in accordance with the state's responsibilities of social, political and economic responsibilities.[39] Violence was being discouraged. Later, the First and Second World Wars in the 20th century influenced violence as an official political tool within systems of government. The churches in Latin America and South Africa learnt to stand firmly for dignity of all human life.[40] Meanwhile, churches continued to remain agents of peace, pacifying political tensions where possible.

During the time of liberation theology, the confrontational approach dominated the scene as a prophetic role of the church. John de Gruchy of South Africa, in support of Dietrich Bonhoeffer, observes that it is proper to disobey civil government in order to obey God, especially because of the unjust laws. This is a kind of paradigm that has generally influenced contemporary Christian civil disobedience. However, to be fair, there are situations when such kind of approach might be appropriate. Disobedience with some responsibility is vital. For Dietrich Bonhoeffer, personal freedom and social responsibility

---

[37] Dietrich Bonhoeffer, *No Rusty Swords*, London: Collins, 1965, 225.
[38] This has been referred to the inevitable logic of the position adopted by most of the reformers.
[39] Dietrich Bonhoeffer, *The Cost of Discipleship*, London: SCM, 1959, 230.
[40] Michaela Davey, *Mastering Theology*, 286.

were supposed to be held together.[41] The reconstructional theology championed by Jesse Mugambi is encouraging African theologians to rethink about their approach to social issues. Reconstruction theologians discourage foreign and western approach to African social issues.[42] In most African cultures a confrontational approach is always discouraged because people are taught good morals and behaviours right from their youth. Without imitating foreign cultures African leaders can promote dialogue more for reconciliation and confidence building than confrontations and violence that are destructive.

The approach of the church to fight against the one-party system of government which was done in the context of liberation theology, whereby churches were determined to help bring about change in Malawi, should now be reconsidered. Their prophetic ministry was meant for the common good; the fight against the tyrannical regime of Dr Kamuzu Banda. Now that we are in the multiparty democracy, churches have to rethink about their approach in their involvement in politics. As Jesse Mugambi argues, the church today must be engaged in reconstruction theology of reconciliation and confidence building.

Conclusion

This chapter has presented and analyzed the activities of the churches and political situation between May 2019 and June 2020. It has justified why the church should be involved in politics. It has also portrayed the biblical prophetic and pastoral roles of the church. In conclusion, the churches in Malawi were involved in politics in a

---

[41] John de Gruchy, *Bonhoeffer and South Africa: Theology in Dialogue*, Grand Rapids: Eerdmans, 1984, 94.

[42] Jesse N.K. Mugambi, *Christian Theology and Social Reconstruction*, Nairobi: Acton, 2003, 132.

partisan manner and because they were involved in partisan politics they contributed to the violence. They contributed to the violence either by keeping quiet or playing a partisan prophetic role to the government or to the opposition. Churches and religious institutions failed to bring reconciliation among political parties. Instead, they widened gaps by siding with a certain political grouping.

With this, it has been evident that there was departure of the church from her proper role during the May 2019 to June 2020 period. It is high time churches started uniting to reflect on what happened and then see how best such situations can be avoided for the stability and development of the country. The Rwanda situation can be avoided only if the church takes a proper lead in guiding the people she serves.

References

Barclay, William, *The Daily Bible Study Bible: Revised Edition*, "The Gospel of Matthew," vol. 1, Chapters 1-10, Edinburgh: Saint Andrew Press, 1975.

Bonhoeffer, Dietrich, *No Rusty Swords*, London: Collins, 1965.

Bonhoeffer, Dietrich, *The Cost of Discipleship*, London: SCM, 1959.

Brown, Robert McAfee, *Liberation: An Introduction Guide*, Louisville: Westminster /John Knox Press, 1993.

Davy, Michaela, *Mastering Theology*, London: MacMillan, 2001.

De Gruchy, John, *Bonhoeffer and South Africa: Theology in Dialogue*, Grand Rapids: Eerdmans, 1984.

Gama, Billy, *The Role of the Church in Politics in Malawi*, Acad SA, 2010.

La Sor, William Sanford et al, *Old Testament Survey: The Message, Form, and Background of Old Testament*, Grand Rapids: Eerdmans, 1996.

Long, Timothy, "Church Politics and the Genocide in Rwanda," *Journal of Religion in Africa*, 31/2, 2001, 163-186.

Mugambi, Jesse, *Christian Theology and Social Reconstruction*, Nairobi: Acton, 2003.

15. The Church in a New Era of Democracy 275

Ross, Kenneth R., "A Practical Theology of Power for the New Malawi," in Kenneth R. Ross (ed), *God, People and Power in Malawi: Democratization in Theological Perspective*, Blantyre: CLAIM-Kachere, 1996, 225-67.

Ross, Kenneth R. (ed), *Christianity in Malawi: A Source Book*, Mzuzu: Mzuni Press, 2020.

Ross, Kenneth R., *Gospel Ferment in Malawi: Theological Essays*, Gweru: Mambo-Kachere, 1995, repr. Mzuzu: Luviri Press, 2018.

Ross, Kenneth R., "The Transformation of Power in Malawi 1992-94: The Role of the Christian Churches," in Kenneth R. Ross (ed), *God, People and Power in Malawi: Democratization in Theological Perspective*, Blantyre: Kachere, 1996, 15-40.

Schwarz, John E., *The Compact Guide to Christian Faith*, Minneapolis: Bethany House Publishers, 1999.

Stott, John, *The Message of the Sermon on the Mount: The Bible Speaks Today (BTS)*, Leicester: Inter-Varsity Press, 1978.

Taylor, Harold, *Tend my Sheep: Applied Theology 2*, London: SPCK, 1983.

Tengatenga, James, *Church, State and Society in Malawi: An Analysis of Anglican Ecclesiology*, Zomba: Kachere, 1996.

Tengatenga, James, "Operation Bwezani: A Theological Response," in Matembo S. Nzunda and Kenneth R. Ross (eds), *Church, Law and Political Transition in Malawi in 1992-1994*, Gweru: Mambo-Kachere, 1995, repr. Mzuzu: Luviri Press, 2020, 101-109.

Ward, Rowland, S., *The Westminster Confession: A Study Guide*, Melbourne: New Melbourne Press, 1996.

Report on National Theology Conference Nkhoma University 24-26 Sept 2020

Introduction

The early 21st century has been, in some respects, a period of expansion and proliferation for theological education in Malawi. New institutions have been formed and older institutions have been revitalized. Yet, an important element that many have been missing is an instrument of unity and collaboration that could bring theologians together for conference and mutual stimulation. It was to meet this need that the decision was taken to call a National Theology Conference, very kindly hosted by Nkhoma University. Originally, it was planned for 5-7 August 2020 which, in a normal academic year, would have been a vacation time for most institutions. This, however, coincided with the rate of coronavirus infection being at its highest point in 2020 so it was necessary to postpone. Thankfully, the prevalence of coronavirus declined, allowing schools to reopen in September and consequently also making it possible for the conference to be held on the new dates of 24-26 September 2020. Despite the disruption and the short notice, the announcement of the plans for the conference was received with enthusiasm.

Since there was not yet any formal organization in place to plan the conference, this was done on an informal basis. Dr Hermann Mvula brought plans that had been on the drawing board at Chancellor College and linked with Prof Kenneth Ross, who returned to Malawi in 2019 to work nationwide from a base at Zomba Theological College, to lead the organization of the event. In terms of resources, Nkhoma University generously took responsibility for administration of the event on their Nkhoma campus, institutions were invited to cover the travel costs of their representatives, and accommodation costs were covered by a grant from the Society in Scotland for the Propagation of the Gospel.

All institutions known to be teaching theology at tertiary level were invited to participate and their delegates were invited to submit an abstract of a proposed paper. Around 20 did so and the resultant papers formed the core programme of the conference. The topics of the papers were such that they fell into three categories: biblical studies, faith and culture, and faith and society. Between plenary sessions to start and finish, the conference ran in these three streams with participants able to choose the one that interested them most or to switch between them if they had interest in one particular paper.

The aim was to provide an opportunity for theologians to present their work and benefit from peer interaction and critique. It was hoped that this would enable Faculty members from a variety of institutions to benefit from professional development, scholarly stimulus and academic collegiality on a nationwide basis. It was also hoped to make a start on charting a common direction for theological research and theological education in Malawi.

Conference Programme

Thursday 24 September 2020

Participants arrived during the afternoon of 24 Sept and shared an evening meal together at the Faculty of Theology before proceeding to the Nkhoma Church for the opening session. Opening devotions were led by Rev Dr Leonard Katundu, Principal of Jehosaphat Mwale Theological College and Dean of the Faculty of Theology at Nkhoma University, who took his text from 1 Timothy 4. Rev Dr Gertrude Kapuma of Zomba Theological College took the chair and offered a prayer for God's blessing on the conference.

Dr Hermann Mvula welcomed all delegates and visitors on behalf of the organizing team and invited the guest of honour, Professor Joseph Chimombo, Vice Chancellor of Nkhoma University, to open the conference. Professor Chimombo indicated how delighted Nkhoma University were to host the event and challenged the conference to examine ways of attracting students to study theology and to consider how best resources could be mobilized to support the development of theology in Malawi.

Rev Dr Gertrude Kapuma took the chair and invited Rev Prof Kenneth Ross to deliver his keynote address on: "Theology in Malawi: Progress and Prospects." This was followed by a period of questions and discussion. The evening was closed with a welcoming address from Rev Vasco Kachipapa, General Secretary of the CCAP Synod of Nkhoma.

Friday 25 September 2020

Opening devotions were led by Rev Luke Limbithu of Malawi Adventist University who based his reflection on 1 Chronicles 21:15-30.

The first session ran in three streams, with papers presented as follows:

1. Biblical Studies: Chair: Rev Luke Limbithu
- Dr Volker Glissmann (Theological Education by Extension), "Fit for Purpose: The Theological Graduate Profile in light of Malawian Grassroots Priorities."
- Dr Stanley Chipeta (Malawi Adventist University), "The Use and Importance of Water in John 13:1-11."

2. Faith and Culture: Chair: Dr Rhodian Munyenyembe
- Dr Joyce Mlenga (Mzuzu University), "The Abiding Influence of African Traditional Religion Among the Educated and Modernized Working Class in Northern Malawi."

- Dr Frank Chirwa (Malawi Adventist University), "An Explication of Selected Sociological Factors Relating to Modernity: Towards Retaining Young People in the 21st century African Christian Church."

3. Faith and Society: Chair: Rev Dr Humphreys Zgambo

- Dr Moses Mlenga (University of Livingstonia), "Cold War Between Reverends and Ruling Elders in CCAP, Synod of Livingstonia: From Ruling to Assistant Elders."
- Dr Hermann Mvula (Chancellor College, University of Malawi), "Separation of Powers: Its Theological Foundations and Implications for Malawi's Governance."

The second session was a plenary in which Prof Klaus Fiedler (Mzuni Press) gave a lecture on "Theological Research and Publication." This was followed by a period of questions and discussion.

The lunch break provided an opportunity for delegates to enjoy a meal together and browse the extensive selection of books on sale from the Kachere Series, Mzuni Press and Luviri Press.

The third session ran in three streams, with papers presented as follows:

4. Biblical Studies: Chair: Dr Gracious Gadama

- Rev Dr Takuze Chitsulo (Zomba Theological College), "The Bible and Socioeconomic Transformation in Malawi."
- Rev Luke Limbithu (Malawi Adventist University), "Covid-19 and the End of the World: A Biblical Perspective."

5. Faith and Culture: Chair: Dr Lawrence Chipao

- Rev Dr Colby Hetherwick Kumwenda (University of Livingstonia), "'I am Married to Jesus': Narratives of Spousal Violence in Ekwendeni, Malawi."

6. Faith and Society: Chair: Rev Dr Hastings Abale Phiri

- Rev David Chuguzeni Kawanga (Synod of Nkhoma), "Apartheid-influenced Theological Principles of Imago Dei among the First Indigenous Christians of Nkhoma Synod."

- Very Rev Dr Timothy Nyasulu (University of Livingstonia), "Pastoral and Prophetic: The Role of the Church in Multiparty Democracy: Malawi Political Context after 21st May, 2019."

The fourth session ran in three streams, with papers presented as follows:

7. Biblical Studies: Chair: Dr Phoebe Chifungo

- Rev Dr Winston Kawale (Nkhoma University), "A Critical Evaluation of Divergent Chichewa Bible Translations of the Tetragrammaton."

8. Faith and Culture: Chair: Fr Francis Bonongwe

- Dr Gerard Chigona, "Relevance of Theology in an Age of Secular Humanism."

9. Faith and Society: Chair: Rev Dr Hastings Abale Phiri

- Rev Dr Gertrude Kapuma (Zomba Theological College), "Pain and Trauma: The Experience of Widowhood."

- Mr Stewart Kapinda (Chancellor College, University of Malawi), "The State, the Church: A Critical Reflection on the Response to Covid-19."

Participants shared an evening meal together before proceeding to an informal session where a representative of each institution gave a brief update, indicating both encouragements and challenges. The evening devotions were led by Rev Bossman Chitheka (Nkhoma University) who offered a reflection on 1 Corinthians 16:20f.

Saturday 26 September 2020

Opening devotions were led by Rev Dr Weston Kapasule who offered a reflection on Ephesians 6:10-20.

Report on National Theology Conference   281

Planning for the Future

Professor Kenneth Ross and Dr Hermann Mvula facilitated a session on planning for the future. It was unanimously agreed that the conference had been a major success and that there was need for an instrument to organize such conferences and other forms of collaboration in future. A wide-ranging discussion included suggestions that there should be an annual conference, an organizing committee, membership of both institutions and individuals, membership fees for the sake of sustainability, and the hosting of a research registry that would keep a record of all research papers produced by member institutions. It was suggested that future conferences might have a main theme but also allow for presentations on a variety of topics, depending on current research interests.

In light of this discussion, it was agreed to appoint a steering group to prepare proposals. It was agreed that these should be circulated to all participants no later than 30 November 2020. With a view to achieving wide representation without making the group too large, the following were elected to serve on the steering group: Fr Francis Bonongwe, Dr Lawrence Chipao, Dr Frank Chirwa, Rev Dr Gertrude Kapuma, Rev Dr Leonard Katundu, Dr Joyce Mlenga, Dr Hermann Mvula (Secretary), Dr Felix Nyika, Prof Kenneth Ross (Chair).

The University of Livingstonia kindly offered to host the next national theology conference in 2021.

It was noted that *Religion in Malawi* had offered to prepare a special issue to publish selected papers from the conference – a hybrid issue that will also be a Kachere book. All paper presenters were invited to submit their revised papers – with no more than 5,000 words and following Chicago-Mzuni style – by 30 November 2020. The papers will be subject to the normal review process and those that are recommended will be published. On this occasion, late submissions will not be considered.

Fr Francis Bonongwe expressed thanks to the hosts, Nkhoma University and Nkhoma Synod for a wonderful and memorable conference; and praised the organizing committee for a job exceptionally well done.

Final Session

In the final session of the conference Dr Hermann Mvula presented a synopsis of Prof Augustine Musopole's paper on "Malawian Umunthu Theology." Prof Musopole had hoped to be present himself at the conference but was unable to travel from Kenya because of coronavirus restrictions. The synopsis provoked a lively discussion and the hope was expressed that it might be possible in future to have a presentation from Prof Musopole himself.

Very Rev Dr Timothy Nyasulu led a closing devotion and the conference concluded with lunch and departures.

Participants

Chancellor College, University of Malawi
1. Rev Fr. Dr Alfred Chaima
2. Mr Stewart Kapinda
3. Dr Mzee Hermann Mvula

Domasi College of Education
4. Dr Gracious Gadama

Malawi Adventist University
5. Pastor Mabvuto Chipeta
6. Dr Frank Chirwa
7. Rev Luke Limbithu
8. Pastor Stain Kamputa

9. Dr Gladdon Thumbalamoto

10. Dr Jimmy Nazombe

Malawi Assemblies of God University

11. Dr Lawrence Chipao

Mzuni Press

12. Rev Prof Klaus Fiedler

13. Mr Hope Kaombe

Mzuzu University

14. Rev Francis Kudzula

15. Dr Joyce Mlenga

16. Dr Rhodian Munyenyembe

17. Dr Felix Nyika

Nazarene Theological College

18. Rev Benson Phiri

19. Rev Farai Manjengwa

20. Rev Joe Lilema

Nkhoma University

21. Rev Bossman Chitheka

22. Rev Maxwell Chowoko

23. Rev Allan Jere

24. Rev Dr Leonard Katundu

St Peter's Major Seminary

25. Rev Fr Francis Bonongwe

University of Blantyre Synod

26. Rev Dr Hastings Abale-Phiri

27. Rev Dr Humphreys Zgambo

University of Livingstonia

28. Rev Dr Colby Kumwenda
29. Dr Moses Mlenga
30. Very Rev Dr Timothy Nyasulu

Zomba Theological College

31. Rev Dr Takuze Chitsulo
32. Rev Dr Gertrude Kapuma
33. Rev Prof Kenneth Ross

University of KwaZulu-Natal

34. Dumisa Mbano—PhD Candidate

University of Pretoria

35. Russel Makonyola—PhD Candidate

Invited Theologians

36. Dr Volker Glissmann
37. Dr Phoebe Chifungo
38. Rev Hastings Bonomali
39. Rev Chiwaya
40. Dr Billy Mayaya
41. Gilbert Njobvuyalema
42. Michael Mkandawire
43. Rev Kananji
44. Rev Chikondi Phiri
45. Dr Gerard Chigona
46. Rev Dr Weston Kapasule

… Appendix: Constitution of the Theological Society

THE CONSTITUTION OF THE REGISTERED TRUSTEES OF THE THEOLOGICAL SOCIETY

Proposed Constitution of Theological Society

PART I
PRELIMINARY

NAME

1. There is hereby established an association whose name shall be **"THE REGISTERED TRUSTEES OF THEOLOGICAL SOCIETY"** (hereinafter referred to as **(SOCIETY)**.

2. **THE AIM AND PURPOSE OF (SOCIETY)**

    The main aim and purpose of the **SOCIETY** is to provide a platform for theological intellectual engagement, support and coordination of theologians or institutions that are delivering theological studies within and outside Malawi.

3. **ADDRESS AND REGISTERED OFFICE**

    The address and registered office which shall be the secretariat of **SOCIETY** shall be P.O. Box 130, ZOMBA, located at Zomba Theological College, Opposite Regional Police Headquarters, Zomba.

4. **INTERPRETATION**

    In this Constitution, unless the context otherwise requires—

    "SOCIETY" means Theological Society of Malawi

    "Board" means the Board of Trustees established

    "Executive Committee" means the Committee established under article 12 of this Constitution

    "Secretariat" means an office with all secretarial work

    "Seal" means the common seal of the **SOCIETY**

Appendix: Constitution of the Theological Society

PART II
OBJECTIVES OF THE SOCIETY

5. The objectives of the Society shall be:-

5.1 To develop a networking system through which members can effectively discuss pertinent ideas and share important information.

5.2 To enhance communication and facilitate team work among members through research collaborations.

5.3 To improve the quality of the work of members through peer review and by establishing a systemized library linkage to ensure that members can have easy access to libraries.

5.4 To foster a culture of writing by organizing meetings specially designed to improve the writing skills of members.

5.5 To establish connections with other theological organisations worldwide so as to widen its members' knowledge on theological issues.

5.6 To enhance faculty development through learning new lecturing techniques from other theological organisations and by supplying external examiners.

5.7 To facilitate the exchange of important and useful information among its members through building connections between those that are near to each other, exchange of lectures, conducting debates on relevant issues and formulating new ways to improve its operation.

5.8 Addressing issues that are of national importance such as giving opinions and advice on matters that affect the nation at large.

5.9 To organize and conduct national and international conferences

5.10 To bring theological perspectives to bear on social, economic and political issues that present themselves in Malawi and in the world at large.

6. ACTIVITIES OF THE SOCIETY

In pursuit of the above objectives the Society shall carry out the following activities;

6.1 Undertake training for capacity building of its members.

6.2 Produce any form of media e.g. reports, journals, periodicals, newsletter, for dissemination of theological information in Malawi or beyond.

6.3 Carry out research on the recent theological trends.

6.4 Work together with Government and other institutions for the furtherance of theological work in Malawi.

6.5 Conduct income-generating activities for the Society

6.6 Do any other activities furthering the above objectives

7. POWERS OF THE SOCIETY

In pursuit of the above objectives the Society shall have the following powers:-

7.1 To employ, orient and train such staff as it may deem necessary for the proper conduct of the Society and lay down conditions of service for such employees.

7.2 To pay any person in its employment such a salary, wage or other remuneration as it may deem fit subject to complying with the statutory minimum wage requirements.

7.3 To purchase, take or lease or in exchange, hire or otherwise acquire any real or personal property, which it considers necessary in the furtherance of its objectives.

7.4 To solicit and receive subscriptions (grants, funds, donations or legacies in cash or kind) from any person or body which it considers necessary for the furtherance of its objectives.

7.5 To invest and deal with money of the Society not immediately required upon such securities and in such manner as may from time to time determined

7.6 To produce and publish any publication of whatever form in the furtherance of its objectives and to disseminate the same.

7.7 To pay costs and expenses incurred in the conduct of the Society.

7.8 To do any such other lawful things as are incidental or conducive to the attainment of the above objectives.

PART III

ADMINISTRATION

8. Membership and Affiliation

8.1 Membership of the Society shall be open to all Malawians and non-Malawians, including institutions, who are interested in the objectives of the Society.

8.2 Any member shall be allowed to terminate his membership but shall not thereafter claim any benefits from the Society as may accrue to a member.

8.3 The members in annual general meeting may decide whether members should be paying an annual subscription fee and if so how much.

8.4 The Society shall have affiliations with other institutions or organizations with similar objectives to its own.

9. MANAGEMENT OF THE SOCIETY
BOARD OF TRUSTEES

9.1 There shall be Board of Trustees consisting of not less than three (3) and not more than thirteen (13) persons who shall be elected by the members at the annual general meeting.

9.2 The Trustees shall elect a Chairperson, vice chairperson, Secretary, Treasurer and Public relations officer from amongst themselves who shall form the Executive Committee of the Society.

9.3 All provisions regarding procedures of the meeting of the Executive Committee shall apply mutatis mutandis to the meetings of the Board of Trustees provided that the Board of Trustees shall meet four (4) times yearly and they shall determine the quorum required at its meetings.

9.4 A member of the Board of Trustees shall hold office for three (3) years and shall be eligible for further re-appointment.

9.5 The initial Board of Trustees shall apply for incorporation of the Association under the Trustees Incorporation Act (*cap.5:03*) of the Laws of Malawi.

9.6 The funds and property of the Society shall vest in the Trustees. The Trustees shall with the approval of the members, purchase, lease or acquire, hold, develop, manage, let, sale, exchange or otherwise dispose of movable or immovable property of the Society and to accept, whether subject to condition or not, gifts, devices and bequests of any such property.

9.7 The Trustees may borrow money on behalf of the Society on such terms and conditions as the Trustees may think fit.

10. VACANCIES ON THE BOARD OF TRUSTEES

10.1.1 A vacancy on the Board of Trustees shall arise upon:

10.1.2 The expiry of the term of office of a member;

10.1.3 Resignation of a member after one month's written notice

10.1.4 The death of a member

10.1.5 A member failing to attend three consecutive meetings of the Board without valid excuse or reason; and

10.1.6 A member leaving the country for more than one (1) year

10.1.7 Incapacity of a member due to sickness or otherwise and in case of the former a medical certificate from a certified medical practitioner shall be necessary.

10.1.8 A member being convicted of a criminal offence or being declared and undischarged bankrupt under the laws of the land.

10.1.9 A member acquiring employment which keeps him/her very busy to an extent that this jeopardizes the operations of the Society.

10.2 A vacancy due to any of the above may be filled at the discretion of the Executive Committee.

11. EXECUTIVE COMMITTEE

11.1 Save as is otherwise expressly provided in this Constitution the management of the Society shall be entrusted to the Executive Committee consisting of:-

(a) The Chairperson

(b) The Vice Chairperson

(c) The Secretary

(d) The Treasurer

(e) Public Relations Officer

11.2 The members of the Executive Committee shall hold office for a term of five (5) calendar years, and shall be elected by secret ballot by members present and voting at Annual General Meeting.

11.3 A member of the Executive Committee shall not hold office for more than two consecutive terms.

11.4 The provisions of Article 10.1 shall apply to the Executive Committee *mutatis mutandis*.

12. APPOINTMENT OF STAFF

12.1 The Executive Committee shall appoint senior staff and junior staff as may be necessary for **SOCIETY's** effective running to meet its objects and when the Executive Committee deems the same to be necessary.

13. MEETING OF THE EXECUTIVE COMMITTEE

13.1(a) The Executive Committee shall meet in ordinary sessions at least once in every three months and such other times as it may determine, or be deemed necessary.

(b) An extraordinary meeting of the Executive Committee may be convened at any time at the request of the Chairperson or at the request, in writing, of any two or more of its members.

13.2 The Executive Committee may, from time to time co-opt any person to attend any meeting for such specific purpose. Such co-opted member shall have the right to speak at the meeting and take part in the deliberations of such meeting but shall not have the right to vote.

13.3 Save as is otherwise expressly provided in this Constitution, the Executive Committee shall determine its own procedure and that of its sub-committees if it would be necessary to set up such sub-committees.

13.4 The Chair person shall preside at all meetings of the Executive Committee, and in the absence of the Chairperson and the Vice Chairperson, the members present at a meeting shall elect from amongst themselves a member to preside at that meeting.

13.5 Voting at all meetings shall be by a simple majority by secret ballot. In the event of a tie in votes, the person presiding at the meeting shall have a casting vote.

13.6 Half of the members of the Executive Committee shall constitute a quorum.

PART IV
DUTIES OF OFFICE BEARERS

14. DUTIES OF THE CHAIR PERSON

14.1 The Chair person shall preside at all General Meetings.

14.2 The Chair person shall, through the Executive Committee, be responsible for the general running and well being of the Society.

14.3 Without derogating from generality of Sub-Article (14.2), the Chair person shall present at the last meeting of financial year an Annual Report which shall contain inter-alia a summary of the activities of Society during the financial year in question and an up to date audited financial position of the Society.

14.4 Represent the Society at external meetings.

14.5 Shall be the one of the signatories of the bank account (s) of the Society.

14.6 Be a member of the disciplinary committee

The Chairperson shall be assisted by the Vice Chairperson in the foregoing and the Vice Chairperson shall perform the duties of the Chairperson in the absence of the Chairperson.

15. THE SECRETARY

15.1 The Secretary shall be responsible to the Executive Committee for:-

(a) Recording and keeping minutes of the Executive Committee Meetings and the General and Extra Ordinary meetings of the Society.

(b) Sending notices of the meetings the minimum being three (3) weeks.

(c) Preparing and keeping a list of all members of the Society.

(d) Handling all general correspondence of the Society.

(e) Being a member of the disciplinary committee.

(f) Any other duties assigned by the Executive Committee Meetings.

16. DUTIES OF THE PUBLIC RELATIONS OFFICER

16.1 The Public Relations Officer shall be the spokesperson of the Society.

16.2 The Public Relations Officer shall generally be responsible for the general publicity of the Society.

16.3 The Public Relations Officer shall also perform such other duties as may be assigned by the Executive Committee.

17. DUTIES OF THE TREASURER

17.1 The Treasurer shall be responsible to the Executive Committee for the control of the funds of the Society.

17.2 The Treasurer shall keep and maintain an up to date records of accounts.

17.3 The Treasurer shall distribute at the Annual General Meeting to all members of the Executive Committee copies of an up to date audited Annual Financial report

17.4 The Treasurer shall prepare a detailed written financial report on expenditures or income incurring events of the Society.

17.5 The Treasurer shall produce annual Budgets in consultation with the Executive Committee.

17.6 The Treasurer shall be one of the signatories of the bank account (s)of the Society.

17.7 The Treasurer shall also perform such other duties as may be assigned by the Executive Committee.

18. BANK ACCOUNT

18.1 The Society shall maintain bank account(s) with reputable Commercial Banks in the name of **"THE REGISTERED TRUSTEES OF THEOLOGICAL SOCIETY" (SOCIETY)**

18.2 All withdrawals shall be made after being signed by two of the following

Executive members; the Chairperson, the Treasurer and the Secretary. Provided that if the amount does not exceed more than MK 100,000 the signature of the chairperson alone shall suffice.

19. AUDITING OF ACCOUNTS OF THE SOCIETY

19.1 The financial accounts of the Society shall be audited by an independent body of Auditors at least once a year and such Auditors shall be as the Board of Trustees may from time to time determine. The Auditors shall be those with proven professional competence and integrity nationally.

19.2 The financial year shall run from 1st March to 28/9th February the other year.

19.3 The financial accounts shall also be subject to such interim audits as appropriate including but not exclusive to the following:-

    19.3.1 At the request of donors

    19.3.2 At the request of the majority of the Executive Committee

    19.3.3 At the request of the members

Appendix: Constitution of the Theological Society 295

PART V
GENERAL MEETINGS

20. ANNUAL GENERAL MEETING

20.1 A general meeting of the Society shall be held every year to transact the following business:-

(a) To receive, if approved, the audited accounts of the Society for the preceding year;

(b) To elect members of the board and executive committees when there is a vacancy.

20.2 Notice of any such Extraordinary General Meeting shall be sent to members not less than fourteen (14) days before the meeting and shall specify the matter(s) to be dealt with.

PART V
MISCELLANEOUS

21. AMENDMENT OF THE CONSTITUTION

21.1 This constitution may be amended by a resolution at any Annual or Extraordinary General Meeting of the Society.

21.2 No such resolution shall be pass unless it carries a majority of at least more than 50% of the voting members.

22. DISSOLUTION OF THE SOCIETY

22.1 The Society may be dissolved by:

(a) Voluntary winding up with the sanction of two- thirds (2/3) majority at an Annual or Extraordinary General Meeting of the Society called for that purpose.

(b) Cancellation in accordance with the provisions of the Trustee and Trustees Incorporation Acts by the Registrar General upon the Association becoming defunct; and

(c) By Order of the Court in case of any serious breach of any of the provisions of the Constitution, the Bye-Laws or Regulations of the Society and/or any relevant law in force.

22.2 On dissolution of the Society the land, buildings or any other property of the Society shall be vested in the registered proprietor of the Society (i.e. the Trustees) who shall also have a lien over all the property still remaining unpaid for by members. The Trustees may appoint an agent (e.g. a liquidator, banker, accountant, solicitor, manager) to manage, administer and dispose of the property of the Society and to present his final accounts and finally to apply the proceeds in satisfaction of the debts and liabilities of the Society.

22.3 After payment of all the debts and liabilities, the remainder shall be given and transferred to any institutions with similar objectives and undertakings as those of the Society.

23. LIABILITY OF MEMBERS OF THE EXECUTIVE COMMITTEE

The Executive Committee shall not be liable for any act or default of theirs or of the Society done in the exercise, in good faith, or within the legitimate functions of the Society.

24. INDEMNITY OF BOARD OF TRUSTEES

In carrying out their duties, members of the Board of Trustees shall not be liable to the Society for any loss which may occur as a result of any investment made in good faith by the Board or occasioned by any mistake or omission made in good faith by the Board or as a result of negligence, dishonesty or fraud of any agent or employee of the Society, unless such loss arises from any dishonesty or fraud of any member of the Board. In this event, the Board shall hold that individual solely and directly responsible and liable for such losses, and the Board will be required to take all necessary civil or legal action to safeguard the reputation and assets of the Society.

25. COMMON SEAL AND A LOGO

25.1 The Society shall have a Common Seal which shall be an embossed circular stamp inscribed with the words "**THE REGISTERED TRUSTEES OF THEOLOGICAL SOCIETY (SOCIETY)**" in around with the words "**(SOCIETY)**" inscribed in the middle. The Society shall also have a logo as approved by the Board of trustees.

25.2 The Common Seal shall be kept by the Secretary and kept under lock.

CERTIFICATION

This is to certify that this is the constitution of the Registered Trustees of Theological Society (Society).

Signed this ....day of............................2020

Dr. Timothy Nyasulu
CHAIRPERSON OF THE REGISTERED TRUSTEES OF THEOLOGICAL SOCIETY (SOCIETY)

Notes on Contributors

Gerard Chigona is a doctoral laureate, scholar and author. Among other tertiary qualifications, he holds a BA (Systematic Theology and Social Political Philosophy), an MA (Systematic Theology), and a PhD (Social Ethics). His academic credentials include research and publication in systematic and philosophical theology, social and political theory, ethics, and cultural anthropology. He has worked in both government and Catholic institutions of higher learning. Since 2017, he has been Governance Advisor at the Embassy of Ireland.

Frank Barden Chirwa obtained his BA/Theology and MA/Theology Degrees at Solusi University in Bulawayo Zimbabwe and a PhD at Mzuzu University. He once served as a District Pastor in the North Malawi Conference the SDA Church, Malawi Union of the SDA Church Education Director, and President for the North Malawi Conference of the SDA Church. Currently, Dr Chirwa is serving as the Head of the Theology and Religious Studies Department at the Malawi Adventist University, Lakeview Campus.

Klaus Fiedler, a Baptist pastor, holds a BA from Makerere, a PhD from Dar es Salaam and a Dr (theol) from Heidelberg University. He served as a missionary in Tanzania, as pastor and editor in Germany, as lecturer and associate professor at Chancellor College, as Professor of Theology and Religious Studies at Mzuzu University and as Guest Professor of Missiology at Evangelical Theological Faculty in Leuven. His passions are postgraduate studies and publishing.

Volker Glissmann is a global mission worker of the Presbyterian Church in Ireland and works as a Programme Developer for the TEE College in Johannesburg, South Africa. He is based in Malawi. He has a PhD in Old Testament from Queen's University Belfast and an MA in Theological Education from the London of School of Theology. He was the Executive Director of TEEM (Theological Education by

Extension in Malawi) from 2010-2018. He is also involved in theological educational consultancy and TEE work globally. He has published a number of articles on theological education.

Stewart Daison Kapinda is a young theologian interested in contemporary New Testament studies in the African context. He is a graduate of Zomba Theological College with a Bachelor of Divinity, Exploits University with a Bachelor of Human Resources Management, and he has finalized his Master of Theology and Religious Studies with the University of Malawi.

Gertrude Aopesyaga Sulumba-Kapuma holds a PhD from the University of Pretoria in South Africa. She took her first degrees at the University of Fort Hare. She is Senior Lecturer in Practical Theology at Zomba Theological College, where she has also served as Dean of Studies. An ordained CCAP minister, she has earlier served as Director of Women's Programmes at Chigodi Women's Centre of CCAP Blantyre Synod and Vice President of the All Africa Conference of Churches. She is the author of several scholarly articles.

Winston Kawale is an ordained minister of the CCAP Nkhoma Synod where he served as General Secretary. He holds a Doctor of Theology degree (Old Testament) from the University of Stellenbosch, South Africa. Dr Kawale is a former Senior Lecturer at Mzuzu University. He is an Adjunct Lecturer, postgraduate studies supervisor and external examiner in several universities. He is an author of several published academic articles, books, and book chapters. Kawale served as Vice-President of the Reformed Ecumenical Council of the Reformed Churches worldwide.

Luke Limbithu grew up in family of five, studied at Newbold College for his Bachelor's and did double major in biblical studies for his Master of Arts with University of Wales – Lampeter in the United Kingdom. He has served as a gospel minister for more than twenty years as well as in administration with the Seventh-day Adventist Church. Currently he is working as Lecturer in Theology & Religious Studies at the Malawi Adventist University.

Joyce Dainess Mlenga, PhD, is presently a lecturer in the Department of Theology and Religious Studies at Mzuzu University. She holds degrees from African Bible College (Malawi), Africa International University (Kenya), and Mzuzu University (Malawi). She once served as the Dean of the Faculty of Education (2007-2015); Dean of the Faculty of Theology (2016-2018); and Deputy Principal (2018-2019) at University of Livingstonia. She has authored a book and several articles.

Moses Mlenga is a scholar, broadcaster and politician. After undergraduate studies at African Bible College (Malawi), he mastered Greek and Hebrew at Africa International University in Kenya and completed his PhD at Mzuzu University. He served as a Lecturer and Dean of Students, before rising to the position of College Principal at University of Livingstonia (2012-2016). He has authored a book and several articles. Dr. Mlenga moved from academics to politics, serving as the Regional Governor of UTM (North).

Augustine Chingwala Musopole, PhD, holds degrees: from the University of Malawi, University of London, and Union Theological Seminary, New York. He was General Secretary of the Malawi Council of Churches (1998-2003); General Manager, Christian Literature Association in Malawi; Assistant Regional Education Officer, Ministry of Education Malawi; and lately Associate Professor (emeritus) Department of Philosophy and Religion, Chang Jung Christian University, Tainan, Taiwan. He is ordained in the Presbyterian Church USA and is author of several articles and books.

Mzee Hermann Mvula is Lecturer in Old Testament Ethics and Applied Theology at Chancellor College, University of Malawi. Mvula is the author of *The Theory, Praxis and Pursuit of Constitutionalism in Democratic Malawi: An Old Testament Ethical Perspective.* He has also published several articles in referred journals and book chapters. Mvula holds degrees from Africa Nazarene University in Nairobi, Kenya and University of Malawi. He served as Head of the Department of Theology and Religious Studies (Chancellor College: 2015-2016), and also as Deputy Director for Kachere Series (2012-2014).

Timothy Kabulunga Nyasulu, PhD, is the Vice Chancellor of University of Livingstonia. He is a graduate of University of Malawi, University of Glasgow in Scotland UK and Trinity International University, USA. He is a former Moderator of the CCAP General Assembly – Malawi, Zambia, Zimbabwe, and South Africa (2013-20). He served as Executive Director of Education in the Synod of Livingstonia. He was also Academic Dean and Vice Principal at Zomba Theological College. He has published a book on Missiology and a number of research articles.

Felix Chimera Nyika (PhD, Mzuzu University) is Senior Lecturer in Church History and Deputy Postgraduate Studies Coordinator at Mzuzu University. He is a graduate of African Bible College (BA) and Trinity International University (MDiv). He also serves as the Lead Pastor of Kairos Christian Center in Lilongwe.

Kenneth R. Ross, a Church of Scotland Theological Educator, is Professor of Theology at Zomba Theological College and Associate Minister of Bemvu CCAP. His recent books include *Mission Rediscovered: Transforming Disciples* (World Council of Churches and Globethics) and *A Malawi Church History 1860-2020* (Mzuni Press), co-authored with Klaus Fiedler. He is Series Editor of the Edinburgh Companions to Global Christianity and Chair of the Steering Group for the formation of the Theological Society of Malawi.

Index

Aberdeen, 54
Adeyemo, Tokunbo, 40
Adonai, 105-108, 111f
Adventist Development and Relief Agency (ADRA), 151
African Bible College, 14, 57, 300f
African Books Collective, 71
African cultural tradition, 199
African Independent Churches, 78
African Theology, 43, 73
African Traditional Religion, 8, 157-166
Age of Reason. *See* Enlightenment
AIDS, 26, 155, 212
Al-Azhar, Cairo, 54
Amanze, James, 42
Ambuye. *See* Adonai
Ambuye Mulungu, 106
Ancient Egypt, 53
Andronicus, 124, 126, 128
Anglican Church, 13f, 78, 185, 263
Antichrist, 136f
Apostellō, 115, 119-122
Apostle Paul, 184, 200
Apostles of the Lamb, 120
Apostleship, 116, 117, 119, 127
Apostolic Church Fathers, 227
Apostolos, 115, 120
Aquinas, Thomas, 178
Aramaic, 100, 115f
Archdiocese of Lilongwe, Roman Catholic, 22
Aristotle, 54, 169, 246

Arius, 42
Association of Theological Schools in North America, 91
Athanasiusses of Alexandria, 42
Atheistic humanism, 171f
Auer, Alfons, 177
Augustine of Hippo, 42, 182, 270
Bacon, Francis, 37
Balaka district, 145
Banda, Hastings Kamuzu, 24, 259, 265, 273
Banda, Joyce, 266
Bantu languages, 94
Baptist Church, 78
Baptist Theological Seminary, 13f
Bar-Jona, Simon, 39
Barnabas, Apostle, 123, 126
Barth, Karl, 37, 49, 168
Bediako, Kwame, 18
Bifurcation of Consciousness, 193
Biographies of People and Parishes Series, 72
Blackman's Church, 15
Blantyre City, 78
Blantyre Mission, 12, 16, 95
Blantyre Synod of the CCAP, 14, 57, 264, 299
Boesak, Allan, 42
Bonhoeffer, Dietrich, 272
Boulaga, Fabien Eboussi, 42
Brunner, Emil, 49
Bujo, Bénézet, 18, 42
Buku Lopatulika, 95-99, 101, 106

Index

Buku Lopatulika mu Chichewa Chalero, 99
Buku Loyera, 94, 96-99, 103-106
Bwana Yesu, 94f, 111
Calvin, John, 226, 228, 252, 265
Cambridge, 54
Camus, Albert, 179f
Cashgate Scandal, 266
Catholic Bishops, 149f, 233
Catholic Commission for Justice and Peace, 151
Catholic University of Malawi, 14
Chakanza, J.C., 19, 55
Chakwera, Lazarus, 266
Chancellor College, 13f, 18, 28, 56f, 276, 279f, 282, 298, 300
Chang Jung Christian University, 25
Chauta, 103-106, 111
Chewa (tribe), 111
Chichewa, 8, 19, 94-101, 103, 104, 105, 106, 108, 109, 110, 111, 112, 280
Chikoya, Lester, 99
Chikuse, Willebes, 95
Chilembwe, John, 15
Chilembwe, Thokozani, 16
ChiNyanja Bible, 95
Chow, Wilson, 91
Christendom, 173
Christian humanism, 170
Christo-Munthism. *See* second Adam
Chrysostom, John, 270
Church and Society, 151

Church of Central Africa Presbyterian, 9, 12, 16, 21, 24, 28, 77f, 225f, 236f, 264, 278f, 299, 301
Church, Henry, 65
Circle of Concerned African Women Theologians, 20, 29
Circle theologians, 29
Classical Greek, 53, 54
Climate change, 139, 187
Comte, Auguste, 167
Constitutional Convention (1787), 247
Coronavirus, 6, 8, 130f, 133, 135-155, 168, 276, 279f, 282
Cyprians of Carthage, 42
Damascus Road, 123
David, 268
Democratic Progressive Party (DPP), 262f, 266
Democratic Republic of Congo, 142
Deuteronomy, 132, 243-249, 252, 254f
Dickson, Kwesi, 42
Dictionary of African Christian Bibliography, 72
Doctrinal orthodoxy, 187
Domasi College of Education, 282
Dual religiosity, 164
Durham, 54
Dutch Bible, 96
Dutch Reformed Church, 23
Early Church, 270
Ebola, 142
Ecumenical Association of Third World Theologians, 24, 43
Eden, 184

Index

Ekballō, 120, 122
Ela, Jean-Marc, 42
English Revised Version, 96
Enlightenment, 36, 46f, 189
Epangelia, 117
Epaphroditus, 123, 125
Epicurean, 169
Epicurus, 246
Epistemology, 39
Epistle of Aresteas, 116
Erasmus, Desiderius, 169
Evangelical Bible College of Malawi (EBCOM), 14
Existential humanism, 170, 171
Exodus, 100, 102, 105, 230, 242f, 246f, 254f
Fall of Man, 174
Fiedler, Klaus, 43
Fiedler, Rachel NyaGondwe, 20, 43
First World War, 15, 37, 272
Flame of love, 132
Fourah Bay, 54
Francis of Assisi, 260
Free Methodist Church, 65
French *La Sainte Bible*, 96
Fuchs, Josef, 177
Galilean mission, 120
Gama, Billy, 264
Germany, 53f, 298
Gethsemane, 184
Global North, 71
Globalisation, 187
Gloria in Excelsis, 185
Great Britain, 143

Greek Community, 228
Gruchy, John de, 272f
Haemorrhage, 132
Hara, Handwell, 55
Heidelberg, 60
Hetherwick, Alexander, 95
Hiebert, Paul, 200
HIV, 30, 155f, 212, 215f
Holy Spirit, 26, 40, 42, 46, 50f, 117, 122f, 126, 128f, 184
House of Wisdom, 53
Human Rights Defenders Coalition, 145, 261f
Inclusive Education, 62
Institute of Public Opinion and Research, 149
International Bible Society, 99
Italy, 143, 169
Jehosaphat Mwale Theological College, 277
Jerusalem Bible, 96
Jesus Christ, 17, 23, 26f, 48, 119, 125, 133, 136, 139, 169, 183, 185, 268
John the Baptist, 13, 118-120, 268
Josephus, 114, 116
Junia, 124, 126, 128
Kachebere Major Seminary, 12, 22
Kachere Series, 18
Kalilombe, Patrick, Bishop, 22, 42, 96, 99
Kalulu Hill, 12
Kamaara, Teresa, 42
Kansas State, 146
Kant, Immanuel, 36f
Kawale, Winston, 99

Index

Kenya, 207, 217, 282
King James Version, 96
King, Noel Q., 58
Kinoti, Hannah, 42
Kipalapala Major Seminary, 12
Kiswahili, 110f
Knox, John, 164, 228
Kumphwefula, 196
Kundecha, Stephen, 12
Langworthy, Henry, 55
Latin America, 272
Latin *Vulgate*, 96
Lay Participation, 78
Leonard Kamungu Theological College, 14
Leviticus, 102
Lex naturalis (Natural Law), 178
Liberalism, 37, 40
Liberation theology, 15, 24, 272f
Likhubula Bible Institute, 13
Likoma Island, 11
Living Our Faith, 149
Livingstonia Synod of CCAP, 9, 14-16, 21, 56f, 62, 95, 225f, 231f, 236f, 263, 279f, 300f
Locke, John, 243, 246, 251
Logical atheism, 171
Lutheran Church, 58, 185
Luviri Press, 19
Machiavelli, Niccolo, 169
Madison, James, 247
Magesa, Laurenti, 42
Makerere University, 54, 59
Makondesa, Patrick, 15, 20

Malawi Adventist University, 14, 197, 278f, 282, 298, 300
Malawi Army, 259
Malawi Assemblies of God University, 14, 283
Malawi Congress Party (MCP), 259, 261, 264
Malawi Electoral Commission, 261, 263
Malawi Gazette Supplement, 144, 146, 154
Malawi Young Pioneers, 259
Malawian Theology, 14, 18, 31, 73, 75
Malembo Oyera, 96-98, 102, 106
Maluleke, Tinyiko, 42
Marx, Karl, 169f
Marxist humanism, 170
Maseko, Dexter, 197
Matecheta, Harry Kambwiri, 12, 16
May 2019 Tripartite Elections, 9, 254, 258, 260, 263, 273f
Mbiti, John, 42
McBrien, Richard, 185
McCracken, John, 55, 62
Mchinji district, 12
Medical Council of Malawi, 232
Medieval scholasticism, 36
MERS, 131, 143
Messiah, 118, 265
Metaphysical atheism, 171
Methodism, 65
Meye, Robert, 91
Mhango, Landson, 53
Milesian philosophers, 169
Minister of Finance, 237

Index

Minister of Youth and Culture, 237
Missio Ecclesia, 263
Mission, 116- 123, 127f
Modernity, 158
Montesquieu, Charles de, 246, 251
Moors, 54
Msiska, Stephen Kauta, 16, 22
Mua, 23
Mugambi, Jesse, 42, 273
Multiculturalism, 195, 198
Multiparty democracy, 258-260, 273
Muluzi, Bakili, 265
Mundua, Victor, 23
Murray, William, 95f
Muslim, 23, 53f, 60, 258
Musopole, Augustine, 24-26, 282
Mutharika, Arthur Peter, 147, 261, 266
Mutharika, Bingu wa, 266
Mwale, Ishmael, 95
Mwasi, Yesaya Zerenji, 15
Mwaura, Philomena, 42
Myth of Sisyphus, 179
Mzuni Press, 19, 283
Mzuzu University, 14, 18f, 53, 56f, 73, 278, 283, 298-301
Namalenga, 104
National Baptist Convention, Inc., 61
National Council for Higher Education, 14
National Theology Conference, 6, 32, 276
Natural law. *See* Lex naturalis
Nazarene Theological College, 283

Nazarene Theological College of Central Africa, 14
Ncozana, Silas, 55
Ndovie, Stanley S., 129
New International Version, 99f
New Jerusalem, 120
New Testament, 8, 59, 95, 98, 100, 114, 125f, 133, 139, 141, 164, 229, 268f, 299
Ngoni (tribe), 16
Niagara Falls Conference, 37
Nicene Creed, 40, 184
Nkhoma Mission, 6, 12, 95
Nkhoma Synod of the CCAP, 60, 95, 280, 282, 299
Nkhoma University, 6, 14, 276-278, 280, 282f
Nyamiti, Charles, 42
Nyamukawala, 12
Nyasaland Times, 15
Obscurantism, 193, 199, 203
Oduyoye, Mercy Amba, 42, 220
Old Testament, 9, 21, 57, 98, 100, 118f, 131-133, 139-141, 244, 247, 268, 298-300
Operation Bwezani, 259
Orthodoxy, 90, 168f
Ott, Bernhard, 90
Ott, Martin, 151
Overtoun Institution, 15
Oxford, 54, 55
Paraclete, 117
Pastoral Letter (1993), 264
Pentateuch, 241-243, 247
Pentateuchal, 254

Pentecost, 117f, 122, 129
Pentecostal, 78
Pentecostal Life University, 14
Person of prayer, 92
Personal integrity, 92
Phiri, Desmond Dudwa, 62
Phiri, Isabel Apawo, 28-30, 42, 55
Pirouet, Louise, 53, 63, 66, 69
Plato, 169, 246
Pneumonia, 132
Pobee, John, 42
Polibius, 246
Postmodernism, 189, 191f
Practical Theology, 61, 260, 275, 299
Pragmatic humanism, 170
Prophet Ahijah, 114f
Prophet Nathan, 268
Prophetic ministry, 273
Protagoras, 169
Protestant churches, 97
Providence Industrial Mission, 61
Rabbinic, 115
Renaissance, 169f
Revised Standard Version, 96
Robert Laws Secondary School, 25
Roman Catholic, 42, 58, 96f, 149f, 227f
Ross, Kenneth, 259
Ruling Elders, 225f, 228f, 231-233, 235-237, 279
Rwanda, 261, 263, 274
Saduccess, 268
Sande, Jonathan, 95
SARS, 131, 143

Sartre, Jean-Paul, 169, 179-181
Satan, 39, 135
Schleiermacher, Friedrich, 37
Schuller, Bruno, 177
Scotland, 12, 277, 301
Scott, David Clement, 16, 95
Second Adam, 27
Second World War, 272
Secular Humanism, 167f, 173-176, 186, 280
Secularism, 37f, 173, 204
Selling, Joseph, 178
Septuagint, 116
Sindima, Harvey, 42
Society in Scotland for the Propagation of the Gospel, 277
Socrates, 169, 177
Sola Scripture, 37
South Africa, 13, 96, 147, 195, 210, 272f, 298f, 301
Spain, 54, 143
Special Needs Education, 58, 62
St Michael and All Angels Church, 16
St Peter's Major Seminary, 12-14, 283
St. Paul, 43
Statham, Todd, 16
Stoic schools, 169
Sub-Saharan Africa, 216
Supreme Court of Appeal, 146, 254, 262
Synod Conference, 235
Synodicalism, 231
Teaching Elders, 225f, 228, 231-233, 235f

Index

TEEM, 13f, 237, 298
Testament of the 12 Patriarchs, 116
Tetragrammaton, 100-103, 105, 109, 112, 280
The Great Commission, 121
The Twelve, 116f, 119, 120f, 125-127, 129
Theological Society of Malawi, 7
Theo-nomous ethics, 177
Thessalonians, 137
Thiesen, Mark, 62
Thomas, Jaison, 75f, 78, 85
Timbuktu, 54
Tonga (tribe), 15
Tongaland, 15
Torah, 247
Transnational modernity, 195
Trauma, 206f, 280
Truth and Reconciliation Commission of South Africa, 221
Tsukuluza, C.J., 129
Tumbuka (language), 270
Tumbuka (tribe), 22, 229
Turner, Harold, 31
Tutu, Desmond, 42
Tyre and Sidon, 119
Ubunthu, 209, 216, 217

UMCA, 11
uMunthu, 26f, 48f
Umunthu, 25f, 44, 47f, 51, 282
United States of America, 61, 143, 146f, 162, 300f
United Transformation Movement, (UTM) 261
University of Blantyre Synod, 283
University of KwaZulu-Natal, 284
University of Livingstonia, 232, 284
University of Pretoria, 284
US Constitution, 240, 254
Villy, Louis, Fr, 96
Virgin Mary, 184
Wendland, Ernst, 94, 104
World Health Organization, 130, 131, 141
Wuhan, China, 143
Wycliffe, John, 227
Yao (tribe), 16, 19
Yehova, 101f, 111
YHWH, 100-106, 108, 111f
Young's Literal Translation, 96
Zomba district, 12f
Zomba Theological College, 13f, 276, 277, 279f, 284, 299, 301

www.ingramcontent.com/pod-product-compliance
Lightning Source LLC
Chambersburg PA
CBHW050858300426
44111CB00010B/1293